IT MANAGER'S GUIDE TO
VIRTUAL PRIVATE NETWORKS

IT Manager's Guide to Virtual Private Networks

David Leon Clark

McGraw-Hill

New York   San Francisco   Washington, D.C.   Auckland
Bogotá   Caracas   Lisbon   London   Madrid   Mexico City
Milan   Montreal   New Delhi   San Juan   Singapore
Sydney   Tokyo   Toronto

Library of Congress Cataloging-in-Publication Data
Clark, David
    IT Manager's Guide to virtual private networks / David Clark.
        p.   cm.
    ISBN 0-07-135202-3
        1. Extranets (Computer networks)—Security measures.   2. Business
enterprises—Computer networks—Security measures.   3. Internet (Computer network)—Security measures.   4. Computer network protocols.   I.
Title.
    TK5105.875.E87C64   1999
    005.8—dc21   99-35354
                                                                        CIP

McGraw-Hill

A Division of The **McGraw·Hill** Companies

1 2 3 4 5 6 7 8 9 0   AGM/AGM   9 0 4 3 2 1 0 9

ISBN 0-07-135202-3

*The sponsoring editor for this book was Simon Yates, the editing supervisor was
Penny Linskey, and the production supervisor was Clare Stanley. It was set in
New Century Schoolbook by Priscilla Beer of McGraw-Hill's Professional Book
Group composition unit in cooperation with Spring Point Publishing Services.*

Printed and bound by Quebecor / Martinsburg.

To Serena, David II, and Stanlyn, "Thanks for being my family." To my surrogate mother, Mrs. Doris Reynolds, "Couldn't have made it without you." To my mother and father, James and Sonia Clark, and my brother, Steven Clark, "We miss you." To my brothers, James, Jr., Christopher, Michael, Ronald, and Dwayne, and my sister, Deborah, "We are family."

CONTENTS

Contents

Contents

Contents

PREFACE

There are a variety of reasons why organizations are so interested in the Internet. Ubiquity is one, scalability is another, and, of course, cost-effectiveness. In response to such ambitions, organizations are wrestling with the challenge of connecting business partners, customers, suppliers, remote field locations, branch offices, and mobile employees directly online to the enterprise network. Most organizations are aware, however, that if the Internet is used as the communications backbone for the enterprise without precautions, the entire network is placed at risk to the wily hacker.

Previously, the choices were obvious. Develop your own private network, hire an Internet service provider (ISP), or use the Internet at great risk. The cost of leased or dedicated lines and dial-in access, supported by communication servers, modem banks, and toll-free numbers, all critical requirements of private networks, can prove to be too expensive and therefore out of reach for many businesses. Similarly, using an ISP could also prove too costly. However, if you consider recent innovations in ease of use and increased functionality, along with the maturation of critical standards for data privacy such as IP Security (IPSec), VPN technology emerges as the clear choice for building a private network, albeit a virtual one, over the public Internet. *IT Manager's Guide to Virtual Private Networks* will guide you with that purpose in mind.

INTRODUCTION

When the Department of Defense (DoD) commissioned the academic research environment to establish a high-speed, open communications backbone that could survive a nuclear attack, Vinton Cerf and the late Jon Postel created the ARPANET. Little did they know that when the network they created switched on in 1969, their academic project would evolve into the Internet, the largest, fastest-growing network in history. Cerf, who worked with Postel on ARPANET at the University of California at Los Angeles (UCLA) graduate school, teamed with Robert Kahn 6 years later to develop the much heralded Internet protocol suite TCP/IP (Transmission Control Protocol/Internet Protocol). To understand the nature of the Internet today, and in particular TCP/IP, a look at the world when ARPANET was still a design spec should provide some insight.

When Cerf, also known as the "father" of the Internet, and the other founders embarked upon development of the ARPANET, their attitudes were cultivated by the free spirited, love-for-one-another movement of the sixties. No institutions embraced these tenets quite like the student body of university and college campuses. The founders, therefore, envisioned a high-speed communications system freely accessible to a community of users where "open" sharing of data would be the norm. Security was of little or no concern in this climate of altruism. After all, they thought, security measures would only hinder creativity and interfere with the free flow of data and ideas. Even in the scientific research environments where they worked, security was never a cause for concern.

The founders saw their dreams materialize when the linking of four university supercomputers created the ARPANET. In fact, the seeds of the Internet were sown when the ARPANET was switched on. What started as an exercise to allow information sharing among scientists spawned two new branch networks in 1972 called CSNet and BITNET (for "Because It's Time Network"). Other branch networks such as Usenet were formed several years later. Usenet was a network of newsgroups that formed to discuss current events and other designated topics. It also provided an unprecedented forum to search for other groups with information and ideas to share. In 1984, a momentous year, the system of branch networks finally became known as the Internet when the branches merged into a homogeneous network of 500 host computers. This latest incarnation continued to grow in the following years and begin to resemble the Internet of today.

And grow it did. In 1989 the World Wide Web (WWW) was introduced, allowing the linking of vast amounts of information among, now, 80,000 host computers. Messages from homegrown email systems and file transfers traversed the new network in a latticelike fashion, becoming a fitting metaphor for the new information superhighway. Computer users, driven by curiosity or a sense of adventure or research, also began exploring the new universe. The first commercial applications began to appear as well. Suddenly, the Internet had become an institution unto itself. The introduction of Hypertext Markup Language (HTML) followed in 1991 and the pièce de resistance occurred in 1993 when the University of Illinois wrote and released the first Web browser. Information and ideas were captured in massive databases and made accessible to the public from anywhere at anytime through an exciting new interface. By 1995, nearly 2,500,000 host computers and 90,000 WWW sites were online. The Internet had become a cybernetic mechanism attracting a community of users from all fields of endeavor. The first cyber radio stations went online, and the first full-length motion picture was broadcast. Magazines and newspapers also began posting their content on their Web sites. It was only fitting that the first cyber rock concert was aired live by the Rolling Stones.

In 1995, use of the Internet by businesses really skyrocketed. Businesspersons, who for the most part had stood anxiously by marveling at the Internet explosion, were no longer able to resist. Over half of the 90,000 Web sites were commercial sites by the end of 1995. Corporate America was able to discern the true promise of the Internet. It was accessible from all over the world (ubiquitous). It could support applications as they increased in size with relative ease (scalable). And, most importantly, analysis had proven that the Internet was the most cost-effective choice for an enterprisewide communications network. As more and more businesses were poised to harvest the benefits of the Internet, however, alarming reports of strange occurrences emerged in the open society of the Internet.

The Internet continued to grow like a coral reef without centralized authority. Between 1989 and 1998, industry research indicated that the Internet grew at 340 percent annually. Somewhere along the way, it attracted a certain community of users who did not share the same spirit of altruism envisioned by the founders and practiced by academic, research, and business communities. As with any free society, the newcomers came partially due to its openness and partially due to the absence of certain rules and regulations. However, they mainly came for mischief and mayhem, perhaps even to wreak havoc. These marauders were the "Hells' Angels" of the information superhighway. Today they are known, almost reverently in certain circles, as wily hackers.

Hacker forays have been plaguing the Internet for nearly a decade. Some exploits have received such notoriety that in Internet pop cultures, hackers have attained rock star-like status. In the beginning, high jinks were limited to macro viruses that cause software to perform computing tasks erratically. Eventually, more sophisticated feats were executed surreptitiously with sniffer software and Trojan horse ploys to steal user passwords. Today, hackers engage in full-scale covert operations with ominous-sounding attacks like Ping of Death, along with session hijacking and backdoor command raids. The National Computer Security Association issued a focus report (August 1997) that sampled a range of U.S. businesses, as well as federal, state, and local governments. Forty-four percent of the respondents reported documented external attacks to their systems. Another study revealed that the U.S. Department of Defense networks are attacked some 250,000 times a year.

Hackers created and are still creating unfortunate circumstances for the Internet. As a result, the Internet has a reputation for severe security problems. In the psyche of corporate managers, the risk of attacks that steal or destroy data, disable protection systems, and shut down entire networks far outweigh the payoff of ubiquity, scalability, and cost-effectiveness. Consequently, avoiding the Internet for important business applications is not a difficult choice to make. A 1998 survey by the Open Group, a consortium carrying the banner for security standards, found that only one in seven companies (14 percent) is willing to link its critical applications to the Internet.

In spite of its reputation for security weaknesses, the potential benefits of the Internet are not easy to ignore. In fact, the potential is awesome. To be painfully obvious, if hacker problems were nonexistent, the Internet would provide an ideal communications infrastructure for enterprisewide area networks. Alternative solutions involving leased lines, public data networks (as distinguished from the public Internet), or Internet service providers (the foundation for private networks) are expensive in comparison. The expense connected with establishing and managing one's own private network is, perhaps, the most compelling reason why Corporate America continues to scrutinize the Internet with raised eyebrow. If somehow the Internet could be harnessed and one's information assets protected from the legions of hackers operating covertly from Internet safe houses, businesses would again gravitate toward the Internet for business-to-business transactions.

Virtual private networks (VPNs) are paving a way for enterprises to return to the information superhighways of the Internet. The advancements and seamless integration of the key technologies of encryption, authentication, and tunneling protocols make it possible to establish secure virtually private networks across the very public Internet. The maturation of critical standards such as Secure IP (IPSec) also plays a key role. In other words, VPNs enable you to build and operate an Internet-based, enterprisewide network fully resistant to hacker attacks. VPNs also provide enterprises a viable alternative to expensive private networks that rely upon leased lines, public data networks, or an ISP. The advent of VPNs signals the beginning of a new era—an era that will see many businesses migrate to the Internet to support mission-critical applications. In summary, VPNs have put the full potential of the Internet within the reach of the corporate networking community. The means to harness the ubiquitous Internet cost-effectively, perhaps, was envisioned by the Internet founders. The means to harness the ubiquitous Internet cost-effectively for *secure* network communications, however, is a fulfillment of the promise.

About This Book

Recent developments in VPN technology and standards are ushering in a new era for the Internet. The celebrated promise of the Internet is ubiquity, scalability, and cost-effectiveness, features that are very desirable for an enterprisewide communications backbone. In recent years, however, the Internet has gained tremendous notoriety for hacker problems. The concerns for security are so deep-rooted in prevailing attitudes that the rate of adoption of the Internet for critical business and government applications is minimal, compared to other alternatives. VPN technology is finally positioned to challenge these mainstream sentiments by fulfilling its promise. The advancements in tunneling protocols, authentication, and encryption, and especially, the seamless integration of the three, make it possible to establish a secure virtually private network across the public Internet.

The purpose of this book is to provide a comprehensive account and reference for network communications by conveying a complete historical perspective and technology review, including standards for interoperability, features, benefits, key industry players, and a methodology for needs assessment. This book is a conclusive reference source for the MIS community and a definitive subject reference for nontechnical professionals as well. Numerous charts, tables, graphics, and illustrations are incorporated to facilitate exposition of subject matter.

Part 1 (Chapters 1, 2, and 3) discusses the evolution of network communications and the driving influences that are reshaping the landscape of enterprise networks or intranets. Upon completion, you will understand how external environmental forces affect internal network communications and why the migration to the Internet is evolving as a necessary, if not natural, phenomenon. Chapter 1, "Private Networks vs. Virtual Private Networks: Exploring Network Security," presents an account of the evolution of intranets and the circumstances that trigger their metamorphosis to private networks, extranets, or VPNs. This chapter also defines the three areas by identifying the characteristics that distinguish one from the other. Chapter 2, "Why VPNs Will Proliferate," delves into the reasons why VPNs are here to stay. The political arena, key players, the historical impact of important tunneling protocols, and the economics of VPNs are fully covered to support the notion that network computing is entering a new era. Chapter 3, "De Facto and Emerging Standards," talks about the important standards that are providing interoperability among competing VPN solutions.

Part 2 (Chapters 4, 5, and 6) reveals the magnitude of potential security problems. This section of the book will prove that hacker attacks are not arbitrary occurrences, as many may be led to believe. On the contrary, security breaches are an orchestrated, deliberate, and ongoing campaign of cyberwar conducted by the wily hacker. Chapter 4, "Hacker Attacks for the Hall of Fame," provides an account of several legendary hacker exploits that have been documented in the media. In Chapter 5, "How They Do It," various hacker attacks and firewall security breaches are categorized by Internet services and protocols such as SMTP (Simple Mail Transfer Protocol, or email), HTTP (Hypertext Transfer Protocol), and TCP/IP. Chapter 6, "When Firewalls Fail: Coping with the Aftermath," discusses what should be done when your firewall is breached and the consequences if remedies are delayed.

Part 3 comprises the next six chapters of the book (Chapters 7 through 12). Chapter 7, "The Technology of VPNs," provides a detailed conceptual and functional overview of VPN technology. Chapter 8, "The Architecture, Technology, and Services of Firewalls," covers the present state-of-the-art, from basic firewall architecture to standard operating features like network address translation. In this chapter, the three main architecture choices used in building firewalls are compared to the Open Systems Interconnect (OSI) reference model for insight into their inherent functionality. This chapter also compares and contrasts the underlying technologies of firewall architectures. Finally, a discussion concerning the standard Internet services and protocols firewalls support completes this chapter's review. Chapter 9, "Innovative Firewall Implementations," is a review of the latest in firewall features and implementations. In it you will be introduced to new terminology, such as firewall "bricks." Chapter 10, "Other Key VPN Technologies," defines VPN and related terms with which you should be comfortable. Chapter 11, "Exploring VPN Security Policy Concepts," provides a bridge from concept to reality by featuring a vendor's actual security management implementation. In the ensuing discussion, you learn how to build a centralized security policy using "rule-base logic" through a GUI interface. The rule base establishes the centralized security policy, which is the framework through which firewall gateways handle data and application policing. Chapter 12, "VPN Performance Considerations and Review," focuses on VPN performance tips and the impact of inherent features of firewall architecture on performance. After reading this part, you will possess a strong working knowledge of VPN technology and understand the significance of building an effective rule-based security policy. You will also see the potential of VPN solutions relative to your own circumstances.

Part 4 focuses on business assessment guidelines that may be used to qualify need areas potentially suited for a VPN solution. Chapter 13, "VPN Implementations: Evaluating Your Business Needs," provides an extensive set of guidelines for the MIS professional. The guidelines walk you through an evaluation of the areas necessary for a successful VPN implementation. Chapter 14, "VPN Business Assessment: Multinational and Large Companies," and Chapter 15, "VPN Business Assessment: Small and Medium Companies," provide guidelines for both MIS and nontechnical executive-level managers. Application of the guidelines will enable you to express business requirements in terms that are easily mapped to VPN alternatives.

Part 5 presents an in-depth look at a variety of vendor solutions available today. Chapter 16, "The Playing Field," is an extensive overview of competing VPN solutions. This section focuses on such critical information as the degree to which standards are incorporated in vendor solutions. Competitive comparison tables are also given to facilitate a review of VPN offerings. The last two chapters, Chapter 17, "Let's Configure a Firewall," and Chapter 18, "Let's Configure a VPN," will walk the reader through the configuration of a firewall and a VPN, respectively. The featured product suite is the popular, Check Point VPN-1, by Software Technologies.

Intended Audience

IT Manager's Guide to Virtual Private Networks is intended for anyone who is interested in leveraging the Internet for enterprisewide communications. This includes chief information officers, MIS professionals, business executives, and consultants employed in small businesses or in medium, large, or multinational corporations. Decision makers at the federal, state, and local government levels are included, as well as associations and other institutions.

Chief Information Officers (CIO) As a CIO, you will find this book very valuable, particularly if you have decision-making authority and responsibility for overall information technology policy and infrastructure for the entire enterprise. You will also find *IT Manager's Guide to Virtual Private Networks* advantageous if enhancing competitiveness and improving information services to both internal users and clients are important strategic objectives.

Executive/Departmental Managers VPN solutions are expressly designed for enterprise organizations that provide sales and marketing, finance, human resources, and manufacturing. If you are an executive-level manager or department head, this book reveals the potential benefits of VPN solutions to your organization. The subject matter is covered in a straightforward, noncryptic manner, which enables you to attain various levels of knowledge, from rudimentary to comprehensive.

MIS/IT Managers For those with direct responsibility for enforcing IT policy and managing corporate IT initiatives, this book introduces you to everything you need to know about VPNs. As a MIS manager, you have the unenviable task of translating business requirements into IT support systems, evaluating the impact of the new solution on the organization, and implementing and managing the technology expansion. If providing secure communications for a mobile workforce, remote offices, or business partners are among your many challenges, this book demonstrates how to meet these and other related challenges with VPN solutions.

System Analysts/Project Managers Systems analysts and project managers have the same interests as MIS managers, and for this rea-

Introduction

son, they will benefit from the full exposition of this subject matter. If you are in this category, most likely you work directly with the tools. The how-to chapters and sections show you what's involved in working with VPN development interfaces.

How This Book Is Organized

IT Manager's Guide to Virtual Private Networks is composed of seven sections: an introduction, five parts consisting of 18 chapters, and an appendix.

Introduction. The Introduction covers intended audience, scope, how the book should be utilized, and conventions employed in the book.

Part 1. Part 1 includes the first three chapters of the book (for chapter headings, please refer to "About This Book," above). This section provides an overview, with philosophical undertones, of the evolution of intranets to virtual private networks. Why VPNs will flourish is discussed next, followed by a complete overview of emerging and de facto standards.

Part 2. Consisting of Chapters 4 through 6, Part 2 delivers a comprehensive overview of hacker attack strategies and techniques and several anecdotes of actual hacker exploits. This section also recommends practical courses of action when firewalls are breached. Web site addresses concerned with firewall security issues are also given.

Part 3. "Going Under the Hood" is the heart of the book. This section, which encompasses Chapters 7 through 12, covers the technology of VPNs from A to Z. It also includes a comprehensive discussion of firewall technology, followed by an insightful review of how firewall systems are utilized to build a centralized security policy. Performance issues are also fully reviewed.

Part 4. This section, Chapters 13, 14, and 15, begins with several case examples geared to challenge and reinforce your knowledge of VPN applications. The reader is also given a comprehensive set of guidelines, categorized by organization size, to assess specific requirements for implementing a VPN.

Part 5. In the final section, which includes Chapters 16, 17, and 18, vendor VPN solutions are reviewed relative to important criteria such as architecture employed, standards supported (encryption and authentication), administration of security policy, ease of use, and so on. This section will also demonstrate how a firewall and VPN are configured.

The featured vendor solution is Check Point Technologies' VPN-1, one of the most popular VPN solutions in the marketplace.

Appendix. This section features a communications primer on a variety of related topics, such as asynchronous transmission mode (ATM), distributed file system protocols, frame relay, gateways, integrated services digital network (ISDN), and networks.

Glossary. The glossary includes many terms you are likely to encounter when working with VPNs.

How to Use This Book

The chapters in this book are thoughtfully presented in order to accommodate various reading styles. Thus, the chapters can be read in succession, or they can be read randomly, as computer books often are. The chapters of each part have been written to be independent of one another. However, for any given chapter, references to information in other chapters are provided when necessary to grasp the topic at hand.

The MIS manager would find it beneficial to read the entire book. When this is not feasible, an MIS manager would find it especially useful to assess the potential of working with an *actual* VPN solution. Chapter 11, "Exploring VPN Security Policy Concepts," and Chapters 16, 17, and 18 focus on popular vendor offerings currently available in the marketplace. These chapters demonstrate how to build a centralized security policy and how to configure a firewall and VPN through the product's graphical user interface. In addition to these chapters, an MIS manager would also be interested in the same chapters that are preferred by CIOs and executives.

System analysts, project managers, and related MIS professionals work directly with technology on a daily basis. Their interests, of course, are comparable to the MIS manager's. And like the MIS manager, the "how-to" Chapters of 11, 16, 17, and 18 should prove to be very advantageous.

Generally speaking, if you are a CIO or senior-level manager considering the power of the Internet for an enterprisewide, communication backbone, there are several chapters to bring to your attention. An area of key concern for a given technology is the maturation and implementation of standards. Standards ensure interoperability, protection of investment, and the ability to choose the best-fit solution from a variety of choices. For a comprehensive review of VPN standards, Chapter 3, "De Facto and Emerging Standards," should be at the top of your list of must-read chapters. For a detailed review of VPN and firewall technology, refer to Chapters 7 and 8. Chapter 11, "Managing an Enterprise Security Policy," is another must-review section. This section enables you to envision the impact of implementing a centralized security policy on your network. Last but not least, a CIO will also find Chapter 12, "VPN Performance Considerations," equally important.

Executive managers may be required to provide an assessment of their organization for inclusion into an overall business plan. If you are an executive with this challenge, turn to Chapters 1 and 2 for an insightful overview and to Chapters 13 and 14 for guidelines to assess departmental requirements. Part 2 (Chapters 4, 5, and 6) is useful to appreciate the risks involved when the Internet is used or planned for the communication backbone of an organization. Finally, a review of Chapters 7 and 8, on VPN and firewall technology, provides departmental managers with the background to talk intelligently with IT managers about VPNs.

DAVID LEON CLARK

ACKNOWLEDGMENTS

Many thanks to Mr. Mathew Davis of the International Society of Performance Improvement, Washington, DC; Ms. Barbara Rose, ICSA, Carlisle, PA; and Mr. Russ Cooper, NT BugTraq Web Site, for your enthusiastic support and expeditious turnaround of permission letters. A special thanks to Ms. Allison Green of Check Point Software Technologies of Redwood City, CA for your thoughtful recommendations and expediency in providing materials for this project.

Also, thanks to my loving wife, Mrs. Stanlyn R. Clark, for the long hours spent editing the manuscript.

From Intranets to Extranets to Virtual Private Networks: A Virtual Evolution

First came LANs, then WANs and now intranets. An intranet is an internal network created from the strategic implementation of certain local area network (LAN) and *Internet* functionality. The internet by default is a WAN. Therefore, an intranet could be either a LAN supporting a few or many users as well as an enterprise WAN supporting thousands of users across a wide geographical area. Think of an intranet as a *private* internet dedicated to an organization's exclusive use. In this part, we explore the important features that makes intranets so attractive. We also look at the environmental forces and chronology of events, which forged the way to this remarkable phenomenon. Next, the metamorphosis of intranets to extranets is discussed along with the implications for security. When security becomes the focal point, characteristics and features of private networks and virtual private networks (VPNs) are compared, paving the way to the feasibility of VPNs as a strategic, enterprise wide communications backbone.

Part 1 also makes the case for why VPNs are here to stay by exploring the political and technical developments that are carving their place as a viable network communications system. Finally, de facto and emerging standards are reviewed in depth to provide insight into the legitimacy of VPNs as a mainstream system.

1

Private Networks vs. Virtual Private Networks:

EXPLORING NETWORK SECURITY

Over a decade and a half ago, enterprises began experiencing unprecedented forces in business environments. The traditional business model and the legacy systems that were so effective in the 1960s and 1970s were no longer effective in delivering mission-critical information in a timely manner. Confronted with evolutionary change, embattled business communities set out on a journey of rediscovery that culminated in a global economy. In this chapter, the evolutionary trends that changed the business communities and led them to new vistas of information systems are explored in detail.

Legacy Systems and the LAN Paradigm

Local area networks (LANs) came into their own in the mid-1980s. Corporate America was looking for ways to distribute processing power to workgroups that were strategically positioned throughout their organizations. Legacy systems composed of imposing mainframes, monolithic databases, and static text-based user interfaces were no longer responsive to the diverse needs of a newly emerging business culture. They were ideal for supporting static, repetitive processes such as double-entry accounting, human resource management, production control, and inventory management. However, like an unending water supply through a sieve, this new culture required information on all fronts. The processes of legacy systems rendered them largely ineffective in meeting the information demands of this new culture. LANs, on the other hand, were the ideal information system. Processing power was distributed to where it was needed most: Workgroups were able to access and process information on demand, share the results with management and peers, and determine the best-possible course of action in response to the requirements on hand.

The concept of the workgroup was visionary yet inevitable, given the evolution erupting in business environments. Gone were the days when businesses could sit back on their laurels and capture market share through the traditional business model, steadily grow the business, and live happily ever after. The traditional model prevailed upon certain recurring business conditions and practices:

1. *Marketplaces are relatively static.*   Uncertainty and risk caused by political influences, regulations, the competition, and lagging market demand are usually manageable within acceptable limits. Market trends and issues are routinely assessed and factored into the business strategy. Through risk management, success in the marketplace could be predicted with reasonable certainty. In other words, "business as usual."

2. *The mission and goals of the organization are the exclusive purview of executive management.*   Once the mission is established, the goals are set forth in a 3- to 5-year business plan formulated by senior management. The rank and file of the enterprise are not necessarily required to know the mission or enterprise-, or macro-, level goals to carry them out. Nor are they consulted for input. Subordinates are expected to execute executive mandates and policy whether the vision of executive management can be discerned or not.

3. *Departments operate within their own organizational silos.*   The interplay of forces within marketplaces tends to pose no threat to organizational infrastructures. The impact on subdivisions, operations, the chain of command, and lines of communication at best are negligible. Reorganizations are conducted in synch with the 3- to 5-year plan. Except for the periodic cross-organizational committee for special projects and capturing certain business opportunities, cross-organizational collaboration is not required for ongoing business operations and decision making. Other than the occasional change in leadership and normal attrition, organizations operate virtually unchanged year after year.

4. *The business culture maintains the status quo.* Professional staff and employees dutifully accept job responsibilities, seldom working "outside the box" or challenging uninspired, run-of-the-mill initiatives. Orders through the chain of command are received and followed like gospel. Productivity is measured more quantitatively than qualitatively. The speed with which enterprise management could harness corporate minions to go to market was the ultimate challenge. If arrival in the marketplace was a preemptive strike against the competition, the traditional model predicted a high probability of success.

5. *Information technology consists of the black-and-white world of legacy systems.* In the pre-workgroup era before distributed processing, the mainframe systems had their heyday. Their legacy, of course, is the monolithic databases. Some found their way into corporate archives, while others still anchor many of today's client/server applications. When one reflects on mainframe systems, huge rooms come into focus, filled with row after row of refrigerator-sized central processing units (CPUs), disk subsystems, and tape storage units humming away in a low-pitched drone with LEDs (light-emitting diodes) constantly flashing. High-speed line printers spit out line after line of black text on white or green bar paper to form massive computer printouts that eventually found their way to various department heads for tedious highbrow analysis. The data-processing shop controlled the information machine, placing it firmly in control of corporate fortunes, or lack thereof. The DP manager possessed great influence and wielded power more like a corporate czar than a department head. The ability to make routine decisions was often tied to the completed analysis of telephone-sized computer printouts.

    If additional information was required outside the scope of the department's regular computer run, department heads submitted formal information requests to the "czar." If "batch jobs" or "adhoc queries" could fulfill the information request, the information would be provided in days or weeks, depending upon where you were in the queue. If, however, more complex analysis was required to derive the necessary information, an additional application would be built. The application development process included design, coding, testing, debugging, compiling, and finally production; a process that could expend 6 to 9 months, especially for the larger applications. If too many information requests came in, preventing the DP shop from fulfilling any one in a timely fashion, unfulfilled requests would be backlogged. Department heads patiently waited for their backlogged enhancements or applications, making certain not to upset the "czar" when routine status reports were requested.

The Traditional Business Model: The End of an Era

Until the mid-1980s, the traditional business model was the archetypal business framework. Unfortunately, the traditional model could not sustain itself, because evolutionary conditions began forcing crucial imbalances. The most significant trend was that markets were no longer static. "Business as usual" was conducted at greater risk to organizations. Companies began to discover that product life cycles were shorter, markets were becoming saturated from competition, market shares were remaining constant or shrinking, and overall growth was stunted or tapering off. As if this wasn't bad enough, companies that were ahead of the curve in their business analysis started moving into nontraditional marketplaces. The opening of auto repair centers by Sears and Roebuck is a classic example. Another example was when AT&T moved into the PC market. These early telltale trends were a foreshadowing of the megamergers, huge divestitures, massive layoffs, and unprecedented product and services diversification efforts that are commonplace in the business world today.

Redefining the Business World: A Manic Moment

When traditional marketplaces started evolving, businesses reacted in a traditional way. Prices were slashed, new products were developed and rushed to market, new and improved versions of established products were released, advertising budgets were increased, marketing staffs were fortified, and sales efforts were increased. However, when none of these heretofore proven strategies resulted in increased or acceptable return on investment (ROI), obviously something unprecedented and perplexing was occurring in changing business arenas.

Overall, enterprises reacted in disarray. Executive management intervened and mandated what seemed like new requirements to department heads. What was *really* happening in markets? Apparently, new dynamics were under way; what were they and what could be done in response? How would they impact the enterprise? What strategies should be instituted to become more competitive? Should we expand into new markets? With these new mandates, executive management was sowing the seeds of a new paradigm shift, a shift from the traditional business model to something more appropriate for the changing times. After receiving these orders, mid-level managers knew something momentous was happening. The traditional model was failing, so a new framework for conducting business was critical, to say the least. New information was needed, sooner rather than later. Consequently, enterprises turned to the corporate information czar, the DP manager.

The DP Manager: From Corporate Czar to Scapegoat

DP shops were inundated with information requests, and the average backlog grew to $2\frac{1}{2}$ years. Almost overnight, the DP manager had gone from a hero of sorts to a corporate scapegoat. In fairness to the DP manager, the inability to fulfill information requests was not so much incompetence as it was an inherent drawback of legacy systems. The application development process of designing, coding, testing, debugging, and compiling was too procedurally-oriented and time-consuming to provide timely responses to the critical information requests of embattled middle management. Even if the DP shop succeeded in placing a new application into service, the rigid process precluded new features from being added in a timely manner. Eventually, the business world and, reluctantly, the data-processing community accepted the sobering reality that mainframes and related systems were too process-oriented and inflexible to keep pace with the information demands of an evolving business community. Fortunately for the business world, the personal computer had arrived.

LANs: A New Information System Paradigm

The personal computer made its debut in the late 1970s for primarily scientific and engineering applications. It only began to flourish after the IBM PC was introduced in 1981. By 1987, all domestic PC makers shipped a staggering 5,460,000 units. With all the PCs in place on desktops and the maturation of local area networking technology and multi-user software, department managers believed that LANs were the potential critical link to migrate an embattled business culture to a new work paradigm. The new business culture demanded strategic information in a timely manner whether they were in the field, headquarters, the warehouse, the shop floor, or at a customer site. LANs provided computing resources at the point of need and the flexibility to support dynamic information requirements on an ongoing basis. Work teams could easily share information, collaborate on critical tasks, provide crucial input to important projects, and derive mutually acceptable recommendations for management.

LANs were also found to be scalable. When work teams added individuals from within or outside of their departments, the expansion was easily handled. Adding a new user to a LAN was a snap. It merely required installing a network interface card (NIC) to a PC to create a workstation (client), which in turn was connected to the information repository (server) via the network's cabling scheme. To complete the process, the administrator would add the new user, or users to an existing user domain or create a new one if necessary. The appropriate LAN applications would be made available to the new users, and the expanded team would be good to go.

The advent of the LAN and its successful implementation earmarked a new era in information systems and the genesis of a new business model. The new information system charged the business climate with a new resolve, providing a platform upon which enterprises could again pin their hopes, pursue their ambitions, and realize their goals. It also regenerated work processes, and in doing so, favorably impacted the organization at all levels. Workgroups acquired the means to *perform* their jobs in business environments being shaped by uncertainty. Executives *performed* their responsibilities with renewed vigor in the face of dynamic, ever-changing markets. Decisions could be made with greater confidence and resolve because the new information system propagated strategic information in a timely manner. The mission and goals of the organization could also be "tweaked" whenever new information suggested that such action was warranted due to current economic indicators. Moreover, mid-level managers *performed* duties with greater acceptance and a heightened awareness of leadership responsibilities, because in the new reality, the means to mine the intellectual capital within organizations were at their fingertips. They also could collaborate with their peers to commission cross-functional teams if present requirements so dictated.

The Performance Model Unveiled

A new business framework was heralded when human resources could again *perform* their respective duties and achieve desired results in response to an evolving business world. This framework was aptly called the *performance model.* (See Table 1-1 for a summary comparison of

TABLE 1-1   Comparison of Strategic Business Model Characteristics.

	Traditional Model	Performance Model	Learning Model
Markets	Static. "Business as usual" ■ Competition main focus ■ Mergers, acquisitions an irregular trend ■ Risk and uncertainty assessed with reasonable effort	Dynamic. Characterized by unprecedented change ■ Mergers and acquisitions, shortened product life cycles, competition appeared from new and nontraditional players ■ Assessment of risk and uncertainty critical to success	Dynamic. Forces of change constant. ■ Megamergers, divestitures, competition from non-traditional players, joint ventures, market dissolution, etc. ■ Risk and uncertainty difficult to assess
Mission and Goals	*Mission:* ■ Defined by executive consensus ■ Based on historical data, market niche, and financial results *Goals:* ■ Formulated by department heads ■ Subordinates consulted primarily in planning stages ■ Occasionally out of synch with the mission of the organization	*Mission:* ■ Established after top-level management collaboration and buy-in ■ Based on current market conditions and anticipation of future trends and developments ■ Modified whenever warranted by business conditions *Goals:* ■ Formulated after critical executive-level review ■ Subordinates are required for routine input after related analysis ■ Established to support the mission	*Mission:* ■ Established after reconciliation of formal external and internal research, executive collaboration and buy-in ■ Based on current market conditions and impact of competition from non-traditional players ■ Depends upon a comprehensive assessment of current risk factors and uncertainty ■ Routinely modified as a strategic requirement *Goals:* ■ Formulated by top managers after all levels of organization conduct business review sessions

Chapter 1: Private Networks vs. Virtual Private Networks

1 1

TABLE 1-1 Continued.

	Traditional Model	Performance Model	Learning Model
			■ Constantly reviewed and modified to account for current business conditions ■ Strongly tied to mission of organization
Strategy	■ Traditional ■ First to market ■ To increase sales, increase promotion/sales staff ■ If strong competition, decrease prices ■ Stay the course if products are profitable, increase advertising for less-profitable, products ■ Increase ROI, employ more resources	■ Evaluate prior period's sales results and future market potential ■ Invest if good market potential; divest if poor ■ Eliminate unprofitable products or services ■ Diversify product mix if market potential exists ■ Expand into new or nontraditional markets if feasible ■ Utilize merger or acquisition to achieve goals ■ Improve profitability, cut costs (e.g., downsize, layoff, spin off assets, reorganize)	■ Sales results barometer of success; if product is profitable, stay the course, if not, change product or go to new market ■ Alternative or potential markets constantly reviewed for entry ■ New markets routinely tested domestically and internationally ■ Unprofitable products and services expediently eliminated ■ Expansion into international markets routine ■ Merger and acquisitions routinely sought to achieve goals ■ To improve profitability/ROI, *rightsizing* routinely employed (e.g., layoffs, divestitures)
Organization	■ Vertical structure with many layers ■ Management and professional staff function mainly within own "silos" ■ Directives/initiatives typically top-down	■ Flatter, fewer layers; matrix structure often implemented ■ Cross-functional management teams ■ Departmental workgroups	■ Matrix structure prototypical implementation ■ Organizations operate as strategic entities or not at all ■ Strategic management teams ■ Cross-functional workgroups
Enterprise Culture	■ Chain of command rarely challenged ■ Directives followed like gospel ■ Maintain status quo ■ Productivity measured by volume of work processed	■ Performance explicitly tied to achieving mission and goals ■ Creative performance awarded ■ Perform responsibilities and tasks creatively and expediently	■ Learning organization ■ Entrepreneurial thinking preferred and awarded ■ Management-led strategic work teams drive the enterprise ■ Professional staff expected to work "outside the box"

TABLE 1-1   Comparison of Strategic Business Model Characteristics (Continued).

	Traditional Model	Performance Model	Learning Model
		■ Management institute creative challenges to stimulate staff ■ Workgroups complete tasks with greater sense of purpose	■ Cross-functional teams standard practice ■ International influences apparent
Technology Platform	■ Mainframe computers, legacy databases, character-based user interfaces ■ Process-oriented, very methodical ■ Character-based non-intelligent user interfaces	■ PCs and personal user software ■ LANs/WANs and multi-user software (groupware) ■ LANs/WANs flexible and scalable ■ GUIs ■ Legacy systems	■ Client/server (sometimes legacy-anchored) ■ Private networks, intranets, Internet ■ Object-oriented multiuser workgroup and database software ■ Multimedia-based software (e.g. HTML, Java)
Information System	■ Centralized data processing ■ Repetitive work processes automated ■ Geared toward heavy routine analysis ■ Information may or may not have time criticality	■ Distributed data processing ■ Provides strategic information at the point of need ■ Supports timely decision making ■ Information routinely time-critical	■ Strategic distributed data processing ■ Strategic information provided globally ■ Available to mobile and remote workforce ■ Available to suppliers, business partners, and perhaps clients ■ Time criticality of information routinely urgent

business models.) In contrast to the traditional model, the performance model operated on the principle of human resource improvement. The die was cast as the paradigm shifted from the traditional model to the performance model. However, it proved to be a sure bet encompassing new ideas, new cultures, new organizations, new resolve, and new market flexibility. As the performance model became firmly entrenched and the focus shifted to performance, a new technology was spawned called *performance technology*.

Performance technology represented a new way of thinking for a new economic era being defined by rapid and unprecedented change. It is the systematic, iterative approach to improving productivity and competence in the workforce to achieve strategic goals of the enterprise. The definitive processes of performance technology consist of performance analysis, cause analysis, and resolution analysis.

Performance Analysis

Performance technology, oddly enough, begins with performance analysis. The first step in performance analysis is defining critical performance requirements relative to an organization's mission and goals. This is a crucial step because without a full account of requisite performance drivers, the organization places its mission and goals in double jeopardy. In order to identify these requirements, the review process begins with the organization's capabilities. The capabilities are thoroughly evaluated to pinpoint current or anticipated deficiencies in workforce performance or competence. The next step, and the critical focus of this particular analysis, involves deriving *two* specific depictions of the workforce.

The first derivation of the workforce describes the *desired* state, or state of achievement. This is a full account, including baseline, of the desired level of competencies and capabilities the workforce should possess to implement the strategy for achieving enterprise mission and objectives. The other derivation, the *actual* state, describes the level of competency in the workforce as it currently exists. The difference between these two states is known as the *performance gap*. The performance gap represents the current or anticipated performance problems that place the mission and objectives at risk. In other words, the performance gap represents an opportunity for performance improvement. Consequently, the ultimate goal of performance technology is to close or remove this gap in the most cost-effective manner.

Cause Analysis

The second phase in performance technology entails *cause analysis*. After the performance gap is identified, the next critical steps seek to identify why the gap exists by isolating the important factors that inhibit desired workforce performance. Before performance technology, solutions to performance problems failed to realize their anticipated goals because such interventions treated only visible symptoms, rather than underlying, deep-rooted causes. Cause analysis is the most vital cog in the performance technology machine because it uncovers and identifies deep-rooted causes. Uncovering such root barriers presents the highest probability of reducing or eliminating performance problems in the workplace. Types of barriers include lack of information or feedback, inability to access strategic applications remotely, ineffective sales or marketing support, or few or no point-of-need job aids. When the barriers to performance are identified, the finding provides the crucial bridge to the next phase of performance technology: the resolution.

Resolution Analysis

Performance technology is inherently a systematic approach to uncovering performance requirements inside the *entire* organization. The real strength of performance technology lies in the fact that every single organizational enclave is channeled through the performance technology apparatus. Therefore, any anticipated *resolution* would naturally be a comprehensive and integrated response to performance difficulties and their causes. At the risk of understating its impact, resolution *analysis* produces a multifaceted, multidimensional solution to enterprisewide deficiencies in workforce performance and competence. In the parlance of performance technology, the performance gap and its causes would be addressed and resolved on every organizational level. Moreover, the process is iterative. Therefore, whenever the mission and goals of the organization change, the routine application of "the apparatus" synthesizes the proper resolution. (See Figure 1-1.) The *post-traditional* business world grasped the process so readily because the success, or lack thereof, was effectively measured in terms of performance improvements and organizational results. The by-products of the new technology were innovative thinking, collaborative cultures, flatter organizations, agile workforces, and new market approaches in the face of dynamic, ever-changing business environments.

Whenever organizational challenges occurred, the performance technology process was the key to ensuring that the workforce was ready to meet them head on. However, there were costs associated with the process and with the development and implementation of the resolution. In fact, cost was a key issue of performance technology, especially in the initial transition period, when a resolution involving the retooling of human resources alone, for example, could require a host of interventions. (See Figure 1-2.) If the evolution in marketplaces would have somehow inexplicably halted, causing business conditions to revert back to the traditional ways, and then just as inexplicably, they resumed again, the application of performance technology would have been an expensive proposition, indeed. So expensive that it would not have

Performance Technology

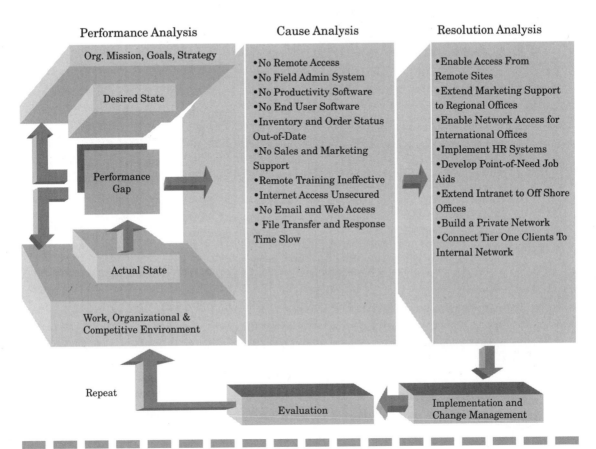

Performance Analysis

- Org. Mission, Goals, Strategy
- Desired State
- Performance Gap
- Actual State
- Work, Organizational & Competitive Environment

Cause Analysis

- No Remote Access
- No Field Admin System
- No Productivity Software
- No End User Software
- Inventory and Order Status Out-of-Date
- No Sales and Marketing Support
- Remote Training Ineffective
- Internet Access Unsecured
- No Email and Web Access
- File Transfer and Response Time Slow

Resolution Analysis

- Enable Access From Remote Sites
- Extend Marketing Support to Regional Offices
- Enable Network Access for International Offices
- Implement HR Systems
- Develop Point-of-Need Job Aids
- Extend Intranet to Off Shore Offices
- Build a Private Network
- Connect Tier One Clients To Internal Network

Repeat

Evaluation

Implementation and Change Management

Figure 1-1   Performance technology.

evolved into a feasible business framework. The fact remains, however, that once the riptide of rapid and unprecedented change had set in, it never receded. The performance model was not a finger in the dike of change, but essentially an evolutionary, if not revolutionary, catalyst for enterprise metamorphosis.

The performance model was precisely what was needed to enable enterprises to effect the changes needed internally to deal with changes encountered externally. Performance improvements and organizational enhancements were inherently permanent, because performance technology remodeled the enterprise infrastructure, processes, culture,

Performance Technology

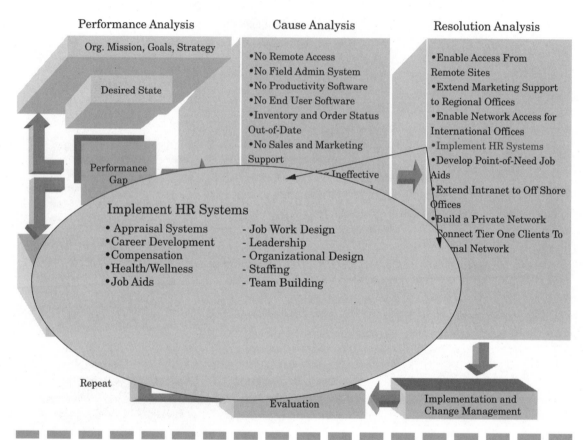

Figure 1-2   Multiple HR systems interventions.

interrelationships, and markets. After each iteration of the process, the resulting incarnation of the organization seemingly operated with greater resilience and efficiency. Resolutions to reduce or eliminate performance gaps in subsequent iterations could be potentially implemented more cost-effectively than previous ones. In other words, the performance model enabled enterprises to reinvent themselves as often as needed, in a cost-effective manner, even if the process required several applications of performance technology over as many business cycles. The point is that the performance model thrived upon implemen-

Chapter 1: Private Networks vs. Virtual Private Networks

17

tation of the most cost-effective solutions. If a potential resolution was believed to be too expensive, then it simply was not implemented.

The New Paradigm in Action

Theoretically, if the enterprise successfully transitioned from the traditional model to the performance model and the culture performed close to the desired state for several business cycles, then design, development, and implementation of subsequent resolutions to new performance problems, by association, should also prove to be cost-effective. You would think a process that encompassed the entire organization would be too massive an undertaking to pull off time and time again, especially with the relentless forces of change lurking ominously just outside the enterprise door. It probably would have been too unwieldy if not for an underlying integral component of performance technology: *the learning system*. The success of performance technology was directly tied to the robustness of the learning system. Performance management could design and implement resolutions to their heart's content. But if the workforce did not gain the skills to incorporate the new interventions in their daily activities, performance improvements would have remained a pipe dream. Furthermore, the focus of the learning system was also required to evolve.

The traditional model treated training as a discrete, one-time event. In contrast, the performance model learning system, or learning model, approached learning as an ongoing process. Therefore, the learning system should be dynamic, in order to create the skill sets of the workforce in a timely manner. It should also be comprehensive, offering a range of training services for consistency and continuity throughout the learning process. And, most importantly, the learning system should be flexible, providing "just-in-time training" at multiple points of delivery.

In the critical transition years when enterprises were migrating from the traditional model over to the performance model, an outstanding learning system was the key driver to performance improvements and acceptable organizational results. The effects of the learning system, under the auspices of performance technology, produced new vistas for organizational growth and achievement. For one thing, a "knowledge" culture was emerging, primed for working "outside the box" and tackling new challenges induced by the rapid forces of change. The performance model culture *learned* to collaborate effectively across flatter organizations. They also *learned* to streamline processes by eliminating those that were not mission-critical or strategic. Modifying the mission and goals based upon ever-changing business conditions was also *learned*. They ultimately *learned* how to reinvent themselves expediently and effectively. Today, this phenomenon is known as a *learning organization*. (See Table 1-1.)

The Learning Organization

The current incarnation of the performance model is the learning organization. A learning organization is characterized by the rapid acquisition and dissemination of information for the purpose of achieving a competitive advantage in dynamic markets. In the culture of a learning organization, employees approach their responsibilities with an entrepreneurial spirit of creativity. They are more accepting of organizational challenges and constantly seeking innovations to resolve them. The business processes are routinely reengineered to support the current mission and objectives of the enterprise. In markets the convergence of international and domestic forces influence enterprises to confront rapid and unprecedented change in a global arena.

A critical benefit and strategic advantage of a learning organization is an agile workforce. The psychology of the agile workforce is by and large creative, collaborative, incisive, proactive, responsive, and persistent. Sustaining such an ideal culture is directly correlated with an effective information machine. Global forces are moving so rapidly that deploying an effective information system is indeed a daunting challenge. Technologies come and go as quickly as a pilot ejecting from a disabled jet fighter. However, the scrutiny and introspection of the agile workforce suggest that the answer somehow lies within computer networking. Ever since LANs and WANs graced the computing world with their evolutionary benefits, networks of various flavors and functionality have been deployed by informationally challenged enterprises. Intranets, extranets, private networks, the Internet, and virtual private networks are the latest of a series of strategic networking implementations that are driving corporate information machines. The balance of this chapter will explore the character and functionality of these information systems, concluding with a transition into the fascinating world of virtual private networks.

Private Networks: Fortresses of Solitude

Private networks are the antithesis of the Internet. Private network use and deployment is expensive; the Internet is not. Private networks are secure, while the Internet is notoriously insecure. Private networks guarantee performance and a level of reliability. The Internet guarantees redundancy (which supposedly would allow it to survive a nuclear attack) and availability. Private networks support multiple WAN protocols; the Internet supports only TCP/IP. Private networks are exclusive, rigid, not easily scalable—a veritable fortress of solitude. The Internet is ubiquitous, flexible, and easily scalable (with VPN technology), with virtually unlimited potential. Taken together, they are the yin and yang of wide area computer networking, where private networks represent the yang. In other words, if private networks are good and desirable, the Internet is the flip side of the same coin. In actuality, the Internet has as much to do with luring businesses to create and adopt private networks as do the benefits of these networks.

Business offices first began accessing the Internet between 1987 and 1989. In 1987, the National Science Foundation (NSF) assumed responsibility for managing the Net's backbone. At this time, the network became known worldwide as the "Internet." The advent of key technologies, such as the introduction of the World Wide Web (WWW) in 1989 and hypertext markup language (HTML) in 1991, fueled the steady acceptance of the Internet by the business community. Gaining commercial support for the NSF-managed backbone was also a contributing factor. By 1995, the use of the Internet by businesses took off. Businesses came calling with great expectations. But almost as quickly as it began, use of the Internet for commerce by many businesses came to a screeching halt. What happened? The hacker. Initially, problems centered on almost innocuous-sounding breaches called "macro viruses," which caused application programs to perform erratically. With greater defiance, hackers initiated exploits that included unauthorized network access, the commandeering of files, illegal funds transfer, various other crimes, and, finally, outright destruction of enterprise data. (Hacker exploits will be covered in greater detail in Part II.)

Today, new viruses are unleashed on the Internet at a rate greater than 200 per month. Coupled with the various classes of hacker attacks and computer crime, the Internet has earned tremendous publicity for security issues. The Internet has become safe through basic encryption for certain electronic commerce (e-commerce). Consumer transactions, such as home banking or retail purchasing of items such as books, music, clothes, computer components, and software are virtually safe. Unfortunately, the secure environment that many businesses need for confidential business-to-business transactions until now did not exist. While awaiting no small miracle of acceptable Internet security, enterprises continue to invest in separate networking facilities for their exclusive use, or private networks. The bottom line is that enterprises had initially cast off their ships of good hope in the vast, seemingly tranquil waters of the Internet, but they were roundly attacked. Now they are seeking more definitive accommodations in private waters.

Private Networks Defined

Private networks are wide area networks (WANs) that connect geographically dispersed LANs, usually between a central office and branch offices and/or remote PC clients in home offices. The connection is usually a main telecommunication line or a backbone consisting of leased lines or dedicated fiber. LAN-to-LAN or point-to-point connections are sometimes handled by frame relay. Ironically, private networks share the same telecommunications infrastructure as the Internet. However, private network lines cost considerably more than standard telephone lines because they are configured for higher speeds and greater bandwidth. Private networks also require another crucial infrastructure component called a *private dial-in access system,* which resides at the central site. Access systems include communication servers, modem banks, and toll-free telephone numbers. Access to the private network from remote locations can be accommodated by standard dial-up or digital telephone lines such as ISDN (Integrated Services Digital Network) or DSL (Digital Subscriber Line) lines. Private networks can be maintained directly by an enterprise or an ISP such as UUNET, CompuServe, GTE, or MCI Communications. (See Figure 1-3.)

Higher performance, speed, and security are obvious advantages of a private network. Private networks also support a variety of protocols such as frame relay, Asynchronous Transmission Mode (ATM), and TCP/IP as well. However, private networks can be incredibly expensive. A large enterprise planning to connect many offices located globally via a fiber-optic telecommunications backbone can literally spend hundreds of million dollars on the resulting private network. Private networks as

Private Network
Fortress of Solitude

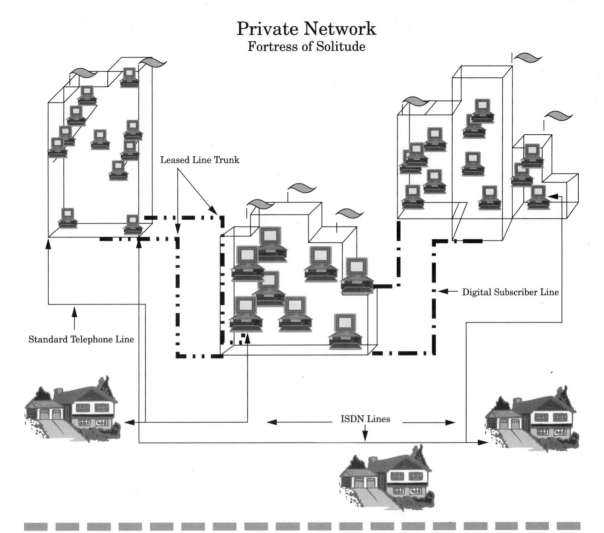

Figure 1-3 Private networking.

fortresses of solitude is a fitting metaphor because once established, they often prove to be too unwieldy and expensive in bringing new locations, business partners, suppliers, or international concerns online.

For example, network hardware such as modems, ISDN switches, and frame relay circuits are constantly being enhanced and upgraded by common carriers. And DSL technology is maturing to the point where they can become a viable alternative for private networks that cover a geographic area the size of a college campus. Similarly, software is also upgraded from time to time. The initial implementation and subsequent upgrades can be tedious and require major effort in terms of human resources and funding. ISDN lines from home offices, for example, can run from $35 to $150 per month depending upon where you live in the United States. ISDN configuration is also very tricky. Although the telephone company from which it was purchased normally configures ISDNs, many markets may not have expertise readily available. In this case, support from a consultant may be required. Point-to-point frame relay connections can run $2000 to $4000 installed and $300 to $500 per month. Installation and monthly fees for leased-line trunks can cost twice as much as frame relay. Adding to the hairiness of private network management is staying abreast of periodic increases of tariffs on a global basis and carrier-competitive offerings.

Private Networking with ISPs

Using an ISP to manage your private network may eliminate the management headaches. However, the cost could still run pretty high. ISP's offerings also include service guarantees for reliability, availability, and quality of service. Such service guarantees are offered at a premium over the standard offering. The biggest disadvantage in dealing with an ISP is that you run the risk of being captive to a single provider. For example, say you use ISP A for frame relay services for your LANs. You want to bring on a business partner located in another part of the country online. However, ISP A does not have a point of presence in that part of the country. Or, worse yet, your partner prefers to go with ISP B for frame relay service. To date there is no automatic or streamlined mechanism, including devices and agreements, for connecting frame relay services between two separate ISPs. This may be available in the not-too-distant distant future, but for now it's feasible to stay with one ISP or carrier.

Thus, whether you build the private network on your own or go with an ISP/common carrier, this is an expensive proposition. Furthermore, even with such potentially horrific financial outlays required for private networks, if the network is exposed to the Internet, the entire private network is at risk to hacker attacks. Although the telecommunications infrastructure is relatively secure, this is not enough to withstand hackers if further precautions are not exercised. This may sound like a poor attempt at humor, given the amount of money that can be shelled out for a private network. Unfortunately, this is no joke. The money you spend should also include other defenses such as a firewall; otherwise, the private network deployed is still at risk to the wily hacker.

Firewalls and Other Perimeter Defenses

Depending upon which side of the fence you are on, a firewall could conjure up either a sense of intrigue, perhaps challenge, or it can impart a sense of security and confidence. A firewall is a gatekeeper, or the first line of defense for protecting an enterprise network from the inside and, especially, the outside of its electronic perimeter. Firewalls check user IDs and passwords of anyone attempting to gain access to the enterprise network from the outside. Firewalls enable access profiles to be established for each individual user. *Access profiles* are privileges to specific areas of the network that enable firewalls to "escort" individuals to the areas of the network that they are allowed to use. For example, a firewall may allow sales personnel dialing in through an outside laptop to access and download sales reports, but it may prevent those same employees from downloading inventory reports because they lack access rights to the information. Since it functions as a perimeter defense, a firewall should be positioned at every node where the network is exposed to the outside world, such as an Internet connection or a router that links a LAN to a WAN. (See Figure 1-4.)

Concentric Layers of Encryption   Firewalls are a suitable complement to the secure telecommunications channels of private networks. Together they provide a reasonable level of security. With firewalls installed, the resulting security walls are fairly high; unfortunately, however, they are not insurmountable. Firewalls rely primarily on passwords for user access. Therefore, the ability to keep out hackers is only as good as the system used for logging onto the network. Too often, the password requirements are much too simple. Given the option to choose a password, most people pick easy-to-guess birth dates, names of close relatives, or their favorite color, for instance. This presents as much deterrence to hackers as a glass door does to a burglar. To ensure maximum security potential, another line of defense should be added at the "front end" of the firewall to form, if you will, concentric layers of encryption. This second line of defense can be created with two-factor authentication methods and/or digital certificates.

Electronic Passports   Two-factor authentication is a user validation method that requires the user to possess a physical object, usually a device the size of a credit card, and something to commit to memory, such as a PIN (personal identification number) code. Usually the

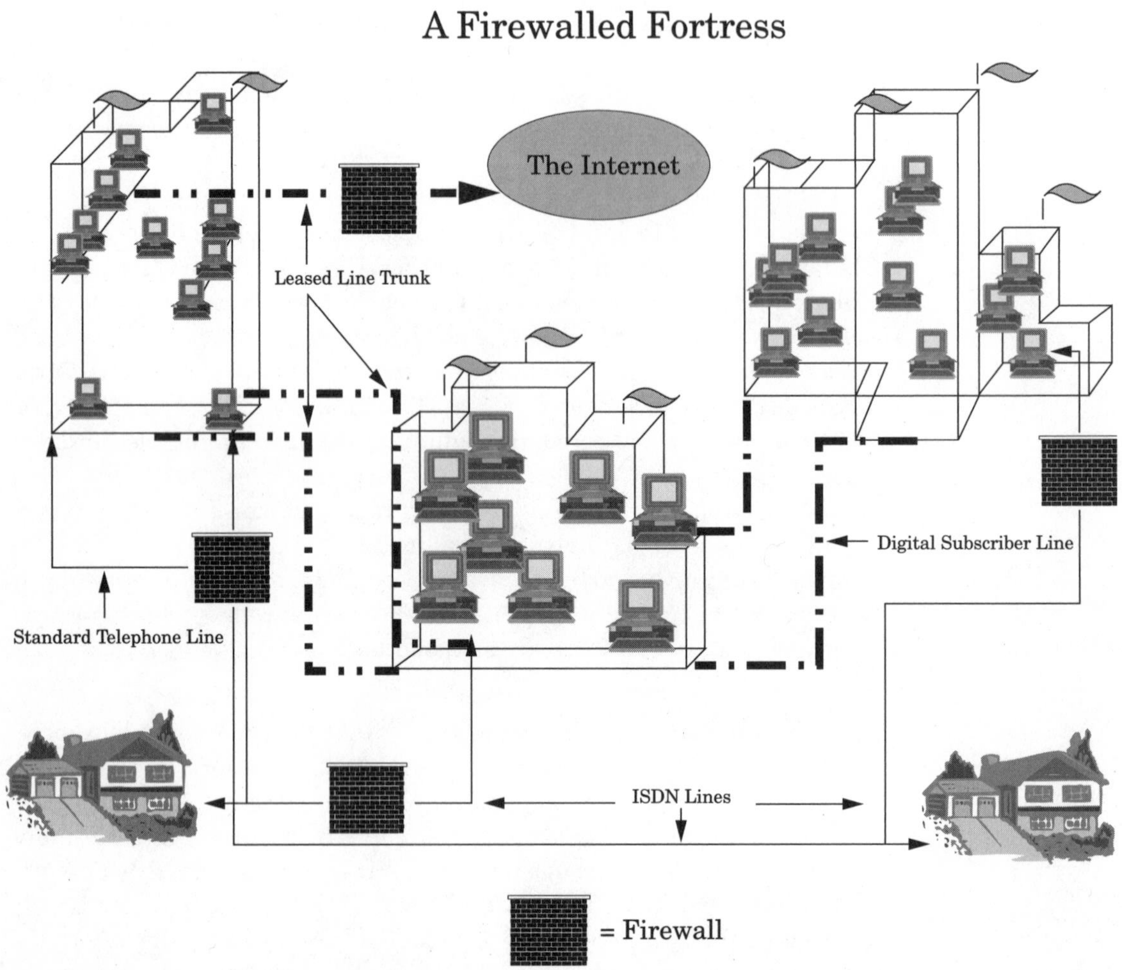

A Firewalled Fortress

Figure 1-4 Private network security.

authenticating card is an electronic device that either generates a new password over a certain time interval, say, every 60 seconds, automatically or when prompted to enter a special code provided by an authentication server behind the firewall. In both cases, the password device provides encrypted passwords, like VPN enabled firewalls, hence, the concentric layers of encryption. *Digital certificates* are effective because they are validated by a third party who has given the bearer of the certificate an unbiased certification of authenticity as to who the individual claims to be. Digital certificates may include additional functionality after authentication by restricting access to only certain areas of the network, much like a firewall. (More on user authentication methods in Chapter 3.)

The Price of Global Privacy

All things considered, a properly fortified private network offers one of the best security environments for business-to-business transactions in a global economy. As with any business decision, there are trade-offs; when considering implementing a secure private network, you should weigh all of them. Not surprisingly, however, private networks and network security are expensive, and implementations at the high end are very expensive. Firewall cost, installation, setup, and routine administration can easily run into millions of dollars. A digital certificate system for a large corporation could command another $180,000 to $200,000. The potential magnitude of the financial outlay for private networks places them conspicuously outside the reach of many organizations. In actuality, there are other more cost-effective solutions for achieving the functionality of a private network without incurring the financial burden. This book, in fact, details one of the most innovative solutions currently available.

Before we get to that point, however, it should be said that there is something inherently suspect with the premise of private networks. If you think about it, the technology cycles of the components utilized in building private networks are askew, perhaps even contrary to their natural order and flow, especially if you consider pricing. In other words, private networks can be seen as a backward progression, or a trend in computer networking moving in the opposite direction of intranet technology trends, for example.

Private Networks: The *Backward* Evolution of Intranets

Given the length of time that key technologies have been around, why are private networks so expensive? For example, leased lines have been around for decades, and so have access technologies, which include communication servers, modem banks, and related software. In contrast, the Internet as we know it today has been in existence a little over a decade. If its fledgling beginnings are considered, you are looking at 30 years. Although the Internet has been around for some time, surprisingly, the enabling technologies, such as the WWW, browsers, HTML, and Java, that are driving the growth and acceptance of the Internet as a viable cost-effective, networking solution have only been in existence a few years.

The Technology Adoption Cycle of Private Networks

Perhaps a brief review of the technology adoption cycle model can provide insight into why pricing for private networks is so prohibitive. In a normal cycle of adoption regarding mainstream technology that has spawned industry, the cycle typically plots a bell-shaped curve. (See Figure 1-5.) Note that in a normal adoption cycle, the price for technology is highest at the "early majority" stage. This is the beginning of the stage commanding the greatest demand for the technology. At this point in the

Figure 1-5
Technology adoption cycle.

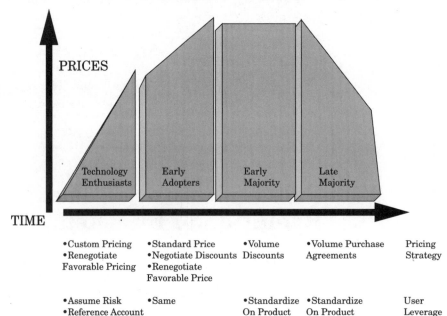

cycle, the majority of the potential buyers are standardizing on the technology. In response to the level of commerce, manufacturers employ a volume discount pricing strategy.

Given the expensive nature of private networks and providers' predisposition for negotiating volume discounts today, the technology adoption cycle for private networks tells us that we are in the early majority stage. If this is true, and given the length of time the suite of technology that makes up private networks has existed, the technology adoption cycle could not possibly map a bell-shaped curve, signifying a *normal* adoption cycle. In fact, the adoption curve would be skewed considerably to the right. (See Figure 1-6.) This type of mapping suggests that private networks took an abnormally long time to catch on. However, this is not the case. Leased lines that function as a backbone to enterprise WANs, coupled with user access technology, have been around for years. In light of these circumstances, the only view that could possibly make sense is that the technology adoption cycle for private networks is *again* under way, producing a normal, bell-shaped curve in the process. In other words, the business world is experiencing another adoption cycle for the technology suite made up of private networks—a technology suite that has already undergone an adoption cycle years ago. The fact that the

Figure 1-6
Technology adoption cycle for private networks.

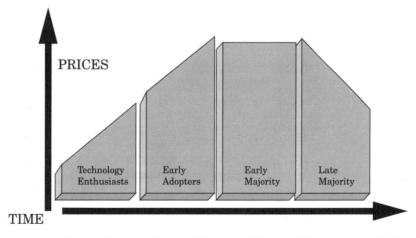

business world deems it necessary to employ private networks today is anachronistic, a backward evolution of computer networking.

To stress this point, intranets incorporate Internet technologies such as browsers, Web sites, and HTML, and therefore provide the same functionality as the Internet, including the use of TCP/IP. IP routing, of course, is an important requirement for many of today's enterprises. Private networks can support IP routing over frame relay protocols. When this occurs, the resulting private network could be construed as a *backward* manifestation of an intranet. What makes intranets so attractive is the relative ease of use, cost, and deployment of the technologies. Using the expensive infrastructure of a private network seems out of line with the inherently cost-effective applications being spawned by the Internet today.

The Impact of Hackers and Other Network Interlopers

The learning organizations went out to the Internet, embraced it, and in the process, learned how to use browsers and develop Web pages with HTML and Java. However, as you would guess by now, hackers chased them away and made it difficult to consider the Internet for business-to-business or mission-critical applications. But when they left, they borrowed the capabilities of the Internet, recognizing the potential for their own internal requirements. Unfortunately, when an enterprise connects its internal intranet to the Internet, it is exposed to the same security risks as organizations with private networks. One school of thought maintains that when an enterprise's intranet is breached, since the technologies are a mirror image of the Internet's, a hacker has an increased ability to wreak havoc in any Internet-like environment. After all, the Internet is where hackers practice their art of intrusion.

The Cost of a Private War

The psychology surrounding private networks espouses the notion of maximum security and reliance on proven technology, albeit old technology. But in fairness to private networks, ISDN capability, and more recently, DSL (digital subscriber lines), firewalls, and GUI-driven applications working in concert provide vitality to a networking solution that is being sustained by and large because of hackers. The lure of the Internet and, more specifically, intranets is strong, and the cost of a private war is beyond the reach of many organizations, so pursuit of a virtual private war is most likely in the cards for many.

For companies that have either instituted a private network or are pondering the potential, the promise of ubiquitous access is also a powerful draw toward the Internet. And in light of the speed of change in today's markets, learning organizations are constantly reengineering their business processes and revamping strategies to compete in a global economy. To achieve this competitiveness, enterprises are looking into methods, including the Internet, for connecting suppliers, partners, and tier one (preferred, or strategic) customers to the enterprise network. The next section explores this interesting trend.

Extranets: The *Forward* Evolution of Intranets

Before we explore the extranet phenomenon, it is important to clarify certain terms that were mentioned in previous discussions. First, try this on for size: All intranets are WANs, but all WANs are not intranets. How's that for paradox! As mentioned above, intranets mimic Internet technology and functionality. But what exactly is the Internet? The Internet is an *open* telecommunication system of technologies and protocols, which allow users on dissimilar computers with dissimilar operating systems to access each other's information sites through graphical interfaces that we know as browsers. The Internet also accommodates file transfer functionality, email, chat rooms, and the dissemination of graphical and multimedia information. (See Table 1-2.) When an enterprise's internal WAN is based on the Internet's technologies and protocols, the resulting network is known as an *intranet*.

Bringing Your Business Partners, Suppliers, and Customers Online

An extranet is established when an enterprise connects *external* organizations like business partners, preferred customers, and/or suppliers to internal applications that run on its *secure* intranet. The linking of separate enterprises into one unified network is revolutionizing the way companies communicate, access information, collaborate, conduct

TABLE 1-2   *Primary Technologies and Protocols of the Internet.*

Protocol/Technology	Description	Function
Microsoft's ActiveX	A relatively new competing standard, based on Visual Basic, for creating interactive multimedia objects.	Enables developers to embed custom-izable ready-made features called ActiveX controls into Web sites.
DNS (Domain Name Service) Protocol	Defines how an application should originate a request for a domain name translation.	Translates Internet domain names into their numerical, 32-bit IP address counterparts.
FTP (File Transfer Protocol)	A protocol that governs the exchange of files on the Internet.	Allows users to upload (send) or down-load (receive) files on demand. Access to service is by password, unless accessing an anonymous FTP site.
HTTP (HyperText Transfer Protocol)	Moderates the exchange of documents on the World Wide Web.	The set of procedures a browser follows when requesting information from a Web site.
HTML (HyperText Markup Language)	Defines the coding method or system of display tags used to create the rich multimedia documents for the WWW.	Essentially a markup language that allows insertion of tags into text-based documents. These tags explain how information should be formatted on screen.
Sun Microsystem's Java	Also a relatively new competing standard for creating interactive multimedia/motion objects.	Used to create a variety of interactive objects, including databases and all media types.
MIME (Multipurpose Internet Mail Extensions)	A standard that allows transfer of binary data (graphics and programs) between users.	MIME is the service that enables the attachment of binary data files to standard email messages.
SMTP (Simple Mail Transfer Protocol)	The protocol for email transmissions.	Governs the transfer of plaintext emails. Works with MIME to support all types of email.
TCP/IP	The main communication protocol for all Internet data traffic.	Enables dial-up (modem) and LAN access to the Internet for any computer running TCP/IP.
IP (Internet Protocol)	This component of TCP/IP establishes the set of rules that separate data into packets for transfer across the Internet.	Transfer data in fixed-sized units called *packets*. Routers on the Inter-net deliver the packets according to the IP address indicated in the header.
TCP (Transmission Control Protocol)	The protocol establishes the temp-orary communication, or "handshake," between two computers on the Internet.	TCP assures, including through retransmissions, that all packets sent between sending and receiving sta-tions are accounted for.
Telnet	Also known as Virtual Network Interface Protocol.	Enables direct connection between computers on the Internet and connec-tion for computers that otherwise could not connect to Internet.

business-to-business transactions, and do business in general. There are a variety of reasons for an organization to extend its intranet for direct access by outside organizations. Access to local and shared files, databases, internal Web pages, and email, for example, increases competitiveness, decision support, client field support, corporate growth, order fulfillment, sales/marketing support, and human resource development. These are only a few of the many advantages and benefits achievable through an extended intranet or extranet. Extranets also tie intranets together with added security and application integration.

A Classic Example

The Automotive Network Exchange (ANX), sponsored by the Big Three automotive manufacturers (General Motors, Ford, and Chrysler), is a TCP/IP-based extranet for linking the Big Three with 8000 suppliers and, ultimately, 20,000 dealers. The ANX, sponsored by the automotive industry's Action Group, went into production during the first quarter of 1998. One of the most critical developments of the ANX pilot project was the successful testing of IP Security (IPSec). IPSec is a maturing standard for managing encryption between to Internet nodes, or *endpoints.* The resulting link, or *tunnel,* between the endpoints is a secure link for data transfer. The success of the IPSec test was a huge boost for establishing a secure virtually private network model for the Internet (more on IPSec in Chapter 3). The ANX automakers estimate that their extranet will reduce manufacturing costs for each vehicle by $70.

The Future of Intranets

Many learning organizations are convinced that extranets are an important new visionary strategy. A recent study by the Gartner Group predicts that more than 60 percent of large organizations implementing an intranet will require extended secure networks during the next 5 years. The report also suggests that security issues would cause barriers to this process in the immediate future, since the Internet is emerging as the clear choice for linking external partners. In the global economy, partners can reside anywhere in the world. Using the Internet may be the least expensive and easiest way to implement a communications backbone for your extranet. Private networks may be too expensive, and ISP point of presence (POP) may be too limited for a given geographical area. With advancements and maturation of standards composing the technologies of VPNs, along with endorsements by the ANX project, the Internet may yet deliver on its promise of ubiquitous, reliable, and secure data communication to the business community.

Virtual Private Networks: Where Extranets End and VPNs Begin

There are a variety of ways to establish an extranet. The following is a list of potential deployment options from least-secure to most-secure communication:

1. Dial-up access through an ISP utilizing the Internet
2. Dial-up access through an ISP utilizing a public data network, i.e., MCI Communications, CompuServe, UUNET, etc.
3. Dial-up access through an ISP utilizing the Internet and user authentication
4. Dial-up access through an ISP using digital telephone lines, i.e., ISDN, DSL, and leased lines
5. Dial-up access through an ISP using digital telephone lines and firewall
6. Dial-up access through an ISP using a VPN

Although the second option is a little safer than the first, neither option protects information as it crosses the Internet or a public data network. The next three options add some additional deterrence to intruders and, with encryption, you could attain a decent amount of privacy. However, intruders could still gain access to the network. Furthermore, options 4 and 5 are private network implementations, which could be overkill or too expensive for many enterprises. As for option 6, this implementation can be supported either directly by an enterprise or through an ISP.

VPNs: An Extranet of Another Variety

This book is mostly concerned with enterprises that aspire to implement, maintain, and manage their own VPN using standard Internet access methods. This is distinguished from using an ISP, which may offer a VPN solution as one of their service offerings. Establishing an extranet with this option is the most secure, because it incorporates tunneling, authentication, and encryption to privatize a communication channel through the Internet. Early on, when VPN technology was just beginning to make inroads, extranet and VPN were used interchangeably. Today, *extranet* primarily refers to an intranet that links external business partners, whereas *VPN* refers more to the method for achieving that end. A VPN, therefore, could be an extranet of another variety or some other WAN application, such as support for work-at-home programs, nomadic users, geographically dispersed cross-functional teams, employees in the field, branch office connectivity, and so on. This book will explore VPNs in their fullest context of application.

Virtual Private Networks: The Magic WAN

If the Internet is the promised land and private networks are other sacred lands, then VPN technology is the magic WAN, because through it, you inherit the best of both worlds. VPNs afford enterprises the security, performance, availability, and multiprotocol environment of a private network over the inexpensive and ubiquitous Internet. For the record, VPNs provide secure data transport links, called tunnels, over the public communication lines of the Internet. (See Figure 1-7.) The secure tunnels are established between two Internet nodes or sites through the technologies of encryption, authentication, and data validation working in concert. VPNs use strong authentication to establish the tunnel, encrypt IP packets or datagrams to scramble the data for protection, then employ data integrity checks to ensure packets arrive at the destination unchanged. In other words, VPNs allow private information to be transmitted over the public Internet without being compromised by hacker attacks. In effect, the Internet is transformed into your very own *virtually* private network.

VPNs and Firewalls: A Marriage Made in Cyberspace

As far as network security is concerned, the protection provided through VPNs is as comprehensive as it comes. VPNs primarily protect data as it tunnels through the communication lines of the Internet. This process, though very effective with information in transit, does

Figure 1-7
Virtual private net-
work technology.

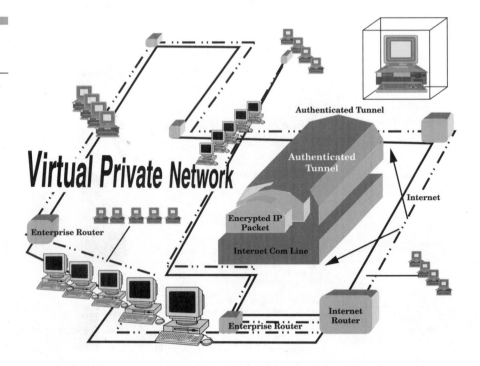

not offer the greatest protection to the network itself. As in the case of private networks, a firewall offers the best potential for VPN security. VPNs and firewalls, working in conjunction, protect data in transit and in residence behind the firewall. (See Figure 1-8.) Firewalls achieve network protection and privacy through access control. Access control specifies the amount of freedom a VPN user has, restricts certain types of traffic, and controls the access of partners, employees, and other external users to applications in various network domains. Thus, not only does access control protect the network's data, it also protects the enterprise's entire wealth of intellectual capital by ensuring that VPN users have complete access to applications they need, but to nothing more. The ability of VPNs and firewalls to protect data in transit and in residence, respectively, makes them a match definitely made in cyberspace.

The Reality of VPNs

VPNs are a major technological advancement and milestone in the evolution of the Internet or wide area networking, depending upon which

Figure 1-8
VPN and firewall
implementation.

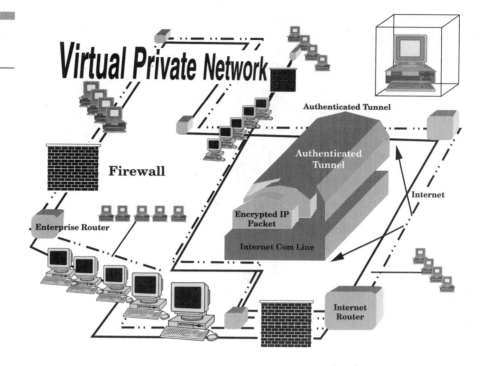

side of the coin you consider. The Internet is already changing the way enterprises do business. The blending of encryption, authentication, and data validation techniques to carve out VPNs on the Internet is truly a remarkable innovation, and VPNs should prove to be an important new catalyst in this change. The manner in which the culture of a learning organization must conduct business in a global economy is contingent upon the reliability, security, and availability of the organization's network. In turn, the VPN itself depends upon how well the technology performs and integrates with technologies of the Internet. As the life cycles of the three basic technologies that make up VPNs mature, the rate of adoption will increase, establishing VPNs in the forefront of WAN deployment.

Critical to this process is the maturation of VPN technological standards. As you know, standards ensure interoperability among competing vendor solutions. The standards of VPNs, though maturing, are basically still emerging, and their implementation into vendor offerings is not completely homogeneous. Consequently, move with caution if you decide to implement more then one vendor offering into your virtual private network. (More on this in Chapter 3.)

CHAPTER 2

Why VPNs Will Proliferate

If you consider the political arena, the major vendors involved, the standards that are emerging, and the economics, it is a foregone conclusion that VPN technology is here to stay. In fact, VPNs will proliferate because of primarily three reasons: maturation of key standards, the strength of the technology, and economic cost factors. This chapter will provide you insight into these and related topics and begin to establish why VPNs are a viable global business solution.

Politics: Who's in the Fray

Encryption, one of the critical components of virtual private networks, is mired in a legal and political mess. This controversy is mainly instigated by Big Brother himself: the U.S. government. Essentially, the U.S. government seriously regrets encryption being in the hands of the public domain. To be fair to the United States though, law enforcement agencies all over the world are dismayed over the widespread use of encryption. France and Russia have banned the use of encryption outright. Great Britain and the European Union are actively pursuing restrictions on encryption that would grant them access to encryption keys. In an effort to control it here in the United States, there are tough laws on the books, strict policies in effect, and proposed legislation in Congress that have the civil liberty organizations up in arms. The United States has either instituted or is trying to institute the following controls:

1. Legislation that makes export of both encryption without a license and strong encryption illegal.
2. Revised legislation providing for the export of strong encryption if "backdoor" access is provided to federal authorities.
3. Pending legislation restricting the right of the public to obtain strong encryption.
4. Pending legislation providing government access to keys (GAK).
5. Pending encryption legislation for key escrow.
6. The FBI has called for a ban on the domestic distribution of any encryption software that bars authorized government access to related messages.

Apparently, the U.S. government and other sovereign states believe that *strong* encryption presents a "clear and present danger" to national security. With industrial-strength encryption, intelligence agencies fear that criminals and especially terrorists could initiate secure communication channels to circumvent investigators. This could mask a litany of organized crime and acts of terrorism, thus posing a serious threat to the security of the entire nation.

There is no law governing encryption key length within the 50 states; however, there is one regarding the use of encryption keys outside of the country. The law stipulates that any encryption software for export must be licensed regardless of key size, and encryption key lengths greater than 40 bits are usually barred from export. *Export* refers to either selling or transmitting of encryption. The U.S. State Department is responsible for processing these applications. In VPN parlance, if you are a multinational enterprise, for example, desiring to configure encrypted VPN channels with overseas offices, you are restricted from using key lengths greater than 40 bits. But here is where it gets convoluted. As a citizen you have a right to apply for the use of encryption key lengths greater than 40 bits in applications planned for overseas transmission. However, these applications are referred to the National Security Agency (NSA), who summarily denies the application. If you think that was convoluted, now try this. If your VPN encryption software is purchased from a company headquartered overseas, then technically you are *importing* software, so the law does not apply. So, in essence, there is a way around the regulation, called the Export Control Act, which was passed in 1994.

We're not done yet, however. The U.S. government is now pushing for government access to keys (GAK). In 1997, the Export Control Act was amended to allow export of encryption software with 56-bit key lengths if the software vendors provide a back door for the government to gain access if so warranted. To prevent any flak over GAK and the right to export *slightly* stronger encryption, the government is proposing a watchdog regulation called *key escrow*. The regulation stipulates that GAK must be implemented within 2 years. Under key escrow, a master key that can decipher all your encrypted messages is divided into pieces. The master key pieces, in turn, are submitted to *two* separate but equal escrow agents for that fateful day. If the federal authorities find "probable cause" that your organization is conducting subversive activities, with a warrant they can obtain your master key. Some business organizations are warming up to the idea because escrow agents can be used as a safe haven just in case a disgruntled employee decides to permanently disappear with the master key.

The government's first attempt at key escrow was as successful as the Edsel. That program, called the Clipper Chip Initiative, was an attempt to induce interested parties to use special encryption developed by, would you believe, the NSA. Clipper is still available today if you do not mind the federal authorities possessing your master key and the NSA knowing your moves. These tough encryption regulations and new initiatives, frankly, have missed the boat. Strong encryption already proliferates outside of the U.S., and shareware programs such as Pretty Good Privacy (PGP) are widely available throughout the world. Given the fact that strong encryption is readily available in the international arena, it's a little absurd that these laws are on the books. So the big question is, will the U.S. government succeed? Most likely, yes. But if civil liberties groups have a strong lobby, that just might be a sufficient amount of opposition needed to thwart Big Brother.

Speaking of Ubiquity...Microsoft

Microsoft's entrance into the VPN game is certainly an auspicious development for an emerging, but strong, industry. Being a software giant, it came in with guns blazing with a VPN tunneling product and the NT operating system (OS), which is fast becoming the de facto standard for vendor firewall implementations. Its VPN solution, Routing and Remote Access Service (RRAS), legitimized the game when it made its debut. RRAS offers the Point-to-Point Tunneling Protocol (PPTP) for tunneling across the Internet. As only a Microsoft could do, RRAS is offered as free download when you buy and implement the NT 4.0 Server OS as your LAN/WAN operating system. RRAS, and in particular, PPTP, is not as robust as, say, IPSec or, for that matter, Cisco's Layer 2 Forwarding (L2F) protocol; not entirely because it is a giveaway, but because it is reflective of the company's Internet strategy.

It appears as if Microsoft's strategic Internet products, such as Internet Explorer and now RRAS, are given away as an add-on or free download. So, naturally, they would not be as robust as an item you would purchase. Furthermore, PPTP tunnels through the Internet's TCP/IP by encapsulating PPP packets with IP. (See Figure 2-1.) This allows remote users to dial into a LAN and directly use protocols like IPX (Internetwork Protocol Exchange), NetBIOS (Network Basic Input/Output System), and NetBEUI (Network BIOS Extended User Interface). These three protocols allow remote users to interact with a LAN's file system, hardware components, and peripherals, respectively, as if they were working locally on the LAN. Although PPTP's initial offering did not provide built-in encryption to tunnel IP and LAN protocols, it still is a nifty approach for a VPN solution. Although the current release of PPTP provides encryption, unfortunately, PPTP possesses some additional drawbacks, like poor user authentication implementation, which could compromise the security of VPN connections. This and other critical weaknesses will be discussed below.

Nonetheless, regardless of the PPTP, NT, or any other product bugs that may creep up in user interfaces, more often than not at inopportune times, Microsoft has the muscle to fix them, as long as they remain

Figure 2-1
PPTP tunneling
process.

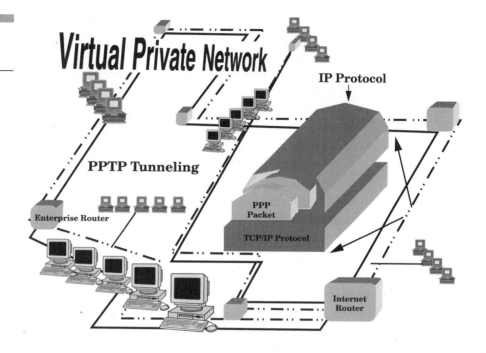

interested in sustaining the product's life cycle. Their presence in any marketplace will be felt; you can count on that. And their financial muscle affords them unlimited resources to correct a problem. So when Microsoft shows up, it's generally a good thing for the user community.

NT: The New Operating System of Choice for Firewalls

The operating system of choice used to be UNIX, but most firewalls sold today run on NT. Earlier releases of NT had security holes, which were corrected in subsequent releases of the operating system. Apparently, software manufacturers are sufficiently convinced that NT is stable enough to now be the platform of choice. Actually, Microsoft has added some new innovations to NT, one of which is called the Network Driver Interface Specification (NDIS). The NDIS is essentially software code or an application programmer interface (API) designed for incorporation into vendors' firewall solutions. Among other things, NDIS is the mechanism that escorts incoming Internet traffic to a proxy, a program, which performs inspection and other duties on Internet traffic. (In this case, of course, the proxy is the firewall.) The NDIS driver also operates in a system execution layer just above the network interface card (NIC). Therefore, potentially hostile traffic never finds its way up to other operating layers such as the network operating system—in other words, TCP/IP or end-user application layers. (For a review on operating layers, refer to discussion on the OSI model in Chapter 8. Another advantage for firewalls based on NT's NDIS driver is speed. The NT operating system barely gets involved in the processing, so the firewalls can perform unencumbered at peak speeds.

In comparison, vendors who build their firewalls on UNIX platforms must hassle with device driver compatibility issues. Additionally, customers are typically forced to purchase UNIX hardware along with the firewall. With NT firewalls, customers are free to choose their own systems. NT definitely appears as the wave of the future. Reviews of vendor products reveal that they have or are planning to have an NT version available. However, vendors are not going to sweep their UNIX versions to the curb anytime soon, because there are a lot of UNIX-based WANs in operation. The handwriting is on the wall, though, and the industry is certainly taking note.

NT Bugtraq Web Site

A true testament of real power in a product is not the economic value it commands but the number of independent concerns that establish support or recognize that product as an institution. NT has become an institution unto itself, and in the process, it has precipitated a host of independent forces such as user groups, consulting firms, Web sites, and media with the common goal of facilitating NT integration into the world of computing. One such independent entity and one of the most comprehensive of its type is the NT Bugtraq Web site. This site is a repository of archives, editorials, FAQs, fixes, and free downloads concerning the security, integrity, application, and problems of the NT operating system. It also tracks the debate between potential and current users and representatives of Microsoft on hot issues and related developments.

Figure 2-2 shows the home page of the NT Bugtraq Web site. The categories listed on the left are the various areas that you can explore at the site. Pictured is the comprehensive list of topics in the December 1998 archives. Figure 2-3 is an example of the type of information that you may obtain at the site.

As you can see, Bugtraq also provides comprehensive coverage on

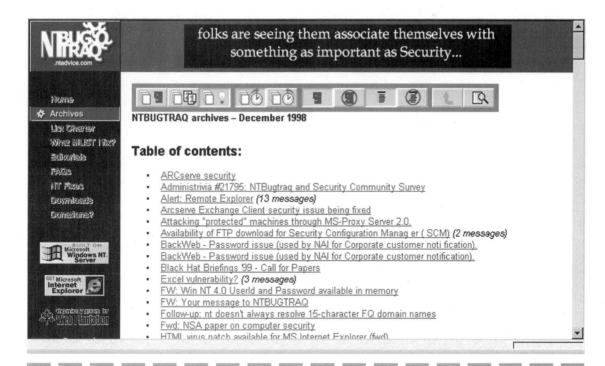

Figure 2-2   NT Bugtraq home page.

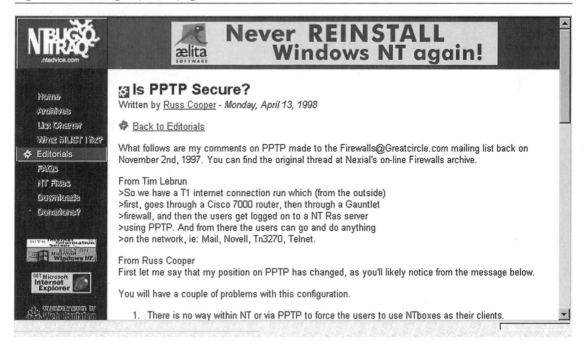

Figure 2-3   Typical NT Bugtraq topics.

related NT subject areas such as end-user applications, computer networking and protocols, industry white papers, position papers, and Internet issues. As indicated above, this is not a Microsoft Web site but an independently run and financed operation. The NT Bugtraq site can be accessed at www.ntbugtraq.com/.

The Debacle of PPTP

Almost since the time it was out of the gate, PPTP has had a rocky road. Encryption options, compared to competing products, were very limited, and overall security could have gotten a considerable boost from some type of digital certificate authentication. PPTP does, however, support Remote Authentication Dial-In User Service (RADIUS), which is a user authentication protocol and an emerging VPN standard. (More on RADIUS in the next chapter.) Available as a free download with RRAS, Microsoft's VPN solution is an attractive option for budget-conscious organizations with basic security requirements. In other words, Microsoft is targeting small- to medium-sized enterprises for their VPN offering.

Although this sounds promising, on the VPN front, PPTP would have been better off if it were missing in action. Unfortunately, reports of its demise were not greatly exaggerated. In June 1998, a group of cryptographers employed by a security consulting firm published a documented discovery of four serious flaws in Microsoft's PPTP. The following flaws were discovered:

1. Weak algorithms that allow eavesdroppers to covet passwords.

2. A design glitch that allows an attacker to commandeer and then masquerade as a legitimate server.

3. Implementation mistakes that allow encrypted data to be recovered.

4. Unauthenticated messages that would allow hackers to crash PPTP tunneling gateway.

The NT Bugtraq Web site was cross-referenced to determine if any additional information could be ascertained to corroborate any of the findings. As a result, specific information was obtained in connection to the first flaw noted above in the Editorial section. In that commentary it was concluded that PPTP cannot be relied upon to be secure because of weak algorithms that may come into play when PPTP seeks to establish a secure tunnel between an NT client and NT server. When an NT client establishes a tunnel with PPTP, it utilizes a certain type of hash value of the password to establish the secure tunnel. When PPTP works with an NT client, the resulting hash value is called "OWF." A hash value, generically known as a *message digest,* is produced by a hashing function. A *hashing function* is a mathematical routine that reduces primarily encrypted information to a smaller size for efficient transmission over the secure channel. In this scenario, the password contains the encryption key that is shared between the client and server to encrypt the data communications involved in the PPTP session. (More on hashing techniques in the next chapter.) As long as the *NT* client uses PPTP's OWF hash value when establishing the tunnel with an *NT* server, the transmission is fine.

A problem arises, however, if a Windows 95 client is utilized to establish a PPTP tunnel with an NT server. When a Win 95 client uses PPTP to establish a tunnel with an NT server, it uses a *different* hash value of the password to establish the tunnel. The hash value that it uses is called "LanMan." Actually, PPTP's OWF hash incorporates the LanMan hash value of the password to create the tunnel. Unfortunately, the LanMan hash of the password uses weak encryption algorithms that are subject to brute-force attacks from hackers. *Brute-force attacks* are a direct assault on transmissions whereby the hacker employs many computers to try every possibility of the encrypted password. In the attacks, hackers would only need about 3 days to crack the encryption and confiscate the password.

The preceding account directly confirms the first finding by the security consulting firm indicated above. It's safe to assume that Microsoft is aware of PPTP's serious drawbacks and has either provided fixes or will correct the problems in a new release. In the meantime, to remedy this situation, use NT clients that have been modified to not use the LanMan hash value when establishing a VPN with PPTP.

Cisco's Layer 2 Forwarding (L2F) Protocol

Like Microsoft, Cisco got into the VPN game relatively early. And like PPTP, L2F has been receiving a lot of attention since 1996. To run properly, L2F requires native support in your router and access server. This should not come as a surprise; after all, Cisco is the IBM of routers. The ability to tunnel layer 2 protocols, such as Asynchronous Transmission Mode and frame relay, is one of the strongest features of L2F. The benefit to you, of course, if your present communications protocol for your

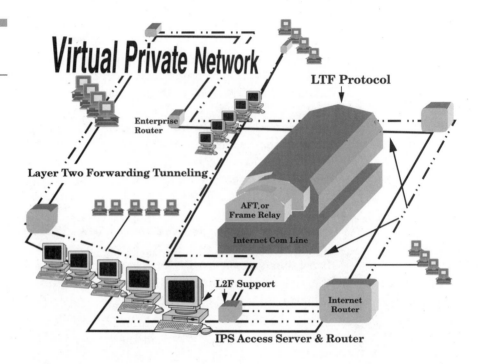

WAN backbone is ATM or frame relay and if you are planning to expand, is that L2F affords you the means to use the Internet as an extension of your current communications backbone. (See Figure 2-4.)

L2F also has built-in authentication capabilities for tunnel endpoints. Believe it or not, the major drawback of L2F is that no standardized encryption scheme is included. Given that encryption should be a standard feature of VPNs, this is similar to talking about confidential business matters in a public place; you never know who is listening. Recognizing the relative merits and shortcomings of each other's tunneling protocols, Microsoft and Cisco decided to merge their competing offerings in the latter part of 1996. The Internet Engineering Task Force (IETF) picked up the ball, and the resulting merger produced Layer 2 Tunneling Protocol (L2TP). (More on L2TP in the next chapter.) All things considered, L2F is basically a forgotten protocol. If mentioned at all it is usually in discussions about the origin of L2TP. Most vendors today implement the IPSec standard for managing encryption between endpoints, especially in light of the critical problems emerging on PPTP. (More on IPSec in the next chapter.)

The Economics of VPNs

VPNs can offer significant flexibility, scalability, and cost savings as enterprises extend their network to include important customers, strategic business partners, and remote employees. Industry forecasts show that more and more organizations are planning to connect their mission-critical applications to the Internet to capitalize on its ubiquity and relative low cost. Privacy through VPNs was the critical missing link for that all-important leap of faith. Large enterprises that made the investment in private networks during the pre-VPN era will first start out with applications in which ubiquitous access makes sense, such as supporting mobile users, telecommuters, or staff on temporary assignments. Successful efforts such as the ANX project demonstrate what a VPN could accomplish on a large scale. From the sidelines, financial institutions, health care industries, and the federal government have been watching the developments with keen interest. In no uncertain terms, the model has been set for similar efforts in the near future. Given the ease of implementation and affordability of VPNs, small to medium organizations should now find the lure of the Internet irresistible for connecting mainstream data networking applications. In fact, industry consultants believe that this segment presents the greatest potential for VPNs over the next 5 years. The bottom line is that all the pieces are in place: the companies, the technology, the solutions and, of course, the Internet. Only time will tell if the marketplace agrees.

CHAPTER 3

De Facto and Emerging Standards

The mission of a particular body of standards, especially in the electronics and computer age, is to achieve the proverbial "open system." The term *open system* is often bandied about, but an example of a truly remarkable open-system achievement is the stereo component system. It does not matter if you buy a Sony receiver, Bose speakers, a Pioneer CD player, or a Panasonic cassette player. When the components are plugged together, there is a high degree of certainty that the system will play. The stereo electronics industry has attained such a complete level of component integration that consumers take it for granted. Not only are standards rarely discussed when purchasing a system, no one really cares about them. Nowhere are standards more important than in the computer field, where achieving the archetypal stereo component open system is too often an elusive goal.

Nevertheless, standards are very important because they ensure interoperability, freedom of choice, and protection of investment. If there is ever a field of endeavor where standards are playing a key role it is virtual private networks. In this chapter, VPN standards are fully reviewed, including emerging and de facto standards. For the purpose of this review, de facto standards refer to protocols and specifications that are popular and readily used but not necessarily sanctioned by any oversight agency. Emerging standards are just the opposite. Their banner is usually carried by an oversight organization, which usually leads the charge for development specifications and compliance policy for an entire industry. In the case of VPNs, the Internet Engineering Task Force (IETF) is leading the charge with several parallel VPN initiatives under way, as discussed below. (See Figure 3-1.) To facilitate discussion, the chapter is divided into four main categories: tunneling protocols, user authentication, data authentication (data integrity techniques), and encryption schemes.

Figure 3-1
VPN standards
universe.

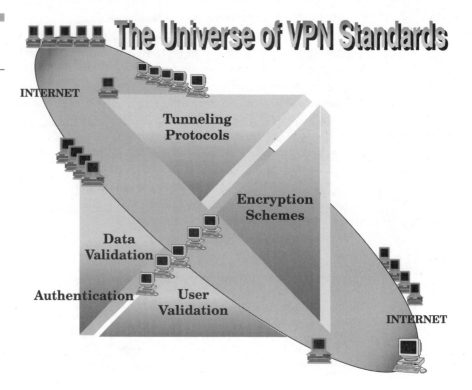

Tunneling Protocols

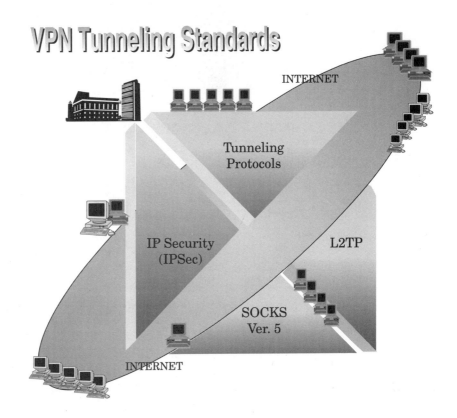

The Arrival of Secure IP, aka IP Security or IPSec

IP Security or IPSec, as it is known almost reverently, was one of the most anticipated, tested, and talked about developments in an industry fraught with good intentions but limited results. The IPSec standard, officially Standards Track RFC 2401 (as of November 1998), is the vehicle that will deliver the promise of the Internet's low-cost, widespread availability for enterprises' mission-critical communications. The construction of IPSec was championed by an IETF working group of the same name. IETF is a large, open, international community of network designers, administrators, vendors, and researchers primarily concerned with cultivating a safe and operationally efficient communications envi-

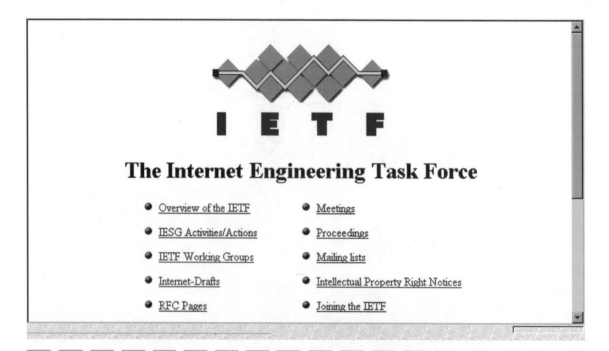

Figure 3-2   The IETF home page.

ronment on the Internet. The actual technical work is performed by "working groups," which are organized by subject matter, for instance, the IP Security working group. For more on the IETF and its working groups, visit the Web site at www.ietf.org/. (See Figure 3-2.)

The goal of IPSec is to provide a security architecture specification that, when implemented, will provide protection for Internet Protocol (IP) communications down to the packet or datagram level. The goal of IPSec also includes providing an efficient process of coordinating encryption between two VPN nodes—in other words, between two security servers or between a host and a security server. The IPSec standard specifies three main categories of security application and control:

1. Security protocols for traffic protection.

2. Incorporation of encryption schemes for data integrity and privacy.

3. Automated and manual key (encryption) management. This latter specification also implies a system of public key infrastructure (PKI)

IPSec Security Protocols and Encryption

IPSec is designed to provide encryption-based security to IP datagrams or packets. (See Figure 3-3.) To deliver security, the IPSec standard specifies two security protocols: Authentication Header and Encapsulating Security Payload.

- The IP Authentication Header (AH) protocol provides data origin authentication, connectionless integrity, and an optional antireplay service.

- The Encapsulating Security Payload (ESP) protocol delivers encryption and limited authentication, compared to AH, to IP datagrams. Like AH, ESP provides connectionless integrity, data origin authentication, and antireplay service. Antireplay service is an important feature for connectionless protocols. This feature provides a barrier to denial of service attacks, which will be covered in detail in Chapter 6.

Figure 3-3
Typical IP datagram formats.

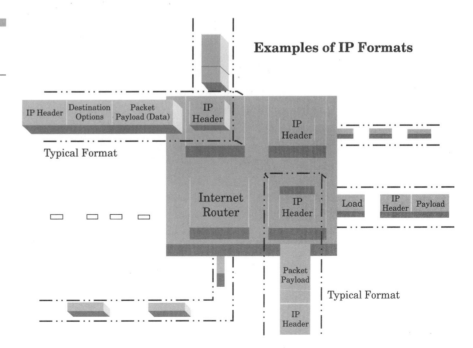

Examples of IP Formats

IP Header | Destination Options | Packet Payload (Data)

IP Header

Typical Format

Internet Router

IP Header

IP Header

IP Header

Load | IP Header | Payload

Packet Payload

Typical Format

IP Header

AH and ESP are the mechanisms through which IPSec delivers security services to Internet-bound IP datagrams. In general, the two security protocols deliver three classes of services:

1. Header authentication and payload (data transported by IP packet) encapsulation to protect "at risk" information fields in IP headers and packet payloads.

2. Authentication and encryption for higher-level connectionless protocols such as TCP and UDP. Connectionless protocols usually do not provide any "successful connection" feedback between sender and receiver. In a *connectionless* transmission, the sender's "protocol" simply dumps the transmission on the communications line. If the recipient's system responds, the connection is successful. If the recipient is offline and no connection is established, or, in the extreme, if the session is hijacked, the original sender of the message will receive no response, hence, connectionless protocols.

3. Self-protection of the actual security agents (parameters), i.e., encryption keys, which negotiate IPSec connections.

IPSec Transport Mode Security Association   In IPSec, when a connection is enabled by either AH or ESP, the resulting connection is called a *security association* (SA). In other words, under the IPSec standard, SAs are specific types of transmissions modes for IP packets. The two transmission modes that IPSec utilizes for security transference are called *transport mode* and *tunnel mode*.

In transport mode, security services are transferred directly to the packet through either an AH or ESP security protocol header. During transmission, the security protocol header is positioned or nested after the original IP header and destination options but before the IP payload or data. In the case of AH, protection is provided to the IP header, selected options, and the IP payload. In the case of ESP protection, only the payload is encapsulated with security services. (See Figure 3-4.) Sometimes IP packets also contain *extension headers,* which usually appear after the base IP header but before destination options. When extension headers are included, AH will also be used to authenticate this portion of the packet.

IPSec Tunnel Mode Security Association   In the case of tunnel mode, IPSec attaches an outer IP header. The outer IP header normally includes the destination of the IPSec processing destination or security

Figure 3-4
Transport mode IP
security.

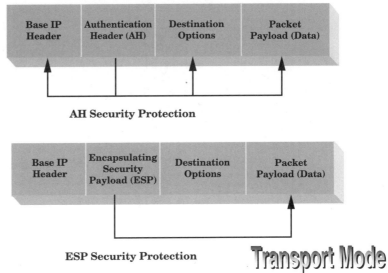

IPSec Security Protocol Services

Base IP Header	Authentication Header (AH)	Destination Options	Packet Payload (Data)

AH Security Protection

Base IP Header	Encapsulating Security Payload (ESP)	Destination Options	Packet Payload (Data)

ESP Security Protection

Transport Mode

gateway. Consequently, in tunnel mode, there are two instances where point-to-point transmission occurs between two security gateways or between a host (client or server) and a security gateway. In contrast, IPSec does not attach an outer IP header in transport mode, because the security associations are usually established between two hosts. (To distinguish hosts from security gateways, hosts usually originate or terminate messages, while gateways transfer messages.) In transmission, the security protocol header is located behind the outer IP header but before the original IP header and associated packet payload. The protection AH provides is similar to the protection it provides in transport mode. Protection is extended to the outer IP header and the entire tunneled IP packet (inner/original IP header and packet payload). ESP, on the other hand, extends security services to the tunneled IP packet only, not to the outer IP header. (See Figure 3-5.)

Standardized packet structure and security associations are one of the major benefits of the IPSec initiatives. A standardized packet structure facilitates interoperation of third-party VPN solutions down to the IP datagram or transmission level. IPSec extends security services at the IP layer, resulting in protection for IP and upper-layer protocols, such as TCP and UDP, as they travel the Internet.

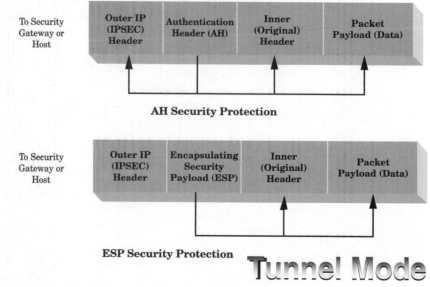

IPSec Security Protocol Services

IPSec Key Exchange and Key Management IPSec's default management system for encryption keys is ISAKMP/IKE (Internet Security Association and Key Management Protocol/Internet Key Exchange). Simple Key Management for IP (SKIP) is optional. Among other things, IPSec key management protocols ensure that both endpoints of the VPN utilize and deploy the same keys for authenticating and encrypting IP packets. They also ensure that keys are exchanged in regular intervals to reinforce the integrity of VPN transmissions on an ongoing basis. With weaker 40-bit keys, changing the key at regular intervals is critical, because, given enough time, a hacker can break the encrypted code. More on key management protocols later in this chapter.

The Layer 2 Tunneling Protocol (L2TP)

Layer 2 Tunneling Protocol is the strategic collaboration between Microsoft's PPTP and Cisco's L2F. (See Chapter 2.) Once they decided to pursue the opportunity, L2TP was left at the IETF's doorstep for certification. Blending the best both protocols had to offer was the driving motivation behind L2TP. One of the strengths of PPTP is its ability to tunnel Point-to-Point Protocol (PPP) across the Internet. PPP provides dial-in connectivity for enterprise LANs. PPTP wraps PPP packets in IP when tunneling over the Internet. For this reason, in addition to tunneling IP, standard LAN protocols like IPX, NetBEUI, and NetBIOS can also be tunneled. IPX, NetBEUI, and NetBIOS protocols deliver file or directory sharing, peripheral support, and hardware support, respectively, within a LAN. The net effect is that a remote user can work in either a regular LAN environment or an intranet environment as if they were locally connected. One of L2F's big benefits was its ability to tunnel "higher-layer" protocols with link layer or layer 2 network protocols such as ATF, SONET, or frame relay. As a result of this strategic liaison, L2TP tunnels PPP packets across a variety of network protocols, including IP, ATM, SONET, and frame relay.

In contrast to IPSec, L2TP does not define any type of encryption scheme for data privacy. Currently, an IETF draft exists to piggyback L2TP tunnels on IPSec security protocols to achieve data integrity and protection over IP networks.

Crossing the Firewall Divide with SOCKS

SOCKS, considered *the* authenticated firewall traversal protocol, was designed and developed by NEC in 1990. SOCKS is now an IETF standard championed by the Authenticated Firewall Traversal Working Group. SOCKS final draft standard was submitted for review in December 1994, and by March 1996, it became qualified for the IETF standards track. Today, the SOCKS standard consists of three companion standards: RFC 1928, 1929, and 1961. RFC 1928 is the actual specification of the SOCKS version 5 firewall traversal. RFC 1929 and 1961 are the standards tracks for user authentication, data authentication, and encryption of SOCKS data streams.

Though SOCKS made its debut before PPTP and IPSec, it did not set the networking world on fire. On the one hand, SOCKS operates in a client/server environment. But in previous versions, the client code had to be recompiled to support the product. On the other hand, SOCKS was designed to tunnel higher-layer protocols like FTP, Telnet, and HTTP. However, before version 5, data streams were unsecured when they traversed the firewall divide. Developers saw these operational issues as barriers to widespread acceptance. Thus, SOCKS implementations were largely overlooked in favor of proprietary solutions, or perhaps more promising standards down the road.

SOCKS version 5 corrects the shortcomings of previous versions of the standard. Not only does it provide authentication and data integrity, but encryption too. In fact, SOCKS offers plug-in support for various authentication and encryption schemes. RFC 1961, which specifies the Generic Security Service API (GSS-API), is the default mechanism for authenticating and privatizing SOCKS datagrams. The GSS-API authenticates both ends of a SOCKS tunnel and then provides privacy though encryption on a message-by-message basis. As a result, SOCKS datagrams are able to cross firewall defenses transparently and securely.

Another new feature is support for UDP. Earlier versions supported another connectionless protocol, TCP. Together with other emerging application layer protocols, SOCKS is poised to facilitate global information discovery. TCP and UDP are the protocols that bring you, for example, audio and video applications and collaborative applications such as video conferencing. If SOCKS had version 5 capability 2 years ago, widespread acceptance of the standard would have been a slam dunk. Nevertheless, the Gartner Group predicts that all leading firewalls will support the product before the end of the millennium.

User Authentication

One of the attractive features of VPNs is the consistent deployment of strong user authentication in competing offerings. User ID and password access are relatively weak authentication in contrast. However, strong authentication methods typically incorporate the user ID/password procedure with other techniques to achieve two-factor or multiple-factor processes, as is the case with RADIUS. This section explores emerging and de facto user authentication standards that are contributing to the openness of VPN solutions.

Remote Authentication Dial-In User Service (RADIUS)

No doubt about it, RADIUS is a strong user authentication system that incorporates a multifactor certification procedure to certify users. The idea behind RADIUS is evolutionary, yet practical, if your organization is planning to connect remote users from field locations, home offices, or mobile units via a VPN. Since RADIUS also requires a Network Access

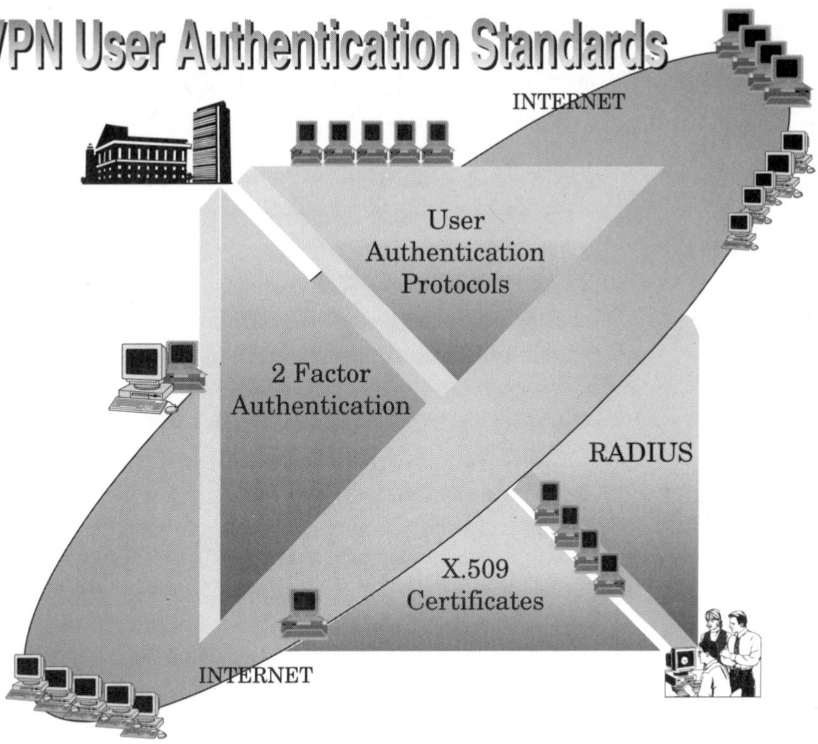

Server (NAS), it is more feasible in installations already equipped with one. Through the user authentication protocol, RADIUS allows you to establish a database of the enterprise's remote users in a server environment. The resulting RADIUS server enables network administrators to manage remote user security, control access to the network's services, and account for how resources are being utilized from remote access points.

RADIUS (IETF Standard RFC 2138) operates as a client/server model. The NAS functions as a client to RADIUS. In this model, the NAS client is responsible for transmitting user access information to the designated RADIUS server or servers, and when a response is returned the client, it responds accordingly. RADIUS servers, on the other hand, are responsible for receiving user connection requests, authenticating the user, and then returning instructions that allow users access privileges to authorized network services.

In general, strong user authentication is synonymous with two-factor authentication. This type of authentication is effective because the user must possess something like a token or smart card and remember something like a PIN code. In contrast, the RADIUS authentication is multifaceted and perhaps the most effective user authentication system available. The protocol's multifactor authentication system includes the following:

1. *A two-factor system possessed by the user.*   In RADIUS, this includes a password and a token or a software utility to generate an encrypted response.

2. *A shared secret (encryption key set) between the NAS client and the RADIUS server and the MD5 message digest.*   The shared secret is used to validate or authenticate the NAS client to RADIUS. Also, the message digest is used to create a hash of the user's password. (More on MD5 later in this chapter.)

3. *An access challenge.*   After client validation, a "challenge" is issued back from RADIUS through the client to the particular user desiring access to the network. The challenge includes a prompt from the NAS client, along with a unique numeric value.

4. *A challenge response.*   To generate an encrypted response, the user enters the numeric value into the token or the software utility. A second access request is generated, with the new encrypted data as the new password. If the new request passes muster, the user gains access to the network.

To put all this in perspective, the RADIUS authentication process works in the following manner: The process begins when a user enters a user ID and password for network access. The NAS client generates an *access request* that includes its own ID, port ID, and a MD5 message digest of the user's password. In response, the RADIUS server validates the sending NAS client using their *shared secret*. If the user is validated on this access server (NAS client), RADIUS looks up the user's access profile in the database. Once the match is found, RADIUS issues an *access challenge* to the user via the NAS client. The access challenge, usually a numerical value, is prepared by the NAS client and forwarded to the user's display monitor. The user, in turn, is prompted to respond. The user enters the numerical value into the *token* or software utility and provides the newly generated encrypted data as a *challenge response*. The NAS client generates a *second access request* with the user's new encrypted response as the new password for the request. If the new user response/password checks out, the user gains access to the network's services. Services can include a variety of environments, including PPP, Telnet, and IP networks. (See Figure 3-6.)

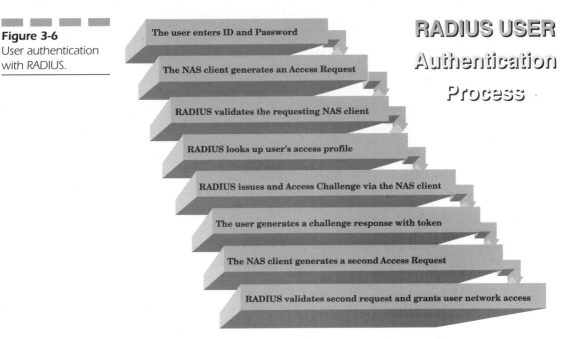

Figure 3-6
User authentication
with RADIUS.

RADIUS USER
Authentication
Process

The user enters ID and Password

The NAS client generates an Access Request

RADIUS validates the requesting NAS client

RADIUS looks up user's access profile

RADIUS issues and Access Challenge via the NAS client

The user generates a challenge response with token

The NAS client generates a second Access Request

RADIUS validates second request and grants user network access

Strong User Authentication

There are many reasons why weak user authentication techniques are a considerable security risk to VPN installations. For one thing, computer users tend to choose passwords that are easy to remember, such as a birthday, pet's name, relative's birthday, favorite color, and the like. Moreover, even when passwords are encrypted, especially with weak encryption, passwords are still at risk to certain hacker escapades such as brute-force and password replay attacks. The strongest economically viable user authentication methods available today are two-factor authentication schemes. As mentioned previously, two-factor systems require two elements to verify or trigger verification of a user's identity. The elements consist of an item that must be physically possessed, such as a token or a smart card (an electronic device the size of a credit card), and one that must be mentally possessed, such as a PIN code. Technically speaking, RADIUS is a two-factor authentication scheme, but it is more like one on steroids.

If two-factor schemes or RADIUS are beyond your current budget, you may find a scheme that is economical, although your options are limited to the garden-variety user ID/password method. If weak authentication is your best choice, at least from the outset, the following suggestions should suffice to make username/password authentication more effective. For a secure password, there should not be any rhyme or reason to it. In fact, the more randomness you employ, the stronger the password. However, whatever is derived should be fairly easy to memorize. Consider the following recommendations:

1. Select an unrelated pair of words from the dictionary at random, and include some special character to create a nonsensical word, such as "#autumn*pottery."

2. For more complex passwords, choose a pronounceable string of incoherent syllables at least eight characters long, such as "ifmaticbo."

3. Another good idea for a password is using the license plate number randomly selected from an out-of-state vehicle, for example.

In other words, use your imagination. Think of the most obscure or remote circumstance, compose a password from it, and in the process, you will be fortifying your password and network's security. Also, be sure to change the password at regular intervals.

Still, if a two-factor system is economically feasible, it is well worth the investment.

Two-Factor User Authentication: SecurID and CRYPTOCard
There are several two-factor user authentication systems gaining in popularity with VPN solutions. Since these systems generally work the same, this section reviews two such schemes that are consistently implemented with VPN solutions: SecurID and CRYPTOCard.

SecurID is the smart card or token component of the ACE authentication system. ACE, developed by Security Dynamics, is a time-based user validation system that works with an authentication server behind the network's perimeter defenses. The ACE SecurID regenerates a six-digit password every 60 seconds. User authentication is typically managed by a firewall that coordinates the security liaison between the user and the ACE authentication server, which is working in tandem with other network security agents, such as encryption, data integrity, and so on.

CRYPTOCard is another strong form of user authentication methodology. Like RADIUS, CRYPTOCard incorporates a challenge/response technique based on passwords generated with encryption. This smart card also works with a companion authentication server component that contains the user access profile database. The server component works in conjunction with a security gateway or firewall to feed a randomly generated numeric challenge issued by the server. When the user receives the challenge, it is entered into CRYPTOCard, which, in turn, generates a *unique* one-time password for the specific session under way. The resulting encrypted password is reentered into the system, and the user gains access to the network. With strong user authentication systems, it is virtually impossible to sustain password replay attacks, because the password is different with each login.

S/KEY S/KEY is also a strong authentication system. The user "possession" item in this case is software instead of a token. S/KEY's client component resides in the user's workstation, and its companion server piece is integrated with the security gateway or host firewall system. To work with S/KEY, the user must go through the security gateway to gain network access. To gain access through the gateway, the S/KEY user must first enter an assigned password and a "seed" value, a type of PIN code, into the S/KEY module residing in the local workstation. In response, the S/Key module produces a one-time password string in the form of six 4-letter words. The user enters the string when prompted by the security gateway or firewall. The user is granted access after validation. (See Figure 3-7.) Like other single-use password schemes, a different password is generated for each new session.

As an extended security measure, S/KEY also provides a unique feature called a *user iteration count*. Each S/KEY user is assigned an access quota

Figure 3-7
S/KEY authentication.

over a certain period of time. The S/KEY system keeps track of each time a user connects, in order to reduce his or her iteration count by a factor of one. When the count is reduced to zero, no further sessions are permitted.

With strong authentication techniques, providers can offer end-to-end security for VPN sessions. As VPN standards continue to mature and make their mark, a new generation of standards appears to be constantly emerging to take their place. This new generation of strong user authentication techniques is *biometrics*. Biometrics, which is beginning to attract considerable interest, authenticates users by validating a scanned thumbprint, retina, or, perhaps, distinguishing lines in the face. We have all seen movies glamorizing the use of biometrics. However, before the technology can make its way from the silver screen to the mainstream, the technology must become more affordable. But for now, two-factor authentication techniques are among the stars of VPN solutions.

X.509 Digital Certificate Standard

Strong user authentication ensures that access to internal networks is safe when crossing a public communications backbone like the Internet. Once online though, data privacy must really count. The X.509 standard is the higher power on validating the identities of computer users. What is implied through the X.509 standard is the premise of a higher authority for validating who you are. The preferred name of this higher authority is *certificate authority (CA)*. A CA is responsible for assigning and certifying public-key encryption keys to VPN users. (See the discussion on CAs in the following section.) CAs issue encryption keys on an object called a digital ID, or *certificate*. A user can only be granted a digital certificate from a CA after proof of identity, which may even involve employing a notary public. The X.509 standard assists in this process in several ways:

1. By specifying the message format and syntax of digital certificates
2. By specifying the manner in which an encryption system should manage certificates
3. By delineating how certificates should be discarded through a mechanism referred to as a *certificate-revocation list (CRL)*

One of the most daunting challenges of the X.509 protocol is achieving interoperability with CRL. Depending upon which CA you use for your digital certificates, you are pretty much relegated to that service bureau's revocation procedures. Similarly, your customers, suppliers, and partners are in the same boat because they are also at the discretion of their CAs. This creates a problem for certificate administration, but more importantly for security. If an employee resigns, gets fired, or retires, it would be helpful to verify that their digital certificate has been invalidated or revoked. Often it may be infeasible for organizations that are connected through VPNs to use the same CA. When multiple CAs are used, there is no automatic method for a customer of one CA to see the CRL of another CA. The IETF, also overseeing this initiative, hopes that this will change with X.509. The X.509 CRL technology is based in part on a system called the *distributed revocation list,* developed by Entrust, located in Ottawa, Canada.

Data Authentication and Integrity

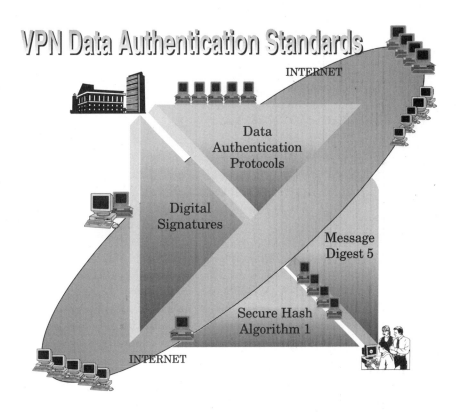

Data authentication is a natural extension of user authentication. From the network's perspective, user authentication says that this person is who he or she claims to be. Therefore, the user may proceed with private communications. Of course, on the Internet, this means the user may proceed with encrypted communications. In the course of ongoing sessions, however, how do you know if the information, encrypted or not, that is received from a user is in fact from *that* user?

With strong authentication and cryptography for data privacy, you may be wondering why there should be a concern. The cause for concern is the wily hacker. A technique hackers successfully employ is the "man-in-the-middle" attack. In this attack, the hacker, who is snooping on a public line, intercepts the exchange of keys for shared secrets between two parties. Afterwards, the hacker sends each of the unsuspecting parties his or her encryption key instead. In subsequent communications, each of the parties thinks that they are using each other's encryption key for private communications. In reality, however, they are communicating with the hacker, because unbeknownst to them, the hacker has become a virtual correspondent who has clandestinely assumed a position between them. Man-in-the-middle and related attacks are the reasons VPNs need data authentication.

The Digital Signature Process

The unsung hero of VPN solutions is data authentication because of two very important abilities:

1. It can prove a message was sent by the sender and was not forged (data authentication).
2. It can verify that a message was not modified or tampered with in transmission (data integrity).

Data authentication is achieved through the use of a digital signature process. One of the premiere digital signature systems, and for all intents and purposes a de facto standard, is one available from the Rivest-Shamir-Adleman (RSA) cryptography system. This system is commonly referred to as the RSA digital signature process. The digital signature method is basically a five-step process:

1. The process begins when a sender decides to send information, a document for example, to a requesting party. Next, the document is encrypted with the sender's private key to create an encrypted message. (See discussion on public and private keys in next section.)
2. The digital signature part of the process begins when the

encrypted message is submitted through a hash function operation. A hash function reduces the encrypted message to a reasonably sized message called a *message digest*.

3. The sender signs the message when the message digest is encrypted with the private key, creating a unique digital signature.

4. The original encrypted message and the digital signature are combined and sent to the requesting party.

5. The recipient (requesting party) verifies the message. Verification is performed as follows:

   A. First, the recipient generates the identical message digest as the sender's with the same hash function.
   B. Next, using the sender's *public* key, the recipient decrypts the unique *signature* embedded in the message.
   C. Finally, the recipient compares the results of A and B. If they match, this confirms that the information was transmitted securely and unmodified.

In addition to transporting encrypted information of all types securely, the RSA digital signature process safely transports public keys. The digital signature process is effective because when the message digest is encrypted with the sender's *private* key, the resulting signature is unique. When received, the recipient decrypts the digital signature with the sender's *public* key. If the message was untouched, the message digests of the sender and the recipient will match. Thus, the digital signature process is a critical requirement when establishing VPNs because it ensures that a sender's identity and related encrypted information is not tampered with during transmission.

Cryptographic Hash/Digest Function

Cryptographic hash functions are the key mechanisms in the digital signature process, which, of course, is essential to data authentication. The two that appear to be most popular with competitive VPN implementations are Message Digest 5 (MD5) and Secure Hash Algorithm 1 (SHA-1). MD5 is a public domain standard for generating 128-bit cryptographic checksums. SHA-1 is a hashing function for generating 160-bit cryptographic checksums for advanced operations. The U.S. Department of Commerce and the National Institute of Standards and Technology (NIST) developed SHA-1 in connection with the Digital Signature Standard (DSS). The DSS never really caught on because of its affiliation with the U.S. government's hell-bent plan to enforce GAK (government access to keys; see Chapter 2). Other hashing functions you are likely to run across include MD4 and CBC-DES-MAC.

Certificate Authorities and Public Key Infrastructure

It goes without saying that if public encryption keys are compromised, then the entire VPN systems falls prey to hacker attacks. The security of a VPN not only relies on encryption keys themselves but also on a secure method of generating, distributing, and managing the keys. Whoever or whatever inherits the responsibility must foster the highest level of trust. Today, this trusted entity is known as a certificate authority (CA). The business of key management by a CA is accomplished through a set of industry guidelines called public key infrastructure (PKI). The CA is usually a third party that issues encryption keys and provides related management services based upon PKI parameters. Conceptually, PKI is an open community of CAs, which primarily employs a hierarchical model to build trust associations where none previously existed.

The hierarchical trust model begins with you. A birth certificate and/or drivers license or some other proof of identity buys you into the trust association at the bottom of the hierarchy. The next layer or organization above you vouches for who you are. In turn, that organization is entrusted by some other organizational layer, and so on. At the top of the trust association is the highest authority. After your identity is established and proven, your encryption keys are issued to you on a certificate called a *digital ID*. The CA certifies your digital certificate by digitally signing your public key with their private key. The next organizational layer up signs the CAs public key, and so on. No doubt, the top organization's key is kept in a vault right next to the Holy Grail. (See Figure 3-8.)

Once the digital certificates are issued, the CA inherits the potentially hairy task of key management; at a minimum, this includes key generation, distribution, revocation, and storage. Vital to long-term success of key management and PKI is the X.509 standard and other PKI systems as well. (See discussion in this chapter.) The X.509 protocol, Standards Track RFC 1919, specifies how key management interoperability is achievable across CAs through a universal certificate format, certificate revocation list (CRL), and cryptographic system management.

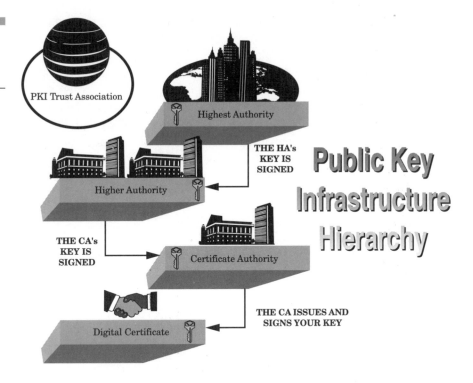

One of the most trusted names in CAs is VeriSign, Inc. Interestingly
enough, VeriSign sells *trust* on three levels, which from a certain perspective is somewhat ludicrous and contradictory to the absolute functionality that CAs should provide. CAs should offer only one level of service, the one that requires a user to produce the proper form of
identification. VeriSign will issue digital IDs based upon an email
address and owner's name, a consumer database, or finally, by proof of
identity. The highest certification service is, of course, the most expensive, with a cost of several hundreds of dollars.

Encryption Schemes

Encryption puts the "private" in virtual private networks. Without it,
information flowing over the Internet or other public backbone will
transmit in cleartext, or plaintext. Encryption is the product of cryptography, and cryptography is the use of specialized programs to scramble
readable data into gobbily gook or ciphertext. The specialized programs

that perform the translation are encryption algorithms. When cleartext is scrambled into ciphertext, it can only be unscrambled with an electronic mechanism called a *key*. The electronic key is a miniature file that ranges in size from 40 bits in length to super-duper lengths of 2048 bits. The process of encrypting plaintext into ciphertext and decrypting it with an encryption key is called a *cryptography system,* or *cryptosystem.* The cryptosystem also includes the human functionality of sending and receiving the encrypted data. Essentially, there are two types of cryptography systems in use: private key (symmetric) cryptosystems and public key (asymmetric) cryptosystems.

Private Key (Symmetric) Cryptosystem

A *private key cryptosystem* employs the same secret key for both encryption and decryption. For instance, the sender can encrypt information with a particular secret key. Anyone with the same secret key can decrypt the message back into cleartext. Symmetric encryption schemes are typically very fast. The most common symmetric key algorithms found in VPN solutions today include RC4, DES, Triple DES, and IDEA. Each of them differs in key length. The longer the length, measured in bits, the greater the strength of the encryption algorithm. The strength of the algorithm refers to the level of effort required to break the system using common hacker attacks. The difference in breaking symmetric keys of 40-bit, 56-bit, and 128-bit lengths is the difference between lifting 100 pounds, 200 pounds, and all of Asia. No wonder the federal government is using its muscle to keep strong encryption on U.S. soil.

If you think 128-bit keys are strong, a 160-bit key (symmetric system) would be classified as military-strength encryption. A *trillion* computers that could each test a *trillion keys per second* would take about *463 trillion centuries* to try all the key combinations in a 160-bit key. Scary, isn't it? In contrast, a standard PC that could test 50,000 keys per second could test all combinations of a 40-bit key in about 255 days. Incidentally, trying each key until the right one is identified is called a *brute-force* attack. Usually, multiple computers with multiple CPUs are harnessed in brute-force attacks, cutting the time needed to break a 40-bit key from hundreds of days down to hours.

Ron Rivest of RSA Data Securities, Inc. created RC4 in 1987. At one time, RC4, employing a 40-bit key, had special export status and, along with a sister product called RC2, was the only encryption algorithm allowed for export. IBM developed DES (for Data Encryption Standard), which the federal government adopted in 1977. DES uses a 56-bit key for data encryption. Using three different DES keys to encrypt a message is commonly known as Triple DES. DES is notorious for succumbing to brute-force attacks. For this reason, Triple DES is more in demand because of greater resilience against such attacks. IDEA (International Data Encryption Algorithm) is a 128-bit key currently in widespread use worldwide. IDEA was developed by James Massey for the Swiss Federal Institute of Technology.

Private key, or symmetric, systems have a glaring weakness. Since the secret key is used for both encryption and decryption, if the key is confiscated, all data processed by the particular key, past and present, is placed in jeopardy. Therefore, extra care should be initiated when working with private key cryptosystems. By practicing a procedure known as *perfect forward secrecy,* where keys are refreshed frequently, hackers would be confronted with only a limited window of opportunity to steal keys, break the algorithm and thus compromise data privacy.

Pubic Key (Asymmetric) Cryptosystem

A *public key cryptosystem* uses a pair of related keys: a private key that is kept secret within the system and a public key that is made available to the public to establish encrypted sessions with the owner of the private key. Two popular public key cryptosystems that are commonly incorporated in VPN solutions today are Diffie-Hellman and Rivest-Shamir-Adleman (RSA).

In a Diffie-Hellman communication between two parties, the public keys of both parties must be exchanged to generate the shared secret between the parties. The shared secret is derived with the private key of one party and the public key of another. This establishes a *two-way* trust model between any two individuals such that no other individual can create or know about the shared secret. (See Figure 3-9.) For example, Tara and Bart want to establish a shared secret for encrypted communication sessions. Tara obtains Bart's public key and Bart obtains Tara's. Tara uses a Diffie-Hellman calculation on her private key and Bart's public key to generate the shared secret key. Bart performs the same procedure with his private key and Tara's public key to generate the identical shared secret key. From this point on, all communications between Tara and Bart will be encrypted and decrypted with the shared secret, which is unique to these two and mutually exclusive to any other Diffie-Hellman key-pair combination.

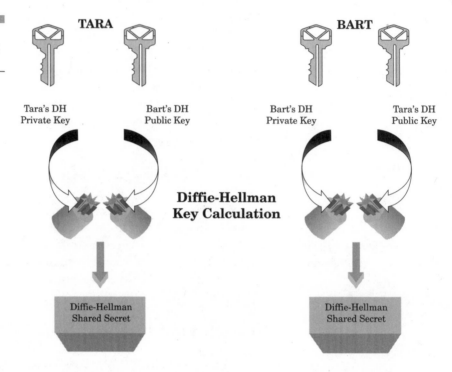

Figure 3-9
Diffie-Hellman public
key cryptosystem.

The RSA public key cryptosystem is the most popular public key algorithm and the de facto standard. RSA, invented in 1977, has experienced widespread acceptance because it delivers both encryption and digital signature capability. (See "Data Authentication and Integrity" earlier in the chapter.) In contrast to Diffie-Hellman, the RSA public key cryptosystem operation hinges upon a *one-way* trust model. Any information encrypted with a sender's *private* key can only be encrypted with the sender's *public* key. Going back to Tara and Bart, if Tara uses her private key to encrypt a message, Bart decrypts the message with Tara's public key. (See Figure 3-10.) A critical success factor for public key cryptosystems is public key distribution. This is why the digital signature process is so important; digital signature certifies the key and ensures that it does not fall into the hands of unintended parties.

The RSA digital signature process can also be used to certify key distribution in a Diffie-Hellman cryptosystem. Common RSA public key sizes include 512 bit, 768 bit, 1024 bit, and 2048 bit. Currently, only the RSA 512-bit key size for public key (*asymmetric* cryptography) is approved for export.

Figure 3-10
RSA public key
cryptosystem.

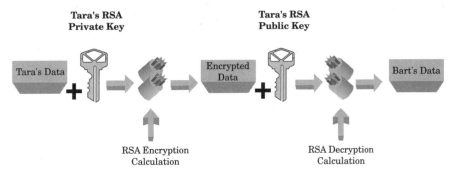

Figure 3-10
RSA public key
cryptosystem.

Key Management Protocols

This section explores the world of key management protocols. Actually, this section is slightly misnamed because of its coverage of Internet Security Association and Key Management Protocol/Internet Key Exchange (ISAKMP/IKE). ISAKMP/IKE is more than a key management protocol. In fact, key management is only a subset of the robust suite of services provided by this promising Internet standard. Perhaps a better name would be, "A VPN Standard for Security Services Implementation and Key Management." Frequently, when reference is made to key management protocols, the discussion tends to include subject matter best labeled by the latter title. However, in this section, when key management is referred to it will only mean "key management." Examples of key management protocols are IKE, OAKLEY, and SKIP.

ISAKMP/IKE—the Mother Lode

ISAKMP, IETF Standards Track 2408, is where the rubber meets the road for delivery of security services for private, secure communications across the Internet. ISAKMP is a comprehensive, modular, flexible, and open system for delivering a variety of security services originated and/or developed in the commercial, federal, and standards organization arenas. ISAKMP is the manager of security associations that protocols such as IPSec establish to transfer security services. It also is the protocol that manages the establishment and subsequent use of public/private key utilization for secure VPN sessions. Specifically, ISAKMP is a framework that defines the procedures for the following:

1. Authenticating a communicating peer

2. Creating and managing security associations (SAs), i.e., specialized communication links that deliver security

3. IP, transport, and application layer security services transference for protocols such as IPSec and other user security services

4. Generating, exchanging, and managing keys

Authenticating Users with ISAKMP   User authentication is perhaps the most important step in establishing a secure communication channel between VPN nodes. Without being able to authenticate the entity at the other end of the connection, the resulting security association and session key for encrypting the current session remain largely suspect. To authenticate users, ISAKMP relies upon a PKI system to generate, verify, revoke, manage, and distribute digital certificates, along with a digital signature algorithm. In addition to users, certificates bind the identities of other entities, including networks, hosts, and applications.

ISAKMP is designed to work with a variety of current and planned CAs and their related infrastructures. Leading the pack is the X.509 standard, developed by the PKIX Working Group of IETF. The U.S. Post Office and the NIST PKI Working Group are also planning separate CA trust associations compatible with ISAKMP. Furthermore, the DoD Multilevel Information System Security Initiative (MISSI) has begun deployment of a CA dedicated exclusively to the federal government. There is also a Domain Name System Security Extensions (DNSSEC) that will provide signed entity keys in the DNS. Where no PKI is utilized, ISAKMP allows the deployment of Pretty Good Privacy's "Web of Trust" user certification process. The Web of Trust process is user certification based upon mutual knowledge associations of user identities. If enough people who know you sign your public key, and the next person's key is signed by enough people who know that particular person, chances are you both have a signer in common. When this is the case, you can be certain the person in question is who he or she claims to be. Therefore, a Web of Trust PKI is feasible within an organization where most of the prospective VPN users know each other.

Applying Digital Signatures through ISAKMP   Also inherent to the authentication process are digital signatures. ISAKMP supports either the RSA digital signature process or the Digital Signature Standard (DSS). Both are based on public/private key cryptography. (See the review of the digital signature process earlier in this chapter.) Note that ISKMP does *not* mandate any particular digital signature algorithm or CA. ISAKMP allows the entity that initiates the communication the ability to select the CA and certificate types. After the CA is chosen, along with related information, the protocol provides the message facility needed to drive the actual authentication exchange.

Security Associations and ISAKMP   Security associations (SAs) are the mechanisms through which ISAKMP delivers security services such as IP layer services (i.e., IPSec). Specifically, it defines procedures and packet formats to establish, negotiate, modify, and delete SAs. An SA is a relationship between two or more network entities, describing how they will utilize security services to communicate securely. In other words, ISAKMP negotiates SAs on behalf of services such as IPSec, or application (user) layer services such as email or file transfer. IPSec security services are channeled through two security protocols: Authentication Header (AH) and Encapsulating Security Payload (ESP). (See discussion on IP security earlier in this chapter.) By centralizing management of security associations, ISAKMP reduces the amount of duplicated functionality within a security protocol. SAs should support different encryption algorithms, authentication mechanisms, and key generation algorithms as well. Consequently, in ISAKMP, SAs are linked with the authentication and key exchange protocol.

IKE vs. SKIP

ISAKMP is most known in the industry for key management services. As mentioned, it does not mandate any specific key management system. Instead, it delineates the desired properties of a key management system that ISAKMP is capable of supporting. For example, desired key management properties include key establishment and exchange, key authentication, and perfect forward secrecy. ISAKMP enables a VPN node initiating communications to indicate which key exchanges (protocols) it supports. After the selection of the key exchange, ISAKMP initializes the messages required to support the actual keys used in encrypting subsequent sessions.

Two key management systems proposed for use with ISAKMP are The internet Key Exchange (IKE), formerly OAKLEY, and Simple Key Management for Internet Protocol (SKIP). SKIP is better suited for small organizations because it is easy to establish and does not require prior communication to establish and exchange encryption keys. In other words, SKIP assumes the encryption scheme operating at the other end of the connection. IKE is better suited for larger, perhaps multinational enterprises/organizations because ISAKMP allows negotiation of encryption schemes, making connections to new sites easier. (See Figure 3-11 for a summary of the ISAKMP process.)

The ISAKMP Process

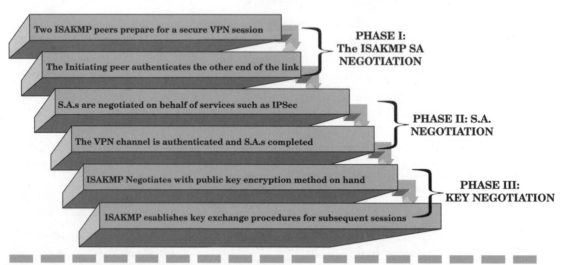

Two ISAKMP peers prepare for a secure VPN session	**PHASE I:** **The ISAKMP SA NEGOTIATION**
The Initiating peer authenticates the other end of the link	
S.A.s are negotiated on behalf of services such as IPSec	**PHASE II: S.A. NEGOTIATION**
The VPN channel is authenticated and S.A.s completed	
ISAKMP Negotiates with public key encryption method on hand	**PHASE III: KEY NEGOTIATION**
ISAKMP esablishes key exchange procedures for subsequent sessions	

Figure 3-11   ISAKMP SA and key management process.

PART **2**

Hacker Attacks and Security Breaches: A Primer

The Internet has spawned new industries, such as Web site development and consulting, and has enhanced established industries, such as retail banking, book commerce, and designer clothes. These industries evolved because of the positive characteristics and potential benefits of the Internet. However, some industries came into being because of the negative forces of the Internet, for example, network security. One of the most important developments, if not innovations, in network security is the advent of virtual private networks. The convergence and seamless interoperability of encryption, authentication, and tunneling protocols are poised to bring the exciting potential of the Internet to the "electronic Windows' sills" of network applications and equip enterprises with the means to fend off the bad guy of the Internet: the wily hacker.

In this part, we explore the diabolical world of the hacker. Why do they hack? What do they have to gain? Some feel that the roots of hacking began in the early days of the Internet, when programmers were looking for shortcuts to fixing source code problems of communication software. Others believe that hacking really began when disgruntled employees of companies and organizations, including universities that were making contributions to the construction of the Internet, left their respective organizations in bad humor. Or, perhaps they hack because of some hell-bent resolve to avenge some professional slight or cold shoulder that was endured during employment.

Notwithstanding these types of hackers, everyone agrees that the real problem is the wily hacker. The wily hacker is organized, perhaps even financed, and hacks because of the challenge of it. Their motivation is comparable to that of adrenaline junkies who climb Mount Everest or parachute off 1000-ft cliffs for that "great rush." Whatever the reason, hacker attacks are real yet surreal, diabolical yet innovative, organized yet covert, and above all, disruptive yet remarkably successful.

In the next chapter we begin with real-world attacks that made the headlines. In the following chapter, how hackers ply their trade is reviewed, along with methods of pinpointing obvious and not-so-obvious clues of undercover activity. The last chapter in this section offers some practical steps to pursue if you feel your firewall has been illegally traversed.

4

Hacker Attacks
for the
Hall of Fame

This section highlights several notorious hacks that are destined for "Hall of Fame" induction. They are real-life accounts that have been documented in the media over the last several years. In every case where hackers breached an enterprise's security they were caught. However, it is important to note the debilitating effects that can be caused by hacker intrusions.

The New Cold War

Détente replaced the Cold War, and, finally, détente itself was supplanted by the promise of democracy. If you were a child growing up in the late 1950s and early 1960s, you might remember air raid drills that were routinely conducted in school. Or better still, you might even have taken home blueprints from school administrators detailing how to construct an underground nuclear bomb shelter in your backyard? Did you think in those days that communism in the former Union of Soviet Socialist Republics would eventually succumb to democracy? Although the Cold War is one for the history books, there is another war being waged—only this time, it's in cyberspace. The new cold war campaign is against the wily hacker. And rest assured, it is a war.

The Economic and Political Reality

In 1996, The American Society for Industrial Security estimated that high-tech crimes were costing American companies as much as $63 billion a year. Surprisingly, in a related development, companies pay millions to hackers each year to keep mum about their success, especially enterprises where network security is included in a service guarantee. (See "Bank of London Held Hostage" below.) Other research has shown that the cost of an effective network security plan for an enterprise with a 50-workstation LAN and Web site could run as high as $100,000. Firewalls alone can run up to $15,000 per site. For all you doubters, do you still think we're not at war?

The federal government has clearly made computer security a high priority. The FBI, the CIA, and the NSA all have small unit operatives dedicated to combating computer security issues and crimes. After Senate hearings on the matter, the Justice Department joined the effort by proposing that it would direct several initiatives to do the following:

1. Commission a full-time task force to study the vulnerability of the nation's information infrastructure

2. Create a rapid response intelligence unit of operatives for computer crimes

3. Mandate that all firms report computer break-ins to the FBI

On another front, MasterCard, VISA, American Express, Microsoft, and IBM joined forces to establish a collective effort called Secure Electronic Transactions (SET). Among other things, the SET Initiative created the specifications for an encryption standard that encodes all credit card numbers and other personal information readable by only the user's and the merchant's (retailer's) bank. In effect, neither users nor retailers themselves can unscramble the information. This ensures that hackers are unable to break through a firewall and read the data in transit across the Internet.

Other companies are establishing emergency response teams to address security issues on the fly, as well as installing firewalls and VPNs to safeguard computer networks for day-to-day activities. The remainder of this chapter features some interesting accounts of successful hacker assaults utilizing a variety of strategies including computer viruses, brute-force attacks, Trojan horse schemes, and outright computer theft.

Speaking of Irony, Russia attacks Citibank

One of the most celebrated attacks on a bank ironically enough was an intercontinental breach launched from a small software firm located in St. Petersburg, Russia. In 1994, a Russian computer expert, along with some accomplices, conducted a series of covert raids on Citibank's New York-based mainframes. The Russians were able to electronically transfer $11 million to bank accounts in Finland, Israel, and California. The bank discovered the theft after the first $400,000 was missing, despite the fact that Citibank's aging computer systems were upgraded to one of the most secure systems in the U.S. banking industry.

The bold Citibank theft was and continues to be mentioned in corporate and computer circles almost every time a company discusses some new Internet banking scheme. The lesson to be learned is, think twice about plugging in another computer service. In other words, thoroughly evaluate an ISP's service, making sure the appropriate security schemes are implemented and available, such as encryption, at a minimum, VPN, or other strong security measures.

If possible, try to avoid expensive private networking solutions such as laying dedicated fiber. Swift, an international banking concern located in Brussels, is spending hundreds of millions of dollars to link member banks with dedicated fiber. Of course, Swift handles nearly $3 trillion in fund transfers a day, so they can afford the ultimate in communications backbone for private networking. However, as presented in this book, even inherently secure channels afforded by solutions like dedicated fiber may not be enough to ward off hacker attacks.

The Sniffer Software Caper

If you look up *irony* in the dictionary, you may find a picture of the Pentagon. Given the fact that the Department of Defense (DoD) commissioned the development of ARPANET, which, of course, evolved into the Internet, it's ironic that the DoD is relentlessly attacked each day through something they were responsible for creating. Attacks on the DoD through the Internet are so prolific and, unfortunately, so common that only about 1 in 500 is routinely reported, according to a Pentagon study.

One of the most daring attacks on the Pentagon involved the use of so-called sniffer software programs. Hackers clandestinely attach "sniffers" to network devices such as routers to monitor information as it flows across the network. One of the U.S. Air Force's top command and control research facilities, Rome Laboratory, encountered this problem in its connection to the Internet. The hackers were able to scan information as it traveled across data switches for passwords that were used to gain access to Rome's internal network. The network was tied to international Web sites. Once inside, the hackers stole tactical and artificial intelligence research. In response to the incident, an official in the Department of Justice suggested that implementing a resolution would be equivalent in scope to the Manhattan Project. VPN solutions might compare in significance, but fortunately, they are not in the same universe when you compare cost.

The Berlin Firewall

Like the Berlin Wall, firewalls can also be brought down if a weak user authentication system is employed. A large, well-known defense contractor of computer services found out the hard way. Using the Internet, two college students hacked their way through the defense contractor's firewall into their internal network. The hackers launched a simple "dictionary attack" with a small program. The program ran through every permutation of potential passwords until one finally allowed them into the network. According to corporate officials, the hackers planned and succeeded in confiscating a list of authorized passwords for profit. Apparently, they were caught when they used one of the passwords to hack into a Cray Research computer owned by one of the defense contractor's suppliers. In an anticlimactic epilogue to the story, both were sentenced to 5 years' probation and 250 hours of community service. The moral of the story is if you are limited to using a weak authentication system such as passwords, establish a policy of constructing strong passwords. (For examples of strong password construction, refer to the "User Authentication" section in the previous chapter.)

The Texas "Firewall" Massacre

Over a year ago, a group of hackers out of the Lone Star State nabbed unlisted telephone numbers and consumer credit information from private networks separately operated by Service Bureau Corporation (SBC), GTE, MCI, and Sprint. In the process, they trashed the networks by wreaking $500,000 in damages. While they were at it, they decided to really have some fun. The FBI got an earful when the intruders rerouted calls from their centers to sex chat lines in Hong Kong and Moldavia. What concerned the common carriers and FBI the most was their ability to gain access and control of core programs, known as "root access." The service bureaus learned that though firewalls are effective, they are not impregnable.

The Bank of London Held Hostage

One of the amazing characteristics of hackers is their ability to hack into enterprises in all fields of endeavor. Even more amazing is their ability to hack into computer and computer services companies such as America Online, Boeing, Intel, Netscape Communications, Rockwell International, and Sun Microsystems. One cannot help but wonder why such companies, with all their computer know-how and resources, do not have ample security measures in place. No doubt this is embarrassing, but this does not signify security weaknesses inasmuch as it indicates the skill level of the wily hacker. Some organizations, such as financial institutions, are so concerned about the negative publicity from hacker attacks that they resort to extreme measures.

According to the *London Times,* embattled financial institutions, including the Bank of London, have even paid hackers more than a half million dollars to keep quiet about computer break-ins. These institutions are using a kind of reverse blackmail to keep hackers from talking to the media. Apparently, such measures seemed warranted to avoid scaring off customers and shareholder complaints. In fact, most companies don't report a successful breach to the authorities. Eventually, domestic and international regulations will come into effect making the reporting of security breaches mandatory.

Sponsored Break-in by RSA

This next account is a fitting way to end this chapter. It contains all the elements of a good story, including intrigue, drama, political statement, incredibility, and irony, because the protagonist in this case is the hacker. In July 1998, RSA Data Security, Inc. of Silicon Valley sponsored a contest to determine who could break a popular encryption standard used extensively by banks, financial institutions, and government agencies. The cryptosystem in question was the 56-bit key Data Encryption Standard known as DES.

The federal government, in its vigorous campaign to keep strong encryption on U.S. soil, has instituted barriers of questionable logic to the exporting of strong encryption. (See "Politics Who's in the Fray" in Chapter 2.) Strong encryption has been classified as keys larger than 56 bits for symmetric keys and larger than 512 bits for asymmetric keys. Federal authorities maintain a tough export policy for U.S.-based companies because of the fear that strong encryption, in the hands of terrorists or other subversives, would place law enforcement agencies at a serious disadvantage. Critics of the policy, however, have argued that strong encryption is readily available from foreign producers. What the policy really does is place users of DES at risk, because the encryption algorithm is too weak to protect the activity of legitimate business users.

Essentially, the contest was sponsored to prove that DES is indeed a weak cryptography system. It was also conducted to convince federal authorities that a determined terrorist group or other criminals could easily break the DES code with a relatively modest financial outlay. The winning contestants were a two-person team (a computer privacy and civil liberties activist and a cryptographer). The two entered a specially designed computer, which they built against a network of almost 20,000 computers, ranging from desktop PCs to multimillion-dollar supercomputers operating together under a distributed processing configuration. The homegrown computer contained about 1000 custom-designed CPUs (computer chips), each designed to test millions of the potential key combinations per second. The computer chips were mounted on 27 motherboards, which, in turn, were installed into several Sun computer chassis.

The resulting computer system was capable of testing *90 billion* different keys each second. More significant, the cost of the custom computer development effort was only $250,000; a paltry figure for some of the well-financed, foreign state-sponsored terrorist groups. The homegrown computer needed just 56 hours to crack the 56-bit key and unscramble the message to win the contest. The computer tested 25% of all the possible key permutations, or a total of 17,902,806,669,197,312 keys. (For the record, this reads: 17 quadrillion, 902 trillion, 806 billion, 669 million, 197 thousand, three hundred and twelve keys.) Incidentally, the decrypted message designated by the RSA judges read: "It's time for those 128-, 192-, and 256-bit keys."

CHAPTER 5

How They Do It

One of the reasons hackers participate in computer crimes, according to the real-life examples in the previous chapter, is for profit. Others are doing it for revenge and still others for the sheer challenge. This chapter focuses on how hackers break into computer systems. The techniques that hackers use to assault your networking environments are in many ways sophisticated, and in other ways they are not. If you fully understand how certain application and operating system software functions, most likely you will know the strengths of a system as well as its weaknesses. For hackers, structural weaknesses in software are the keys to the promised land, because the weaknesses of the software are the objects of exploitation. As the chapter unfolds, practical defenses to these attacks will also be given as a counterbalance.

How Firewalls Are Breached

Not long after firewalls began to receive mainstream acceptance, the first reports of hackers successfully breaking through firewall defenses began to emerge. As a perimeter defense mechanism, firewalls are placed at every critical juncture where the network is exposed to the outside world, such as an Internet connection communications server or a router that connects a department LAN with the enterprise WAN. Since they are positioned on devices that are adjacent to the outside world, hackers were able to discern this functionality and mount a counterstrategy using sniffer software programs. Sniffer programs positioned strategically on Internet nodes filter password information as it traverses a switch or router en route to a firewall access port of an enterprise network. When firewalls rely only upon weak authentication or nonencrypted authentication, a firewall's ability to keep out intruders is only as good as the identification system employed to log into the network.

Brute-Force and Trojan Horse Attacks

Brute-force attacks were another early favorite of hackers when firewalls became a mainstream security solution. Brute-force attacks involve harnessing a computer or computers to cycle through every permutation of potential possibilities of either encrypted password or encrypted data, such as a cryptography system's public key. Today, many organizations utilize strong authentication techniques to certify user access. Since strong authentication, for the most part, employs some form of encryption, brute-force attacks are infeasible for the average hacker because of the considerable computing resources needed to test billions of combinations per second to break the encrypted data. Though the average hacker may not have a battery of computers at his or her disposal to launch brute-force attacks, don't underestimate the hacker's resourcefulness in this regard.

In contrast to earlier implementation of firewalls, today's best systems do not allow incoming messages to touch the rest of the network, because each message is fully inspected before it is allowed to proceed. If the message does not conform to access rules, the message is routinely dropped. This is a key functionality because another favorable attack mechanism of hackers is email. Hackers attach malicious code to email such that when the network operating system processes it to determine the email's destination, the errant code instructs the operating system to create a new name and user password. Afterwards, the hacker is able to access the network at any time. Fortunately, firewalls that inspect all incoming messages render this Trojan horse-like attack largely ineffective.

Java Applets and ActiveX Controls Security Holes

With the advent of Java applets and ActiveX controls, hackers gained renewed life in regard to their ability to breach perimeter defenses. Although Java applets and ActiveX controls are exciting multimedia development tools for the Internet, they became notorious for riddling firewalls with security holes. Internet browsers such as Internet Explorer and Netscape Navigator version 3.X and above contain built-in "virtual machines" to run Java applets and ActiveX controls. Unfortunately, hackers have discovered a variety of security flaws in both systems. To exploit such security flaws, hackers use Trojan horse attacks, for example, to steal passwords or set up user accounts including passwords that will allow them to slip through perimeter defenses. Future releases of both development suites undoubtedly will correct security problems. Until then, the best firewalls allow you to turn off Java applets and ActiveX controls. The trade-off is that you give up fun multimedia effects for a secure networking environment.

Telltale Signs That You've been Breached

Thus far, you have seen that even with the preemptive security afforded by private networks or networks protected by firewalls, such security measures might not provide sufficient protection against hacker attacks. This factor in itself may be the justification that you need to extend or augment your network with a VPN. Regardless of your level of security, how would you know if in fact your network were hacked? Though there are a variety of indicators, you are most likely to encounter any of six telltale signs that hackers have set up shop in your network:

1. *Unknown accounts appear in your system seemingly out of thin air.*
   If you are an administrator responsible for adding new users, it's a
   strong possibility that hackers created a backdoor into your network. Most likely a Trojan horse rolled in with an email, a Java
   applet, an ActiveX control, or when someone was browsing a rogue
   Web site.

2. *Excessive logon failures appear in log reports.* Sometimes hackers
   are long on patience and short on discretion. With enough knock-
   ing, hackers can sometime force doors on your network to open. As
   a rule of thumb, allow each user a certain number of logon attempts
   over a certain period of time, say, over an hour or half day. When
   that number is reached the account should be deactivated and reac-
   tivated when the user initiates contact in person. This should not
   become an administrative headache, since authorized users typically should never reach the maximum logon amount.

3. *Unexpected crashes or reboots of the computer.* Some intrusions
   require the addition of new code to the computing environment,
   followed by a reboot to execute it. Sometimes operating systems
   are unstable, like certain versions of the Windows operating system, and you grow to expect system crashes. However, if your
   server, for example, crashes unexpectedly or reboots itself, what
   happened?

4. *Missing logs or gaps in records.* Hackers cannot cover their
   tracks by erasing them with a tree branch. Sometimes the only
   means at their disposal involves deleting parts of files, which
   leaves obvious holes. The resulting gaps in records become the telltale tracks of those elusive hacks.

5. *Heavy traffic during nonpeak hours, such as after midnight.*
   Have you noticed a considerable amount of file transfer activity
   out of your Canadian office, although it is a small operation? Or
   better yet, do the information requests not match up with the function of the office? Is the traffic load normal? If not, why do your
   graveyard-shift processing loads exceed the daylight loads?

6. *System logs that suddenly fill up faster than normal.* Depending
   upon the company, these critical logs are generally spare. If a
   hacker is masquerading as a system operator, this will be reflected
   here.

Although the preceding items are definite indicators of possible
attacks, other signs may exist as well. In general, hackers tend to work

their art of intrusion between the hours of 6:00 p.m. and 8:00 a.m. on Saturdays, Sundays, and national holidays. Anytime you notice an unexplained but consistent pattern of activity in your network, check it out. It might be readily explained. Then again, it just might be that fiendish interloper of your network neighborhood.

Popular Attacks

In this section, we'll take a close look at how hackers attack the design flaws and inherent weaknesses of key Internet protocols, including TCP/IP and SMTP, and application layer services such as Java and ActiveX. To obtain a more complete understanding of the attacks, the discussion reveals how hackers gain access to your networks from the packet and/or operational level of the protocols. It should not come as a surprise that attacks are launched on this level. Bear in mind that hackers are computer techies, either self-taught or college-educated, and perhaps current or former computer professionals. Hackers possess keen knowledge of the inner workings of Internet protocols and appear to be driven to find that obscure security flaw or inherent weakness to exploit to gain illegal access into places where they are not allowed. Hopefully when we're done, you will be better equipped to prepare your VPN solution to fend off hacker assaults.

IP Address Spoofing

One form of address spoofing begins when the hacker gains access to a network utility called the Routing Information Protocol (RIP), which is used to disseminate routing information to the network. Typically, when a network receives information from RIP, the information is not verified. As a result of this shortcoming, a hacker can send bogus routing information to a target host let's say (A) that the hacker is looking to deceive or spoof. The counterfeit information is also sent to each of the gateways one would encounter along the path to the target host A. The bad routing information that the target host A and gateway(s) receive usually represents a path to a dormant or unused host (B) on the network. (Usually an idle workstation.) Thus, any packets defined for host B would be routed to the hacker's computer instead, though the target host A and the gateway think the traffic is going to host B, a "trusted" node on the

Figure 5-1
IP address spoofing
attack.

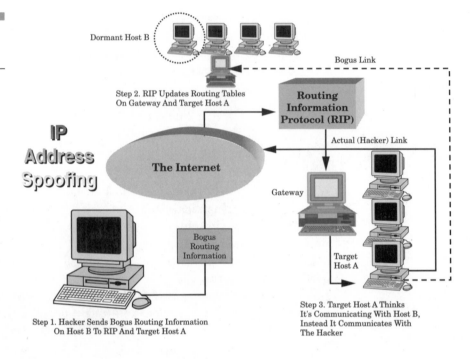

network. Once the hacker is able to substitute his or her workstation or host for an actual host on the network, host spoofing is achieved. Protocols or services that rely on address-based authentication are then effectively compromised. (See Figure 5-1 for a summary of this attack.)

IP Address Spoofing with Active Host

The IP address spoof above enabled the hacker to achieve host spoofing on the targeted host's network, using an idle host or workstation. The hacker could also realize host spoofing utilizing an active host or workstation. In order to compromise an active host, the network must have a feature turned on called *IP source routing*. Assume that the hacker submits routing information on compromised active host B to the RIP. The RIP, in turn, updates the routing tables of target host A and its gateway. Now when target host A communicates with active host B, the communication goes through the hacker for inspection and possible alteration, allowing the intruder to capture passwords and other sensitive data. When the hacker is done confiscating all the information he or she

Figure 5-2
Spoof attack using an
active host.

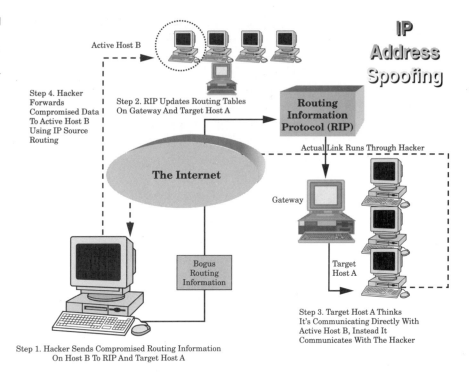

Figure 5-2
Spoof attack using an
active host.

Active Host B

IP
Address
Spoofing

Step 4. Hacker
Forwards
Compromised Data
To Active Host B
Using IP Source
Routing

Step 2. RIP Updates Routing Tables
On Gateway And Target Host A

Routing
Information
Protocol (RIP)

Actual Link Runs Through Hacker

The Internet

Gateway

Bogus
Routing
Information

Target
Host A

Step 3. Target Host A Thinks
It's Communicating Directly With
Active Host B, Instead It
Communicates With The Hacker

Step 1. Hacker Sends Compromised Routing Information
On Host B To RIP And Target Host A

prefers, the communications link is completed when the intruder forwards the compromised information packets to active host B using IP source routing. (See Figure 5-2.) Fortunately, IP address spoofing or host spoofing is easily handled through firewall security policy functionality as a standard feature. (See Chapter 8 for a review of firewall operation.)

IP Source Routing

Of all the shortcomings of the IP protocol, IP source routing is perhaps the easiest to abuse. Say, for example, you have an originating host B seeking to establish a session layer or TCP open request for return traffic with target host A. The IP source packets from the originating host B use a certain path to target host A. Assume that target host A uses the *same* path that host B uses to return the requested data but in the reverse order. Suppose the originating host B, utilizing IP source routing capability, specifies another path to the destination host because the automatic route is inactive. As a result, information replies from target host A might not reach the originating host B if host A's replies travel across a new pathway. In other words, since the original automatic pathway from host B has changed, the pathway for host A's return replies *back* to host B is uncertain.

Enter the wily hacker. At this point, the hacker can come in and supply *any* IP source address desired, including the source address of a trusted host on the network in question. With hacker-supplied IP addresses, the replies from host A acquire a definite pathway—not to host B, but to a host chosen by the hacker. Therefore, any facilities available to the host (computer system) assigned to that IP address also become available to the hacker. (See Figure 5-3.) Though IP source routing is tricky to defend, a VPN's security server gateway can establish a policy option to reject external packets claiming to be from the local, internal network.

Java and ActiveX Attacks

One of the bothersome injustices in the world is the exploitation of security flaws found in Java applets and ActiveX controls by hackers. Hackers exploitation of the software's security flaws has become so notorious that when you browse sites where objects are blinking or flashing,

Figure 5-3
IP source route attack.

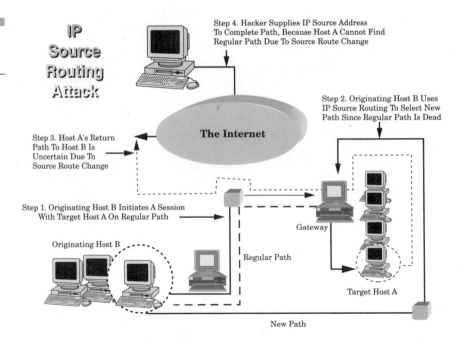

instead of saying "oh wow," you say, "oh no" (or perhaps something a little stronger). Without a doubt, hackers have made it risky to enjoy the rich multimedia effects in Web sites that incorporate Java applets or ActiveX controls. For instance, to interact with a Web page that calls Java applets for multimedia effects, compatible browsers such as Internet Explorer or Navigator version 3.X or higher must download the "object libraries" to a workstation in order for the Web page to run the Java applets. Web pages are usually constructed with HTML, and HTML calls Java applets through mechanisms known as *tags*. The applets use the object or class libraries, which are compiled Java source code, to feature the full-motion animation that makes Web pages fun to view through your browser.

On a rogue Web site, a site compromised by hacker presence, hackers covertly attach Trojan horse programs to the object libraries. When a user's browser interacts with a site, the Trojan horse slips into the user's system with the class libraries and stays dormant until the right keystroke and/or mouse-click combination activates the Trojan into action. Once the Trojan swipes the user's password and delivers it to a safe haven for hackers, a hacker can use a dictionary attack or a brute-force attack, if it's encrypted, to derive the correct password.

Another hacker technique exploits a certain workstation configuration featuring, for example, Microsoft's Internet Explorer browser operating under NT client software. In this scenario, hackers write a simple ActiveX control using the "PWDump" command code and subsequently embed the resulting control to a Web site running other ActiveX controls. At this point, the Web site in question becomes a rogue Web site. When an administrative user operating under the above configuration browses this site, PWDump extracts hashed passwords out of the system software. The hacker, in turn, identifies the actual password after a brute-force attack.

To avoid this scenario, special administrative procedures can be performed with NT. To find out what you can do, contact Microsoft or the NTBugtraq Web site at www.ntbugtraq.com/. In the meantime, VPN solutions allow you to strip tags from HTML documents that call Java applets and ActiveX controls. Until security improves with future releases of the development suites, stripping tags and applying other VPN security measures are your safest courses of action.

How Sniffer Software Programs Work

It may come as a surprise that sniffer programs are as commonplace as network routers. Sniffers are a network software utility used to analyze network traffic. Normally, the programs compile too much data to be useful to hacker shenanigans. However, they are attractive to hackers because they are equipped with an application programmer interface (API). Through the API, sniffers can be programmed to monitor and search for data consisting of certain patterns, such as passwords. Since sniffers, more often referred to as "packet sniffers," are regular tools in the hacker's bag of tricks, you can be certain that they are widely used throughout the Internet.

When data traverses the World Wide Web of the Internet, it may cycle through several routers before reaching its destination. Along the way, it is a foregone conclusion that the data typically pass through a poorly secured system. Obviously, poorly secured systems invite the wily hacker to set up shop and install a packet sniffer. Once in place, the packet sniffer examines all the data streaming through the system, including account and credit card numbers, passwords, corporate information, and the like.

As each new generation of sniffer programs emerges, it poses more serious risks to TCP/IP communications (Internet data transport) security. A fundamental shortcoming with IP is the lack of any mechanism to verify where packets actually originate. All packets have source and destination addresses, but nothing exists natively in IP that authenticates the source or destination of the IP packet. You have seen how IP addresses can be spoofed through the Routing Information Protocol (RIP) and how hosts can be spoofed through source routing. If the flaw did not exist, such attacks could not occur. A packet sniffer also takes advantage of this flaw, since it can be used to detect valid Internet connections. Once detected, the packet sniffer allows the use of some other IP weakness to hijack the connection by interposing the attack between the client and the server. In effect, all subsequent information in the session can be intercepted, saved, and printed.

TCP Attacks

TCP "sequence number prediction," one of the more sophisticated hacker attacks, usually leads to host spoofing. A normal TCP connection establishment sequence requires a three-way handshake between an Internet client and server. The connection sequence begins when the client selects an initial sequence number, ISN(C). In response, a server on the Internet acknowledges it and sends its own sequence number, ISN(S), in return. The three-way handshake occurs when the client acknowledges the server's response with ISN(C-ACK). After the three ISN messages are exchanged, data transmission begins between the client and server. The exchange can be shown schematically as follows:

1. Client sends ISN(C).
2. Server sends ISN(S) in response.
3. Client sends ISN(C-ACK) for client acknowledgement
4. Three-way handshake is completed.
5. Client and server engage in two-way data exchange.

In a TCP connection, the server ISN is generated randomly. A timing mechanism increments the ISN number by a constant amount on an ongoing basis. When a client seeks to initiate a connection, whatever is the incremented ISN as of that particular time becomes the ISN(S) in the connection sequence. A sequence number prediction attack occurs after a hacker observes a normal session between a trusted host and server on a given network. Once the hacker determines a server's ISN number and the timing constant that is continually added to create it, the next ISN number can be calculated with a high degree of confidence, hence, sequence number prediction. When the ISN that is slated for the next TCP connection attempt can be predicted, the attack unfolds in the following manner:

1. Hacker sends ISN(IC), which impersonates trusted client.
2. Server sends ISN(S), which was predicted by the hacker.
3. Hacker sends ISN(IC-ACK) to acknowledge receipt.
4. Three-way handshake is completed, and trusted client is summarily spoofed.
5. Hacker and server engage in two-way data exchange.

Before clean data transmissions can occur between the hacker and the spoofed server, the hacker must perform one other housekeeping chore to cover his or her tracks. Though the intruder hijacks the session, the server thinks it's communicating with a trusted host. In fact, the trusted host actually receives the message from the server. In response, the trusted host, not really understanding the reason for receiving an unsolicited connection response, attempts to reset the connection instead of sending an acknowledgement as per a normal sequence. Knowing why the server is attempting the connection request, the hacker bombards the trusted host with a battery of successive connection requests. The bombardment overflows the queue and the server's connection response is eventually lost.

Ping of Death

"Ping of death" is not some Shakespearean nickname for one of his sinister villains; instead, it is a denial of service ploy used by hackers. If they can't steal from you or trick you into submission or surreptitiously gain access to valuable computing resources, the next best thing is bringing you down. Denial of service is not sporting in any way—as if hacker attacks could ever be. Such attacks are designed to remove an entire site or an entire network from service. Unfortunately, denial of service can only be treated. To eliminate it would require a complete overhaul of the Internet's operational design. In some documented attacks, these ploys have nearly driven enterprises out of business because they can literally interrupt service for weeks at a time.

Ping is an Internet service that investigates the validity of an Internet connection between two communicating hosts by sending a message from one to another for confirmation. By default, ping messages are designed to be 64 bytes or less. Hackers, in their infinite wisdom, discovered that by sending ping messages greater than 64 bytes, it's possible to bring down computers connected to the Internet. They simply crash. Sustained bombardments of ping result in continual denial of service and possibly, figuratively speaking, "death." Again, denial of service attacks can never be eliminated, but they can be opposed through router utilities and VPN solutions.

Other Attacks

Other attacks include some that are launched against Simple Mail Transfer Protocol (SMTP), which transfers email from computer to computer. Two popular SMTP attacks include "buffer overrun" and "backdoor command raids." A buffer overrun is a typical email attack where someone's mailbox is flooded with a constant barrage of emails until the system goes down. Backdoor command raids are usually launched through email attachments. Trojan horse programs are secretly embedded in the email such that when you double-click on the email listing, the Trojan slips through a back door in the program attachment and reads your passwords or instructs the system to set up a new user account.

Still another attack is "Web spoofing." Web spoofing is a relatively new attack where a hacker breaks into a Web site to compromise hyperlinks that take you from the current site to another. For example, suppose a site's Web page contains a hyperlink to a certain WWW site, and a hacker who has piggybacked his or her Web site's WWW or URL (Uniform Resource Locator) to the URL for the legitimate site compromises this hyperlink. When a hacker attaches his or her URL to the legitimate one, the hacker's cannot be seen. Thus, when an unsuspecting Web surfer double-clicks on the link, instead of being connected to the legitimate Web site, the surfer is whisked off to the hacker's site instead. The hacker's site, of course, would resemble the legitimate commercial site. So when a surfer decides to make a purchase, credit card numbers and other personal information can be confiscated. The scary thing about this is, if the site provides encrypted transactions, which are verified by a lock or key icon on the Web browser, the surfer will think the site is perfectly safe when, in fact, it is not. Unfortunately, Web spoofing is transacted through Java applets and ActiveX controls. Since there are basically no comprehensive remedies for them, your only option is to strip off Java applets and ActiveX controls with your security gateway.

Recommended Web Sites

Now you know how they do it, at least for the most popular attacks. For the wily hacker, cyberspace is a lot like the old frontier in the late 1800s. In the Old West, men usually took matters into their own hands. Sometimes rules and regulations and the men that enforced them had to cover vast territory that took them days, maybe weeks, to cross. Of course, most tried to live as law-abiding citizens, but too many did not. If you substituted the references to the Old West with "Internet," you could be describing the situation on the information superhighway of today. Unlike the Old West, which eventually gave way to industrialization and manifest destiny, hacker problems won't be eliminated so systematically. In fact, hackers will be here indefinitely.

In the meantime, VPN solutions will provide the bridge over these crime-infested waters. If there are security flaws or weaknesses in tunneling protocols, encryption, and authentication, hackers will find them—just as they found weak encryption schemes and firewall vulnerabilities and used brute-force or Trojan horse attacks to break in. Due to the sophistication of security solutions and protocols of today, it is imperative to keep abreast of the intricacies of security issues and developments to maintain top-level security for your network computing environment. Be sure to regularly consult several Web sites, trade journals, forums, and the like and keep track of security developments and issues

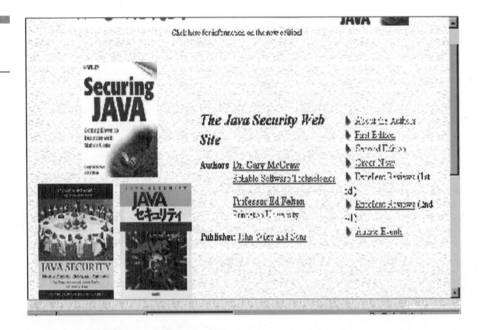

as they happen. Two excellent Web sites that convey comprehensive sources of information on hacker and security issues are the Java Security and ICSA Web sites.

The Java Security Site   The Java Security Web site is a comprehensive information source for a variety of Java security issues, problems, developments, and other related aspects of the security universe. (See Figure 5-4.) It features descriptions and reviews of the latest books, white papers, and articles on security concerns. The Web location also features the latest research and the anticipated impact of the research on related security problems. A section for FAQs is included, along with the specific enhancements and corrections that new releases of commercial implementations will deliver for combating prevailing security issues. The most dynamic section found at this site, however, is the "Java Security Hot List." The hot list delivers an up-to-the-minute descriptive list of hostile applets that users should be aware of, related fixes, and how to avoid them when surfing the Internet. The Java Security Web site can be accessed at www.rstcorp.com/java-security.html.

The ICSA Site   The International Computer Security Association (ICSA) Web site can be accessed at www.ncsa.com or www.icsa.net/. (See

Figure 5-5
ICSA, the security
assurance home
page.

Figure 5-5.) ICSA (formerly the National Computer Security Association) is one of the world's foremost authorities in certifying computer
products for Internet application development. ICSA is an independent
company that is also successfully leading the security industry in establishing best practices for Internet security assurance. ICSA certifies the
full complement of security products and application suites, including
antivirus, firewall, cryptography, filtering and monitoring, biometrics,
and even Internet and Web sites. It also certifies commercial products
for compliance to industry standards such as IPSC, IKE, or MD5 hashing algorithm. The ICSA Web site features all the latest certification
efforts that are currently under way. It also maintains a list of company
products that have been successfully tested and certified. For a listing of
certified VPN products, visit the Web site.

CHAPTER 6

When Firewalls Fail: Coping with the Aftermath

If a chain is only as strong as its weakest link, then a firewall is only as strong as its weakest "brick"—or something like that. Like any technology, firewalls are not perfect. And since they are user or administrator installable, it is virtually impossible to anticipate every aspect of potential installation scenarios or security considerations when preparing a firewall for duty. (See Figure 6-1.) Although firewalls are technically not a native component of VPN solutions, together they propose a remarkably robust security solution for enterprise networks. However, firewalls must be installed properly for every given situation, and it is safe to assume no two are exactly alike.

Figure 6-1
Managing initial fire-
wall setup.

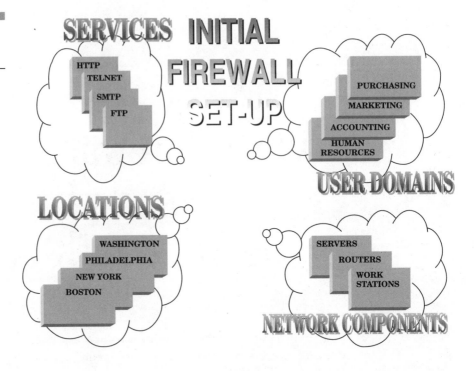

Figure 6-1
Managing initial fire-
wall setup.

There are two important requirements for setting up your firewall to function optimally. First, it must be physically installed properly. This may include installing to a server unit and numerous network routers—some local, perhaps most remote. And second, it must be configured correctly as the enterprise's security gateway. This might include setting up more than one physical gateway in several locations. (This second requirement is covered in detail in Chapter 8.) This section identifies several situations and related circumstances concerning firewall failures and what you should do about them.

Refiguring Your Misconfiguration

If you consider the number of services intranets can provide, and the number of ways these services can be combined into a particular solution for a given enterprise network, firewalls can be configured with virtually an infinite variety of options. Unlike jet pilots who can make up time in the air after a late departure, it's a mistake if you plan to configure and administer your firewall on the fly. The initial configuration effort must include the most comprehensive account of your networking environment as possible. Although this could prove to be a tedious, time-consuming project, it is unwise to deploy a basic firewall configuration initially with the idea that the comprehensive one will be deployed at a later date. By the time this is done, intruders may have already compromised your network.

The default state for some firewalls, out of the box, is to drop all incoming packets. At the opposite end, the firewall can be set up to allow all traffic through. It's safe to say most will find an implementation along this spectrum. Many firewalls, though high, are scaled because some class of service was allowed that ultimately proved to be a channel for a hacker attack. Policing all the services each individual may eventually want to run through the firewall could also prove to be a tough, time-consuming responsibility. For this reason, a thorough assessment of current and future requirements must be determined during planning stages. And once the firewall is in operation, a strict policy for adding new services must be followed. To maintain a safe networking environment for the entire enterprise, management on all levels must be apprised of the security policy for its buy-in and support. This support is just as important as the initial firewall setup. Without it, some department managers, periodically, may request services to be allowed through the firewall that are not sanctioned by enterprisewide policy.

Apathy: The Fastest Way to Get Burned

One of the cardinal sins of network computing is taking a firewall for granted—that is, ignoring it and assuming that it is doing its job. Once in place, firewalls provide real-time monitoring of network activities, including logged-in users and status of security gateways. Mounting a constant vigil to monitor the status of an enterprise network can be a mundane, uneventful activity; however, it is a necessary one. Real-time monitoring responsibility may often lull network operators into complacency or perhaps even apathy. However, at those times when you least expect it, such moments become prime opportunities for the hacker to strike. To maintain the integrity of the security, the network manager's responsibility is to make certain that this task is approached with due diligence.

Another problem network managers may run into is not having sufficient time or resources to monitor firewall activities. In addition, the resulting reports (i.e., login or usage reports) must also be systematically reviewed to ensure the security system's effectiveness. If, in fact, either time or lack of resources is an issue, monitoring activities can be divided and shared among the networking or MIS staff as additional responsibility. In effect, each individual would be required to spend only a few hours with such a routine task. Since hackers tend to attack during non-prime-time hours, including weekends and holidays, covering these periods of relative inactivity is essential.

Dial-in for Firewalls

Another way firewalls can be broken into is through modem banks that organizations maintain for dial-in access by mobile users or remote offices. Enterprises that maintain modem banks in connection with a private network are particularly at risk, as are those companies that outsource their private network to an ISP's public data network, distinguished from the public Internet. If your organization invests a lot of funds in a firewall or pays a premium to get this service through an ISP, it is imperative that you institute the proper security measures if you support your own or that you verify the security measures your ISP has in place for theirs. One of the many advantages of VPNs is forgoing the need and expense of maintaining modem pools or communication servers to support remote dial-in access (see Chapter 1). Since most major firewall vendors offer a VPN solution in connection with the firewall component, the combination is typically very effective against intruder strikes.

Incoming Traffic: The Smoke Alarms of Firewalls

You knew this was coming. Where there is smoke there is not necessarily fire—unless, of course, we are talking about firewalls. In the previous chapter, six signals of firewall breaches were discussed. Metaphorically speaking, those six signs can be considered firewall smoke alarms, which are peculiarities suggesting the possible compromise of a network's security.

Certain incoming traffic may also pose a potential threat to the network behind the firewall. One of the evolutionary features of firewalls is access control. Access control allows incoming traffic to only interact with certain areas within the network. For example, remote-marketing offices may access sales training information or check purchasing reports for order status, but they cannot review financial data. Or, if you allow email from outside the demilitarized zone (i.e., outside the firewall) to be processed by the enterprise mail server, you need to be concerned about possible SMTP attacks, as discussed in Chapter 5. Also, placing Web site servers that were developed with Java applets or ActiveX controls might lead to a breach with Trojan horse attacks even though the Web site is positioned outside the demilitarized zone.

Fortunately, firewalls offer application proxies, which inspect application-level services like SMTP, HTTP, and Telnet, before information is allowed to selected parts of the network. Overall, application proxies working in conjunction with a VPN offer a pretty formidable security protection system. Application proxy concepts are discussed in detail in Chapter 8.

Software Upgrades: Fuel for Firewalls

Upgrading the firewall is a critical process in maintaining the long-term viability of the enterprise's security system. For one thing, it keeps you ahead of the game, since hackers are always on the prowl. Firewall vendors routinely enhance product offerings by adding new features that increase functionality and correct security holes in earlier releases. New releases also include on-the-spot fixes that firewall manufacturers provide to correct all types of problems encountered by the customer base in between official releases of the product. Hackers may see a firewall as an enterprise's way of throwing down the gauntlet, thereby motivating them to develop all new methods of attack, especially if established ones no longer prove to be effective. Consequently, expediently upgrading your firewall in connection with new vendor releases is a critical safety requirement for the long-term security of the enterprise's network.

Key Firewall Web Sites

Three Web sites you should visit for information on firewalls and security are as follows:

1. *www.clark.net/pub/mjr/pubs/fwfaq*—This is the official site for FAQs about Internet firewalls.

2. *www.clark.net/pub/mjr/pubs*—This site includes vendor-neutral or unbiased editorials and presentations about firewalls and security. An excellent information source to visit routinely.

3. *www.gocsi.com*—A newsletter, published by the Computer Security Institute, may be accessed at this site. This newsletter and other publications produced by the institute are a good source for learning about the extent and cost of computer crimes. The publications also provide comparison matrixes of all types concerning firewalls.

In addition to these sites, your firewall vendor most likely has a Web site. Vendor sites are an equally good source of information on firewall security. Although these sites may not be as unbiased as the three sites given above, some vendors do an excellent job in providing comprehensive information on firewall security. As you know, the more perspectives you experience, the more knowledgeable you become on the subject matter.

PART 3

Going Under
the Hood

Welcome to the exciting world of virtual private networking. Part 3 takes you in for a close look at VPN operational features and functionality and provides an overview of how the components of VPNs actually work. Until this point, you were provided with a bird's-eye view of the building blocks of VPNs. Now you will see how those building blocks plug and play to establish secure channels across the public Internet, and you will fully understand how VPN component integration is designed to work. With this knowledge you will be in a favorable position to evaluate VPN functionality in terms of your own potential requirements.

In Chapter 7, the operational characteristics of VPNs are discussed to show how they engage the Internet to provide private communication channels. In Chapters 8 and 9, we look at the architecture of firewalls in detail, along with innovative firewall products. Chapter 10 focuses on other key VPN functionality to broaden your horizon. Chapter 11 explores how VPN and firewall technologies are harnessed to create an enterprisewide security policy using "rule-based logic." Finally, performance considerations are reviewed to provide some guidelines for evaluating and monitoring VPN performance.

CHAPTER 7

The Technology of VPNs

Tunneling, encryption, and authentication protocols are the primary technology platforms on which VPNs are built. Within each of these three technology classes, security administrators can choose from various options to deploy the VPN. The options that are available, however, depend upon which VPN components are made available through competing solutions. For example, IPSec, LT2P, and PPTP are options for tunneling. Most vendors have either implemented or are planning to implement IPSec for tunneling. Others have based their tunneling on PPTP, despite PPTP's weak support for encryption and strong authentication. Still others incorporate a proprietary tunneling protocol. In some cases, vendors that started out with a proprietary tunneling protocol may also offer an "emerging standard" such as IPSec to broaden their solution's market appeal.

This chapter will discuss the operational features of the most popular building blocks that VPN vendors have to choose from for their respective VPN products. Many of the integral components of VPNs provide similar functionality, while some are better suited for certain other tasks. For example, L2TP is best suited to provide remote dial-in for users crossing the Internet for a frame relay, X.25, or other packet-switched network. Packet-switched networks are WANs that convert network traffic into basic units, called *packets,* for transmission across a communication line. The switching occurs at network routers, which determine the path of least resistance for the destination of a given packet.

Private Information Highways

Figure 7-1 demonstrates the concept of private information highways across the information superhighway of the Internet. There are two

Figure 7-1
Virtually private information highway.

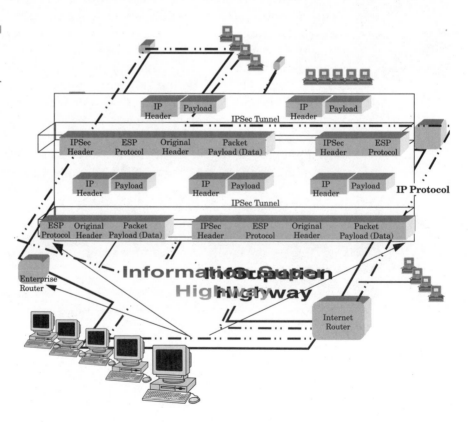

types of virtually private highways or connections that can be established: a client-to-LAN connection or a LAN-to-LAN link. (Actually, a third could be created from a combination of the two.) In a client-to-LAN link, the VPN endpoints consist of an end-user workstation and LAN security server or gateway. The ultimate destination, of course, is the application server behind the security gatekeeper, usually a firewall or other security gateway providing a similar function. In a LAN-to-LAN connection, the VPN endpoints are two security gateways that are handling private communications between users on two different LANs positioned behind their perimeter defenses. The destination application for users on either LAN could be email, Web browsing, video conferencing, file transfer, or establishing new DNS entries for entities connected to the WAN.

In Figure 7-1, PPTP or L2TP—if the WAN protocol were frame relay or ATM—could have also created the resulting virtually private highway.

How Do They Work?

When a connection between two VPN nodes is established, the VPN tunnel actually performs like a router on top of the Internet protocol. If the destination address of a packet is targeted for a VPN end node, generally speaking, the tunnel server or *originating* security gateway performs several operations:

1. The tunneling protocol attaches an "outer" header to the original packet. The outer header contains the address of the VPN node that terminates the tunnel.

2. The tunnel server or security gateway selects the appropriate encryption key for authentication and encryption operations. Each resulting tunnel uses its own encryption key.

3. The original IP header and the packet payload or transport data are encrypted. In the case of IPSec, the outer header, put in position by IPSec, is also authenticated.

4. The tunneled (authenticated and encrypted) IP packet is routed over the Internet to the VPN destination endpoint. The endpoint could be a host, such as a remote user workstation, or another security gateway. (See Figure 7-2.)

Figure 7-2
Establishing a secure
VPN tunnel.

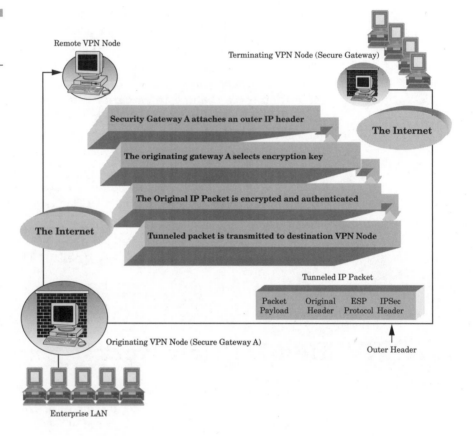

Dynamic Exchange through Public Key Algorithms

The cryptosystem incorporated by the VPN dictates which formal encryption scheme is utilized between the two tunnel endpoints. If a public key cryptosystem is used, the options usually include either a Diffie-Hellman or RSA public key exchange, or both. (See Chapter 3 for a discussion on cryptosystems.) Each remote user in a client-to-LAN VPN connection and each user communicating through a LAN-to-LAN VPN link possesses different encryption keys for establishing encrypted tunnels. In fact, the number of potential keys increases exponentially with each new VPN participant, including a site or a node. For this reason, a critical success factor in VPN deployment is an automated key management system. Key management systems specify how keys are created, distributed, revoked, and refreshed. (Key management systems are discussed in detail later in this chapter.)

Weak vs. Strong User Authentication

There is a critical dependence between a secure VPN tunnel and user authentication. Therefore, it is important to establish a high degree of confidence that a user, at the source or originating VPN node, is who he or she claims to be. However, when a weak authentication login scheme is in effect, such as user ID and password, the security of the resulting tunnel is at risk unless extra precautions are taken. The extra precautions entail selecting passwords that are not easy to guess (easy-to-guess passwords include birth dates, favorite colors, and pet names). Instead, passwords should be chosen at random, perhaps from a dictionary, employ special characters such as ampersands or asterisks, and never be written down around the workstation. (See "user authentication" in Chapter 3.)

Strong authentication that employs a challenge-response system or generates a new password at specific intervals ensures the highest level of security for VPN tunnels. Strong user authentication is virtually foolproof against password attacks of the brute-force and dictionary kind, and perhaps even resistant to certain Trojan horse ploys that instruct administrative systems to clandestinely set up a user ID and password of the weak-authentication variety. While the administration and management of strong authentication schemes are more expensive, the ability to deploy secure private information highways across the Internet makes the trade-off worthwhile.

Progression Authentication Techniques

Typically, when considering authentication, one thinks of user authentication and data authentication. In addition to regular authentication, however, some VPN vendors offer other innovative techniques such as client (host) authentication and session authentication. In *client authentication,* a particular individual user is validated to use a specific remote or network workstation. (See Figure 7-3.) After a remote or network VPN user is authenticated, the user's ID and password are mapped to the IP address of that user's remote or network workstation or host computer. In this situation, if the user attempts to access the network from

Figure 7-3
Client (host)
authentication.

another workstation or host, because this workstation has a different IP address, access to the network is summarily denied.

Session authentication can be seen as an extension of client or host authentication, or as a progression of user authentication. If user and client authentication is successful, the next authentication challenge is at the session level. In session-level authentication, a user is given access rights to certain applications on the network. Thus, when subsequent sessions are conducted, the user may only engage those network applications where access rights were granted. For example, if a user is granted access to email or the internal Web server, any attempt to use other internal applications, such as FTP or UDP, is blocked by the security gateway.

Figure 7-4 summarizes the progression levels or concentric layers of the authentication process. With user, client, and session authentication progressions, the resulting VPN tunnel is guaranteed the highest level

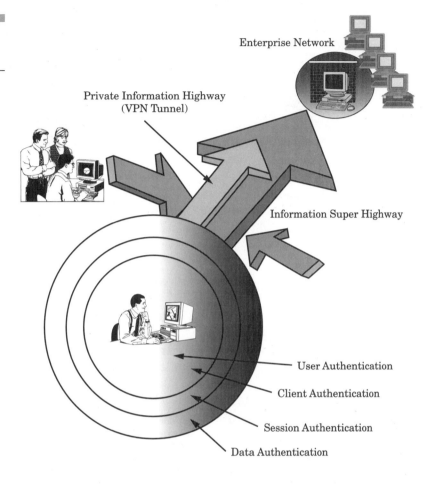

Figure 7-4
Concentric layers of authentication.

Enterprise Network

Private Information Highway
(VPN Tunnel)

Information Super Highway

User Authentication

Client Authentication

Session Authentication

Data Authentication

of security. The next section discusses the impact of data authentication techniques in establishing secure VPN tunnels.

Data Authentication (Integrity Check)

Data authentication is the fourth and final layer in the metaphorical model for authentication. (Bear in mind that client- (host) and session-level authentication may not be available through a particular vendor. If you are interested in these features, you should query your prospective VPN vendor.) After each successive level of authentication is attained, data authentication ensures that the actual VPN data is not tampered with while in transmission.

In a resulting VPN system, data authentication is typically applied in two situations. In the first situation, your certificate authority (CA) employs a data authentication technique to certify a given user's encryption key set. The user receives the encryption key set on a digital certificate. The certificate is authenticated with a technique known as the *digital signature process.* (See discussion on digital signatures in Chapter 3.) In the digital signature process, the CA signs or validates your key with their private key. Given that each encryption key is different, the resulting procedure produces a unique message, called a *signature,* that is produced by hashing the encryption key and encrypting the results. The unique signature that is produced at the CA is also reproduced at the potentially new VPN endpoint, or where the key is to be placed in service. If the two messages are identical when compared at the VPN endpoint, the encryption key set was not tampered with en route from the CA to the VPN node.

The other situation where data authentication is utilized is in regular VPN transmissions. When data leaves a VPN node that originates a transmission, the digital signature process is used to authenticate data transmitted via a VPN tunnel. Data authentication is typically applied at the packet level by the security association established by the tunneling protocol or at the application level by the user. Usually, data authentication at the packet level is handled transparently to the user, between the security gateway and the originating VPN endpoint. Insofar as authentication goes, data validation is the icing on the cake for assuring secure private VPN tunnels. At a minimum, your VPN vendor should offer strong user and data authentication. If other forms or authentication are offered, so much the better for your VPN.

Size Does Matter

If there is ever a situation where size does matter, it's encryption. The size of encryption keys matters so much that the federal authorities have enacted laws restricting the use of strong encryption outside the United States. (See "Politics: Who's in the Fray" in Chapter 2.) In regard to a symmetric, or private, key cryptosystem, software applications or cryptosystems that employ keys greater than 56 bits are barred from export. Typical private key or symmetric key sizes are 40 bits, 56 bits, 112 bits, 128 bits, and 160 bits. To deploy an application for overseas service requires licensing by the State Department. You may apply for 56-bit key use. The resulting application, however, is remanded to the

National Security Agency for approval. Generally, applications for overseas service requesting the use of keys greater than 40 bits are denied. The Export Control Act of 1994 was amended to allow export of 56-bit keys, if the software vendor includes a back door that can be accessed by federal authorities if necessary. The federal authorities allow 2 years for compliance. A proposal in Congress lays out a plan for housing backdoor keys in an escrow system called government access to keys (GAK).

In an asymmetric, or public/private, key system, only 512-bit keys are approved for export. Public/private key sizes of 768-, 1024-, and 2048-bit keys are considered to be strong encryption. Regardless of the politics surrounding encryption, the larger the key size, the stronger the encryption. Since encryption plays such a vital role in a VPN system, deployment of strong encryption ensures greater privacy and greater resilience against hacker attacks. (See Figure 7-5.)

Figure 7-5 suggests that encryption plays a critical role in VPN systems. It is an integral component in strong authentication systems, such as RADIUS and CRYPTOCard, a smart card device. In strong authentication methods, encryption is incorporated to generate user passwords in ciphertext instead of cleartext. RADIUS also uses encryption to

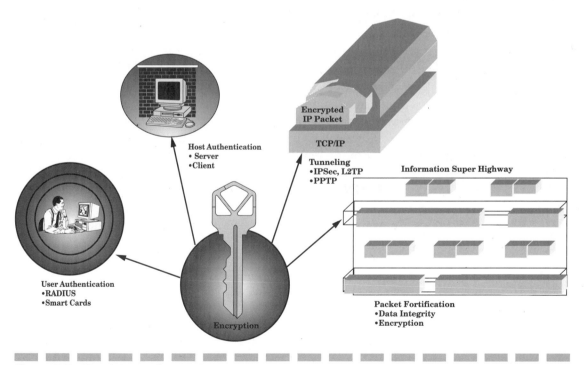

Figure 7-5 The vital role of encryption.

develop a shared secret to validate the network access server with the RADIUS user authentication server. Encryption plays a key role in data authentication, as well specifically anchoring the digital signature process. IPSec uses encryption to fortify packet payloads and IP source and destination addresses. In addition, single encryption key sets can be bound to a server or other hosts including security gateways.

If you are planning to build VPN connections to service overseas applications, a very important technique to consider is *perfect forward secrecy,* a procedure that ensures that *ongoing* encryption operations, for example, key generation, do not compromise *existing* encrypted information. If routinely practiced, perfect forward secrecy can be an effective deterrent against hacker attacks, regardless of key size, because encryption keys are replenished regularly, thereby preventing hackers from having sufficient time to do their thing. For example, in a Diffie-Hellman cryptosystem, perfect forward secrecy is inherent to the encryption process. Whenever one of the parties of a two-way trust model changes, the resulting shared secret changes. When that happens, perfect forward secrecy is attained because, in going from one key exchange to the next, a distinct level of independence from the previous exchange is created. This process is effective because no shared secret remains on a network long enough to be compromised by a hacker.

IPSec (IP Security) Encryption Technology Implementations

What makes the IPSec tunneling protocol so desirable is its ability to deliver a comprehensive level of security to the packet level. Authentication and encryption services are delivered to specific areas of the IP datagram operating structure, including IP headers and payload data. (See Figures 3-4 and 3-5 and the discussion on IP security protocols in Chapter 3.) IP security services are administered through the Authenticating Header (AH) protocol and Encapsulating Security Payload (ESP) protocol. AH and ESP deliver security services to two types of VPN transmission modes: transport mode and tunnel mode.

In transport mode (VPN transmissions between two hosts), AH provides two key data validation services:

1. Authentication of the IP source address in the packet's IP header.

2. Data integrity checking for connectionless upper-layer protocols such as UDP and TCP. Connectionless protocols communicate by

dumping their data payloads on the Internet. Confirmation of a successful transmission occurs when the receiving host responds to establish a regular session. If the receiving host is not available or activated, the originating host receives no response. For this reason, TCP and UDP are called "connectionless" protocols.

AH connectionless integrity service lends connectionless protocols a helping hand by ensuring that communications are not tampered with during transport mode communication.

In transport mode, ESP provides confidentiality or encryption to the packet payload or upper layer protocols only and basically does nothing for the IP header. In tunnel mode, however, ESP provides encryption services to the original IP header and to the packet payload as well. In this mode, IPSec also attaches an *outer* IP header, which is the IPSec processing destination of the tunneled or encrypted packet. To secure the outer IP header, IPSec utilizes AH to authenticate it to the receiving VPN security gateway. AH also authenticates the *inner* IP header and the packet payload of the "tunneled"(encrypted) IP datagram. Therefore, AH delivers the authentication services to the tunneled IP datagram, and ESP delivers the confidentiality or encryption services. When IPSec uses both AH and ESP to fully secure an IP datagram, this technique is referred to as "AH encapsulating ESP." For a summary of this technique, see Figure 7-6.

Figure 7-6
AH encapsulating
ESP for full packet
security.

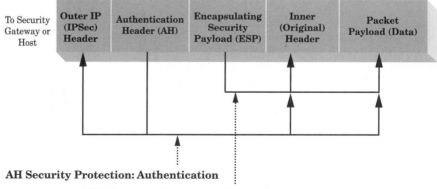

IPSec Security Protocols Services

| To Security Gateway or Host | Outer IP (IPSec) Header | Authentication Header (AH) | Encapsulating Security Payload (ESP) | Inner (Original) Header | Packet Payload (Data) |

AH Security Protection: Authentication

ESP Security Protection: Encryption

Tunnel Mode

When AH encapsulates ESP to fully secure an IP datagram, more IP overhead is naturally required and a given IP packet is larger compared to when either AH or ESP is used alone. (Note that IPSec requires either AH or ESP for transport or tunnel mode transmissions, not both.) However, if VPN traffic is a concern, IPSec allows limited authentication capability through the ESP security protocol in tunnel mode. ESP also provides payload-padding service, which is used to conceal the actual size of a packet during transmission.

An important note: When selecting a vendor that claims that their VPN is IPSec-compliant, verify if the services from both AH and ESP security protocols are available and perhaps even what transmission modes are supported by the product in question. If only ESP encapsulating transport transmission mode is offered, then you know that only host-to-host security is supported and no portion of the packet is authenticated to guard against packet tampering during transmission. In this IPSec solution, you will also know that only data from higher-layer protocols are encrypted, leaving IP addresses open for compromise. Therefore, make certain to clarify two things: which VPN transmission mode and which security protocols are supported. The best IPSec vendor implementation would offer tunnel mode AH encapsulating ESP, in addition to several other IPSec security association options.

One of the key dependencies in administering the robust security services of IPSec is the cryptosystem used or encryption keys employed by the VPN solution. In the next section, ISAKMP/IKE, the default key management system, is reviewed to reveal how IPSec deploys and manages encryption keys.

ISAKMP/IKE Key Management and Exchange between Endpoints

As implied by its name, Internet Security Association and Key Management Protocol (ISAKMP) (Standards Track 2408) defines procedures and related specifications for managing security associations and encryption keys. It does *not* provide specifications for key exchange or mandate any specific key exchange. However, the Internet Key Exchange (IKE) is a proposal that recommends the OAKLEY key exchange as the default system for ISAKMP. SKIP (Simple Key Management for Internet Protocol) is also a key exchange specification primarily geared for basic VPN installations.

Based on network requirements, an ISAKMP-compliant firewall or security policy database allows network administrators to specify the specific key exchange protocol available to network users. Key exchange protocols like IKE, working in conjunction with ISAKMP, facilitate exchanges based upon public-key cryptography systems such as RSA or Diffie-Hellman algorithms. ISAKMP also allows the VPN installation to specify the certificate authority and/or public key infrastructure (PKI) that will be supported by the network. Examples of PKI include X.509 specification or PGP's Web of Trust. In other words, ISAKMP allows administrators to specify how keys are put into place from a CA. Implied in this process is a user authentication phase, which includes use of a digital signature algorithm to authenticate users being assigned to key pairs. Once the key exchange type (i.e., IKE), CA and PKI, or certificate types are identified to ISAKMP, the protocol automatically executes the steps required to authenticate VPN users. See Figure 7-7 for a graphical depiction of this process.

Figure 7-7
SAKMP's role in user authentication process.

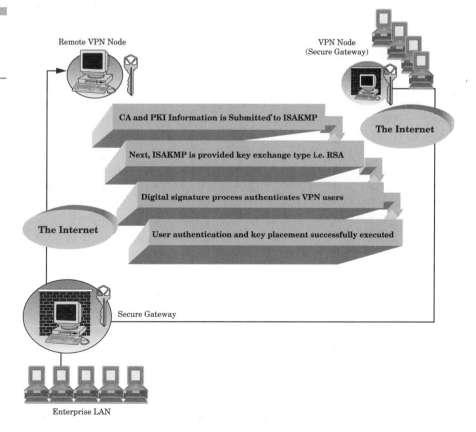

Figure 7-8
ISAKMP key
generation and SA
establishment.

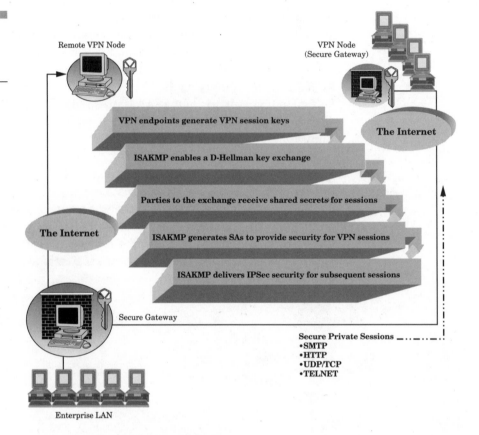

After user authentication, ISAKMP, through IKE, is ready to facilitate the actual exchange of keys to be used for generating subsequent encrypted sessions. For example, a Diffie-Hellman key exchange can be initiated through ISAKMP/IKE to generate the shared secrets between VPN endpoints. Once the shared secrets are generated, they, in turn, can be utilized to encrypt subsequent sessions between the VPN nodes. After key establishment/generation, ISAKMP next creates the security associations that will deliver the authentication and encryption services down to the packet level by AH and ESP. (See Figure 7-8 for a summary of the actual key exchange and SA establishment.)

ISAKMP provides one other beneficial service worth mentioning. The ISAKMP services described above can be summarized into primarily three phases: authentication, key exchange, and security association establishment. ISAKMP links these three activities in such a way that a given session is resistant to connection hijacking. This linking prevents an intruder, for example, from waiting for the authentication phase to be completed and then jumping in to spoof a legitimate host by completing the process with the next two phases of key exchange and SA establishment. ISAKMP also provides a barrier to successful man-in-the-middle attacks.

Finally, IPSec supports both manual and automatic key management systems such as ISAKMP/IKE. In a small VPN installation, the network administrator can provide a centralized key-issuing authority. The administrator can go from workstation to workstation and install keys generated from a PGP system, for example. The subsequent session keys generated and exchanged can be managed without too much effort. However, as you approach 100 users who desire to exchange keys among themselves, the number of potential keys to manage can approach more than 4500. This is where a key management system like ISAKMP/IKE or SKIP would come into play. Widespread deployment of IPSec mandates that an automated key management system is utilized to maintain the integrity and security of the network on an ongoing basis.

Layer 2 Tunneling Protocol (L2TP)

L2TP is the precocious offspring of PPTP and L2F. (See discussions on L2TP in Chapters 2 and 3.) And the proud guardian of the protocol is the IETF. Like PPTP, L2TP provides dial-up VPNs by tunneling layer 2, or link-layer, protocols through the Internet using PPP. Like L2F, but unlike PPTP, it does not depend on IP to tunnel layer 2 tunneling protocols of other packet-oriented network media such as frame relay, X.25, or ATM. (See Figure 7-9.) Combining the best traits of its predecessors, therefore, L2TP provides dial-up VPN capability by using PPP to tunnel link-layer protocols from remote users to corporate sites. However, PPP provides weak authentication for the dial-up user. In addition to supporting PPP authentication, L2TP supports strong authentication with RADIUS as per L2F.

Making a clean break from its predecessors, L2TP will provide data authentication and privacy with IPSec security services. Thus, when L2TP tunnels ATM, frame relay, or X.25, packet headers and payloads will also be authenticated and encrypted in the comprehensive way that IPSec protects IP packets. L2TP server and firewall implementations are starting to emerge in vendor offerings. Soon to follow will be a breadth of client implementations that are L2TP-compatible. This

Figure 7-9
L2TP Tunneling link-
layer network
protocols.

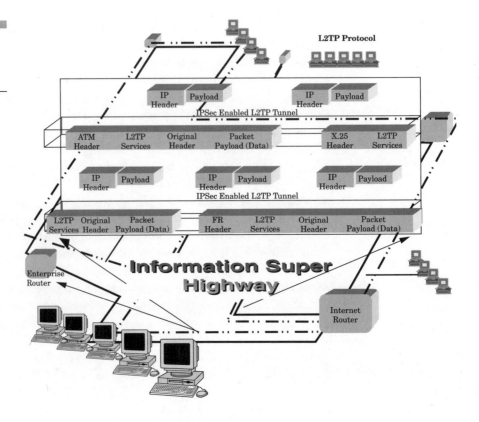

extends the attractiveness of VPN solutions and firmly establishes a
cost-effective alternative to private networks that support such networking protocols.

SOCKS Regaining Its Footing

When client/server information systems evolved beyond the physical
boundaries of department LANs and enterprise WANs, the computer
networking world discovered that a global economy had sprung up, forcing client/server requirements in unprecedented ways, such as between
the networks of various organizations. When client/server requirements
started crossing organizational boundaries, and when the Internet
became the threshold for access, perimeter defenses such as firewalls
eventually became the norm for network security. The premise behind

SOCKS grew out of the need for client/server relationships to cross firewall security systems in the most fine-grained manner as practical. Also, access by clients to server objects behind the perimeter defenses must be controlled and perhaps even authenticated. Earlier SOCKS protocols such as version 4 embodied these ideas, but certain operational shortcomings, like the need to compile TCP-based applications to utilize SOCKS security services, was a barrier to widespread use. (See the discussion on SOCKS in Chapter 3.) The release of SOCKS version 5 corrected such shortcomings and is perhaps providing a toehold for SOCKS to regain its footing.

SOCKS version 5 is a tunneling protocol designed to provide transparent firewall traversal for TCP-based client/server applications such as Telnet, FTP, and HTTP. SOCKS version 5 also contains support for UDP-based client/server applications such as videoconferencing and related audio and video applications as well. SOCKS offers plug-in support for various authentication methods and key management schemes. When a TCP-based client wishes to establish a connection with a network host behind a SOCKS-supported firewall, it must enter into a negotiation for authentication. Currently, SOCKS authentication is based upon user-level authentication as opposed to packet-level authentication, such as IPSec. Authentication can be based upon simply a user ID and password or other methods that deliver more-comprehensive security features such as encryption and data integrity. In the initial-connection phase, both ends of the tunnel are authenticated. Afterwards, the client and SOCKS server reaches an agreement on how messages will be secured. In other words, a security context is established between client and server for the delivery of security services similar to the security associations (SAs) of IPSec. Subsequently, the tunnel is established and the resulting session ensues. SOCKS *unidirectional security architecture* effectively restricts one's exposure to attacks from the network that terminates the tunnel.

And that's basically it. Whether the new version of SOCKS will allow it to regain momentum remains to be seen. In the meantime, many popular firewall vendors have pledged their support for SOCKS in future releases of their respective products.

8

The Architecture, Technology, and Services of Firewalls

This chapter explores firewalls, in context with VPNs, at the implementation or security gateway level. In contrast, the previous chapter explored VPNs at the network and packet level. Firewalls are a critical component in the solution mix of vendor VPN solutions because they provide access control to network applications and services. Coupled with authentication, data integrity, and tunneling, a VPN-enabled firewall solution offers network administrators the strongest form of network security.

In this chapter, the three types of firewall architectures are reviewed and compared in terms of their features and advantages. To facilitate this discussion, an overview of the OSI model is provided as a backdrop to the functionality of packet-level versus application-level firewall systems. Standard features that firewalls offer right off the shelf are also fully reviewed, along with the services they make available to VPN installations.

Mapping the Open Systems Interconnection (OSI) Model

The OSI model comes close to being the sacred scrolls of network communications. As its name suggests, the OSI model, which was developed in the early 1970s by the International Standards Organization (ISO), based in Paris, is a conceptual framework designed to provide developers of network protocols with a scheme for achieving interoperability among competing products. The OSI model was crafted to govern the creation of network hardware and software components that communicate with each other regardless of the manufacturer. The ISO was able to map all network functionality into seven categories graphically represented by a seven-layer stack. This stack is often referred to as the "OSI protocol stack" or, metaphorically, as the "seven-layer cake." (See Figure 8-1.)

Each layer interfaces with the one immediately above it and below it, except for the two at the bottom and top of the stack. In a network communiqué between sender and receiver, the protocol stack represents how data communications should be processed from what the user sees on the display screen to what is required to transport it across a communications medium. Each layer on the sending system corresponds with the same layer on the receiving system. The receiving device, however, must perform everything in reverse of the sending system to reconstitute the message from the base transmission format to one that can be seen and processed by a user at the receiving node. (See Figure 8-2.)

On the sending system, the application layer begins the process by treating the messages or data packets being prepared for transmission. Each subsequent layer receives the data from above it and adds the necessary information of its own before passing the message packet on to the next layer. The process continues until it reaches the physical layer, where each message packet is relayed to the actual transmission medium.

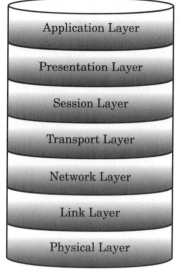

Figure 8-1
The OSI reference model.

The OSI "Seven Layer Cake"

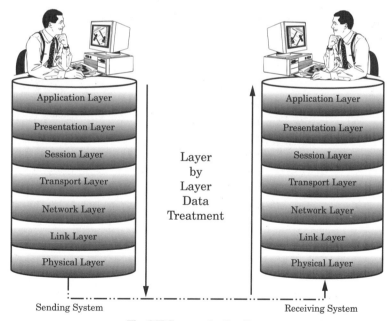

Figure 8-2
The OSI Model's basic communication framework.

Layer by Layer Data Treatment

Sending System

Receiving System

The OSI Communication Process

The matching protocol layers on the receiving machine repeat the process in reverse by removing from each incoming packet any "treatment" its corresponding layer on the sending system applied to it. As a result, each layer on the receiving system is only concerned with and receives what was transferred to the packet by the corresponding layer on the sending system. The message packet becomes smaller and smaller as it moves from one layer to the next, until the user on the receiving end can interact with the message in the manner intended by the application.

The OSI model delineates a general task-oriented description for each of the seven layers. The layers run from the lowest (layer 1) to the highest (layer 7). The lower a layer, the closer it is to the underlying transmission medium.

Layer 1 is the *physical layer*. This layer furnishes the instruction set of the signaling and connections required for the packet to traverse the given communications line. This layer does *not* include the physical communications line itself.

Layer 2 is the *link layer,* sometimes referred to as the *data-link layer.* This layer prepares message packets into a format required for transmission. It also counts message units in the queue and checks each one for errors. Next, each message unit is placed on the transmission medium, like boxcars on train tracks, and the medium whisks the packets off to the receiving unit. At the other end, the receiving system, like the station manager of a train terminal, confirms arrival with the sending system when all message packets are successfully received. In the event some message units are "derailed," the receiving system coordinates with the sending system for a retransmission.

Layer 3 is the *network layer.* The network layer is responsible for *real-time* routing of message packets between sending and receiving systems. This layer also assigns destination addresses to packets formed at the transport layer. Choosing the optimal communications pathways is predicated upon network traffic, conditions, and delivery priorities of a given message.

Layer 4 is the *transport layer.* The transport layer, as its name suggests, prepares messages for transport by fashioning data from the upper layers into self-contained packets suited for transmission. In the event of network failure, the transport layer performs a virtual routing operation locally by choosing alternate routes for a retransmission or by saving the message units until the network comes back online. In this regard, it provides similar functionality to the network layer. Going back to our train analogy, when a transmission is successful, the receiving host acts like a freight yard inspector by inspecting each of the message unit "boxcars" to ensure that each arrived intact (i.e., in the proper format) and in the right order. This operation is critical when communication is between dissimilar computer systems.

Layer 5 is the *session layer*. The session layer establishes, manages, and terminates connections between two applications or portions of the applications communicating across a network. It also passes calls from application programs to other service components in the network and performs security, name recognition, and logging functions, as well as housekeeping and administrative chores.

Layer 6 is the *presentation layer*. This layer is concerned with how applications should appear and work. The presentation layer is commissioned to format data and files to appear the way the application intended. This layer is the home of control codes, special graphics, and character sets. It is also the home of software controls for printers, scanners, and other related peripherals. Depending upon the software, this layer may provide encryption and special file formatting.

At the top is layer 7, the *application layer*. This layer is concerned with what the user can see and therefore control, including operating systems and application programs. Layer 7 is also the realm of file sharing and transfer, print job spooling, email, Web browsing, and personal productivity software.

Table 8-1 provides a summary of the OSI reference model seven-layer structure.

Packet-Filtering Approaches

When implementing a VPN, it is a foregone conclusion that a firewall should anchor your implementation for the highest level of network security. In this section, the architectures of firewalls are covered to help you gain insight into their inherent advantages and disadvantages and how one type versus another would impact the security of your network. There are basically three architectures in use today for firewalls: packet filtering, circuit-level gateways, and application proxies. In addition, there are two types of packet-filtering systems: simple and stateful architectures.

Simple Packet-Filtering Systems

Packet filtering has been a basic feature of routers almost since inception. When firewalls emerged, it seemed natural to base development upon simple packet-filtering capability. As you might guess, packet-

TABLE 8-1   OSI Reference Model Feature Summary.

OSI Layer	Function	Where Located	Examples
Application layer (Layer 7)	▪ Provides what user sees and works with	In application software	▪ NT operating system ▪ JAVA applets ▪ Home pages and Web sites, HTTP ▪ Email, SMTP
Presentation layer (Layer 6)	▪ Formats display screens and files ▪ Controls peripherals ▪ Provides encryption	In application software	▪ GUIs ▪ Printing service and utilties ▪ Distributed file systems, e.g., Internetwork Protocol Exchange (IPX)
Session layer (Layer 5)	▪ Establishes, manages, and terminates connections ▪ Provides logging and administrative functions	In network operating system software	▪ NetBIOS
Transport layer (Layer 4)	▪ Performs like network layer, but locally ▪ Provides virtual routing or saves data when network fails ▪ Performs quality control ▪ Ensures data is received in right format and order	In network operating systems of network hosts	▪ TCP ▪ UDP
Network layer (Layer 3)	▪ Provides real-time routing of network message packets ▪ Selects optimal route ▪ Prioritizes message routing	In network routers, switches, or NICs (exists out in the network)	▪ IP ▪ IPSec ▪ PPTP
Data-link layer (Layer 2)	▪ Message formation and queuing ▪ Error checking ▪ Disaster recovery ▪ Retransmission	In network operating systems or integrated circuits on NICs	▪ L2TP ▪ Frame relay ▪ ATM, X.25
Physical layer	▪ Provides instructions for electrical signaling and connecting	In circuit boards and NICs	▪ Printer ports ▪ NICs ▪ Digital and binary coding

filtering systems operate at the network layer of the OSI reference model. This stands to reason, since routers and firewalls operate out in the network. (See Figure 8-3.) Packet-filtering systems work by distinguishing packets based upon IP addresses. Others operate by selecting specific bit patterns, such as those found in certain data fields. Still

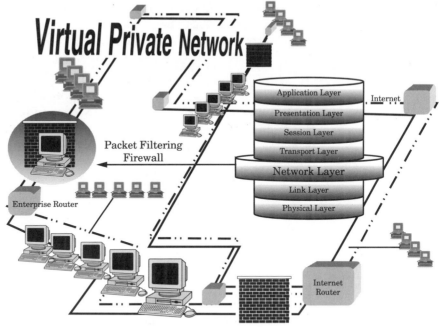

Figure 8-3
Mapping packet-filtering firewalls to the OSI model.

others work by filtering a combination of the two from IP packets. Since simple packet-filtering systems access such a limited amount of information to determine if a packet should be admitted or denied, they are not effective against certain IP-level attacks such as IP source routing. (See Chapter 5.) These architectures also proved to be ineffective against hacker attacks that operate on the application level, such as Trojan horse attacks.

Simple packet-filtering systems do not automatically hide network and system addresses from public view or the demilitarized zone. In addition, they are difficult to initialize and manage. Thus, because of these shortcomings, they are inherently less secure than other architectural implementations, such as those that incorporate a combination of packet-filtering and application proxy techniques.

Stateful Packet-Filtering Architecture

Stateful packet-filtering firewalls are an innovative extension of ordinary packet-filtering architectures. Stateful packet-filtering architectures extract *state information* such as IP addresses, application port numbers, and data context information from incoming packets seeking to traverse the firewall. The extracted information is placed in *state tables* that are used to evaluate subsequent incoming packets. In general, firewalls utilize *rule-based* security policy databases to evaluate incoming packets. (More on rule-based security databases in Chapter 11.) State tables provide firewalls a convenient alternative to constantly having to reference the security policy database (SPD) to evaluate each incoming packet. In other words, state tables are used to track connections in real time by foregoing the need to consult the rule set in the SPD for each network-bound packet.

In large VPN installations, evaluating and logging each incoming packet against a dynamic list of connections in real time may prove to be too CPU-intensive to maintain optimal network performance. To prevent potentially severe network degradation, a feasible number of security gateways should be employed, with the proper load balancing, to ensure an effectively operating firewall-based VPN. Like simple packet-filtering systems, stateful inspection systems can prove to be ineffective against application-level attacks and routing-based attacks. Also, like ordinary filtering architectures, they don't automatically perform address hiding. System administrators must manually configure all the addresses to be "hidden" or translated. To ensure the ultimate in firewall security, some vendors who utilize stateful inspection architecture also employ application-level mechanisms such as proxies in their firewall/VPN solutions. For the best network security, make certain that the system you consider includes both packet-level and application-level security.

Circuit-Level Architecture

Circuit-level gateways typically operate at the OSI model's session level. (See Figure 8-4.) However, like stateful firewall systems, they also utilize state tables to process incoming sessions on real-time connections. After state tables are built, circuit-level systems compare subsequent connection attempts such as UDP or TCP against the state information listed in the tables. Based on this information, connection attempts are either allowed or denied.

The circuit-level approach does, however, possess some inherent weaknesses. Since it operates at the session level, firewalls based on this approach are subjected to any kind of traffic being allowed to pass through. The otherwise-protected network may prove to be susceptible

Figure 8-4
Mapping circuit-level firewalls to the OSI model.

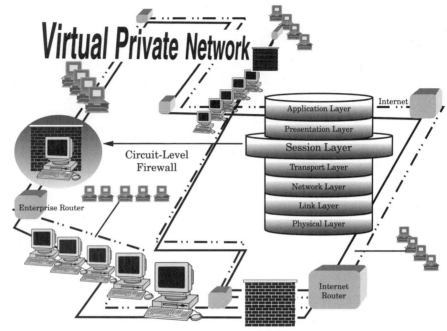

Enterprise Router & Firewall

to attacks that exploit the firewall's lack of contextual information. Also, firewalls that incorporate circuit-level architecture alone may not be robust enough to resist network- (packet) or application-level attacks. Therefore, it is very important to know what you are getting into when you break open the shrink-wrap.

Application Proxy Approach

Firewalls that are based on *proxy* architecture typically operate at the OSI model's application level. (See Figure 8-5.) Since application proxies administer their rule base in the SPD at this level, one school of thought contends that it is optimal for snaring hackers. Proponents of this approach maintain that many hacker attacks are eventually manifested on the application level. Furthermore, the firewall proxy has plenty of "contextual data" to run against its rule base to determine which connections will pass muster. Since application proxies evaluate data in context to each other, application proxies can make access decisions based on a variety of factors. Consequently, the evaluation factors are very effective in weeding out intrusive data.

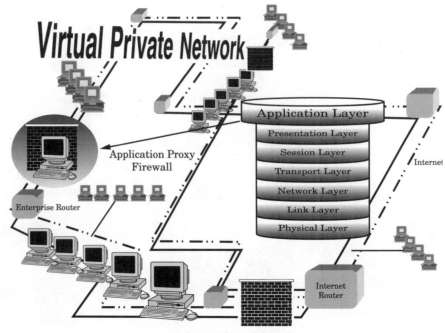

Application proxies perform the following functions:

1. Examine packet contents
2. Allow or deny connections based on IP address, time, and type of service
3. Monitor direction of service, i.e., FTP, HTTP
4. Log all session data
5. Provide automatic address hiding

Application proxies, though effective, are still vulnerable to certain IP or network-level attacks. When implementing VPNs, firewalls based upon this architecture should also include some type of packet-filtering mechanism to guard against attacks, which may arise from VPN tunnels with exposed IP addresses.

Of all the potential architectures available to firewall implementations, application proxy-based firewalls tend to receive the nod over competing architectures in administering security. The ability to evaluate contextual data on the application level presents the ideal approach in detecting hacker intrusions. However, since hackers are just as cunning with their attacks on TCP/IP and especially IP, the best application proxy firewall solutions on the market also employ some packet-filtering mechanism to dispense an optimal level of network security. Similarly, popular firewalls that are based upon stateful inspection architecture tend to incorporate application proxy mechanisms as well. In fact, the trend for firewall providers appears to be combining both packet-filtering and application proxy capabilities in their offerings, at least for the most popular firewall systems. Examples of two such systems are VPN-1 (formerly FireWall-1) by Check Point Software Technologies and the Raptor Firewall (formerly Eagle Firewall) by Axent Technologies.

Stateful Inspection Technology

Check Point Technologies VPN-1 (formerly FireWall-1) is one of the most popular stateful packet-filtering systems available today. In VPN-1, the Inspection Module handles packet-filtering duties. The Inspection Module operates just below the network level in OSI parlance. Recall that in the network layer, hardware and software either physically operate out on the network or are concerned with network operations. In other words, routers, switches, and gateways are examples of components that operate at the OSI model's network layer. Since firewalls are deployed on the perimeter of networks, it makes sense that they should operate at this layer. Therefore, VPN-1 can intercept all packets before they reach the operating systems and application software executing in higher-level protocols in upper layers. No packet is passed through VPN-1 destined for the upper operating layers, unless it complies with the enterprise security policy. (More on building an enterprise security policy in Chapter 11.)

After the security policy is built, it is deployed at the perimeter of every LAN or subnetwork in the enterprise WAN. (See Figure 8-6.) Once in place, VPN-1's Inspection Module can go to work.

The Inspection Module investigates incoming transmissions at the packet level; because of this, it has access to the raw message layers composing the packet. The Module analyzes packet areas such as headers, perhaps extended headers, and payload data to extract "state" information such as IP addresses, application port numbers, and specific bit-patterns in the data. If the packet complies with an access rule that, for example, allows certain packets from an IP address to arrive on a particular application port, the Inspection Module performs two operations:

Figure 8-6
A VPN security policy
deployment.

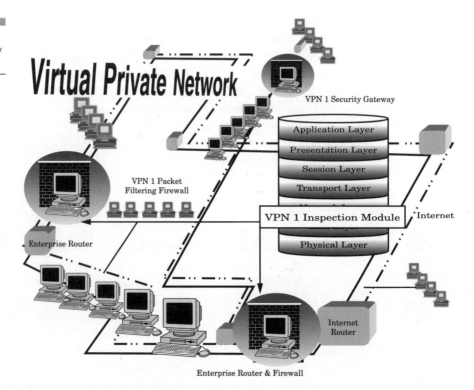

Figure 8-6 (continued)

1. Passes conforming packets through to destination hosts behind the firewall.
2. Updates dynamic state tables with the state information extracted from the initial packet(s). State information will be utilized to evaluate subsequent incoming packets. (See Figure 8-7 for a summary of this process.)

The default state is to drop all incoming packets. However, after configuration, the Inspection Module will drop only those packets that do not comply with the security policy.

The Inspection Module also manages "stateless" connections originated for UDP sessions, also known as connectionless protocols. The Module performs the same functions as it does normally, except that it builds state tables from information extracted from the packet's *application* content. The information from the stateless protocols is used to establish an application pattern of sorts, much like application proxies do with context data from higher-level protocols. When state tables are populated with stateless information, the Module monitors the session

Figure 8-7
Inspection module
compliance
operations.

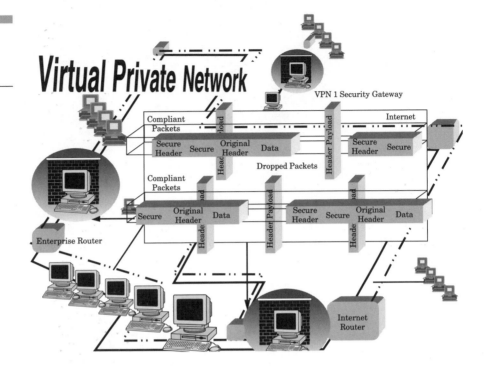

Figure 8-7
Inspection module
compliance
operations.

by checking each packet's application content against the state tables, until the UDP or another stateless protocol session runs its course.

Application Proxy Technology

The Raptor Firewall by Axtent Technologies is one of the most popular application proxy-oriented firewall systems in the marketplace. As mentioned above, application proxies operate at the OSI's model application level, and the Raptor is no exception. (See Figure 8-8.) Regardless of the architecture employed, firewalls enforce network security through a centralized security policy. (Security development and management will be covered in detail in Chapter 11.) All connection attempts through the firewall will be processed based upon the access information provided by the rule base, which is used by mechanisms called *security proxies* to enforce network security. The *security proxies* sift through contextual data in the connections before deciding what connection attempts are allowed to pass.

Figure 8-8
A VPN application
proxy deployment.

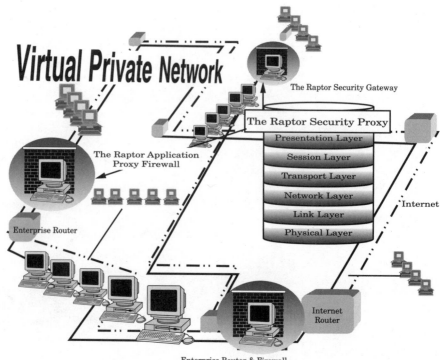

Figure 8-8
A VPN application
proxy deployment.

One of the nice features of the Raptor that is worth mentioning is automatic address hiding. The Raptor automatically conceals the topology and IP addresses of internal networks from public viewing. The Raptor's security proxies protect the source IP addresses of internal hosts by substituting the true IP source addresses with the IP address of the Raptor firewall. As a result of this nifty feature, it virtually eliminates spoofing of internal hosts because their addresses are never seen or encountered on the Internet.

Standard Features

Firewalls are mainly known for controlling access to secure network applications. However, firewalls provide a number of useful features such as address hiding, address translation, antispoofing, and event logging as part of the standard feature set. Some firewall solutions may offer more features than others. Also, some may offer features that are connected to the underlying architecture used by the firewall. For the most part, however, the features that are offered all relate to the main functionality provided by firewalls: access control.

Network Address Translation

Network address translation is one of a series of features that protect IP addresses of internal hosts from the outside world. The IP address could either be invalid or a secret address of a network object, such as a workstation, or of an entire network itself. Despite the fact that internal IP addresses could be invalid Internet addresses, internal network hosts can be accessible from the Internet, and internal hosts, in turn, can connect externally to the outside world. In support of network address translation (NAT), firewalls allow setup of a rule set for this feature for inclusion in the overall rule base of the centralized security policy.

NAT can either be automatically configured, translating the IP addresses of all network entities, or selectively configured, where the IP addresses of certain hosts or entire networks are hidden from the outside. Typically, automatic configuration is a straightforward, uncomplicated process. The network administrator activates the feature through a firewall's GUI interface by responding to prompts in a dialog box. The administrator is prompted to enter information such as `add automatic address translation rules`, (to rule base) or indicate the valid IP address to be used for the translation. When the screen is completed, the firewall adds the newly generated NAT rule set to the overall security policy rule base. From this point on, the IP addresses, whether invalid or secret, of every network entity will automatically be translated to the valid address, usually the IP address of the security gateway that houses the overall rule base.

In selective configuration, a separate NAT rule can be generated for any internal host. This provides complete control over the process. Selective configuration requires knowledge of the logic of the firewall's rule base. Table 8-2 is an example of a rule-base set for NAT. Item number 2 states that all illegal source addresses of packets originating from "Ournetwork" are translated to valid source address "Legal addresses." The destination and services allowed for the *newly* translated packet remain the same as destination and services allowed for the *original* illegally addressed packets. Finally, the rule set is installed on all security gateways.

Firewalls that offer this feature may also provide several choices for operating modes. In Check Point Technologies' VPN-1, these modes can

TABLE 8-2   Network Address Translation Rule Set Example.

	Original Packet			Translated Packet			
No.	Source	Destination	Service	Source	Destination	Service	Install On
1	Ournetwork	Any	Any	NAT	=Original	=Original	Gateway
2	Illegal addresses	Any	Any	Legal addresses	=Original	=Original	Gateway
3	Any	Legal addresses	Any	=Original	Illegal addresses	=Original	Gateway

be classified as dynamic or static. A NAT dynamic mode translates all illegal addresses of a given network to a single valid address, typically one for a security gateway. This is a form of address hiding. (This feature will be discussed further in the next section.) A NAT dynamic mode is useful when desiring to keep secure the IP addresses of many users on a specific LAN. Static mode, on the other hand, allows for a one-to-one relationship when assigning legal addresses to illegal ones. Static mode is useful when attempting to hide the address of a single host, such as an internal Web server.

Address Hiding

Operating on the OSI model's application level, application proxy firewalls, such as the Raptor Firewall by Axtent Technologies, employ an interesting approach in the application of this feature. Address hiding is a key feature in eliminating spoofing attacks. In order for spoofing attacks to succeed, the hacker must learn address and perhaps topology information about the network and then use this information to gain unauthorized access under the pretense of a trusted host. Application proxy architecture guards against address or host spoofing in two ways. First, the proxy approach hides the structure of the network from the outside world by forcing all traffic to connect through the firewall. Second, the firewall automatically drops any packets that contain the address of any of its internal host systems that arrive on any of the network's external access ports. These attributes make it difficult for potential intruders to gain access to the protected network.

In the Raptor Firewall, the address hiding operation begins when an internal host attempts a connection to the outside world. The connection attempt is forced to the Raptor Firewall for processing by one of its security proxies for applications such as FTP, SMTP, or HTTP. Functioning

Figure 8-9
Example of a firewall
address hiding
operation.

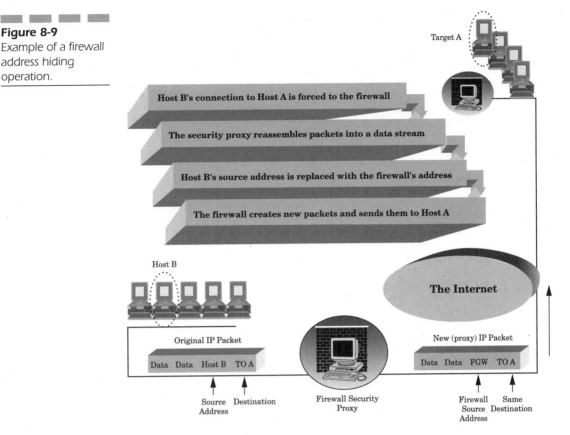

under the underlying operating system, the security proxy reassembles
the IP packets from the internal host into a data stream for the proxy
operation to occur. When the data stream is fully reassembled, reflecting
its true context, the security proxy creates *new* IP packets and rewrites
their source address with its own address. The Raptor Firewall reestab-
lishes a "proxy" connection to the original destination and sends the
newly addressed packets on to the receiving host. (See Figure 8-9 for a
summary of this feature.) In address-hiding scenarios, the destination of
the original connection attempt remains the same. The source of the
communication, however, is the firewall gateway (FGW).

Address Transparency

Occasionally, the need may arise for outside hosts to interface directly to
firewall-protected internal hosts without having to experience the

"delayed" effect of going through an enterprise firewall. If the rule base in the security policy has been implemented efficiently, the delay, of course, is barely perceptible. However, if a particular host such as an internal Web site or email server is frequented a lot from external sources, the delays can be noticeable. For this reason, firewall solutions allow access to such internal hosts without the intermediary proxy or inspection steps, which could cause processing delays in connecting to a very busy host.

Although this feature traverses the firewall transparently, as if it were not there, external systems accessing internal hosts must still be authorized and governed by a rule set. Address transparency is a practical feature with potential for definite application. However, when the feature opens internal hosts for seemingly direct connections, although access is governed by a rule set, the resulting connections are not as secure as if they were individually inspected or proxied, even when authentication is required. Therefore, address transparency should be used for connections with trusted external sources such as with a business partner or client. As an added safeguard, this feature should be used in conjunction with a VPN, as packets that are tunneled with encryption and authentication should provide the security net to stave off attacks from the Internet.

Access Control

Access control is the primary reason why firewalls have become so popular. While VPNs protect data in transit, access control through firewalls provides protection to the network itself. This functionality dictates the level of freedom a VPN user has in a network and controls the specific applications a user can and cannot access. Access control not only provides protection for the network's data but also for the network's entire repository of intellectual capital. Because of the inherent data integrity and privacy functionality of VPN-enabled firewalls, the secure private communication channels provide a cost-effective communications backbone to enterprise partners, suppliers, clients, remote, and nomadic users.

System Load Balancing among Gateways

The ability of a firewall to physically work on multiple servers simultaneously, creating as many enforcement points, is a key advantage for dispensing optimal network security. Firewalls that facilitate distribution of the processing responsibility of a single enterprise security policy across multiple server platforms also support a centralized control mechanism. In the Raptor Firewall, for example, the IP addresses of multiple enforcement points are mapped to the DNS name of a central enforcement point. This process decreases the time required to set up user access, because all clients can be assigned to one access point.

Check Point VPN-1 handles load balancing in an effective manner. Like the Raptor, the processing load is distributed among multiple points and controlled by a central unit called a Logical Server. Also like the Raptor, users are only aware of the Logical Server as the security gateway. (See Figure 8-10.) To activate the service, the network administrator uses VPN-1's rule-base system to define a rule that directs connections to the Logical Server. The Logical Server handles the connection attempts by utilizing one of several load-balancing *algorithms*.

Figure 8-10
Example of a firewall load-balancing feature.

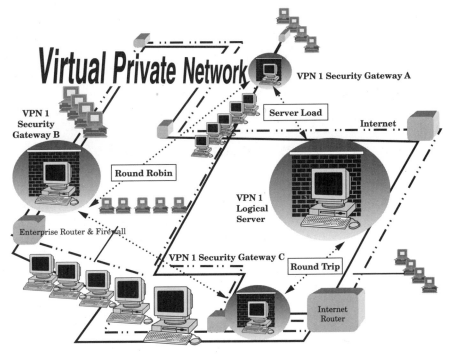

The Logical Server can choose from the following set of load-balancing algorithms:

1. *Server load.* VPN-1 queries servers in real time to determine which one can best handle the next connection attempt. For this to work, each server requires the use of a load-measuring agent.

2. *Roundtrip.* VPN-1 uses ping to ascertain the roundtrip times between the firewall and each of the deployed server gateways and chooses the server for a given situation with the shortest roundtrip time.

3. *Roundrobin.* VPN-1 automatically assigns the next security server on the list of available security servers.

4. *Random assignment.* This is self-explanatory.

5. *Domain name proximity.* VPN-1 simply assigns the "closest" server in connection to domain name.

In response to a connection request, VPN-1 decides which of the servers in the group will fulfill the request, using the load-balancing algorithm mapped to the Logical Server. VPN-1 also allows the security modules, working in conjunction with the Logical Server, to automatically share and update each other's stateful inspection tables. If any one of the security gateways stops functioning for some reason, another one takes over its processing duties. Since the servers are constantly updating each other's state tables, the replacement security gateway can seamlessly take over the failed gateway's network connections, thus the user never notices an interruption in service.

Event/Connections Logging

Event logging is one of the quintessential features of firewalls. Through this feature, every actual and attempted connection attempt is monitored in real time. It also provides alerts for suspicious or potentially intrusive connections. Significant network events, such as system failures or new security module installs, are other activities supported by this feature. The type of information you may monitor on the screen may be customized based upon your security needs. Fields can be displayed or hidden, and certain activity can be color-coded for ease of tracking. Reports generated in response to the network monitoring functions are typically customizable too.

In connection with this feature, firewalls provide mechanisms such as system status windows that allow administrators to check the operational status of every security gateway in the network. Other information that event and connections logging may provide includes excessive logon failures, increased spikes in network activity from certain hosts, and unusual login times for certain users. Real-time events and connections logging are some of the most important services provided by your firewall because it is the window to your network's activity. However, these features can be taken for granted because of the constant vigil that must be sustained to work with the features properly. If these features are approached and managed proactively, they can be the most instrumental activities for maintaining a secure networking environment.

Antispoofing Feature

When your network is accessed from the *outside* on an *external port* with a source IP address that is *internal* to your network, guess what, you've just been spoofed. Somehow, an intruder has confiscated the IP address of one of your trusted internal host computers and is trying to set up shop in your network by masquerading as the trusted internal host. IP address or host spoofing is easily detected with the right security features in place. However, without them, when a hacker is able to ascertain the source IP address of a trusted host, it's virtually impossible to prevent spoofing attacks. So your main challenge is keeping your internal IP addresses off public transport mediums like the Internet. This can be achieved through address hiding as indicated above or through encrypting the IP addresses with VPN tunneling.

Antispoofing works a little differently than the other two features. Antispoofing features, per se, do not keep IP addresses off public networks. However, if an internal IP address is compromised and arrives on the internal network from external access points, such connection requests are summarily denied. Antispoofing is a standard feature of firewalls that merely requires you to turn the feature on. If this feature ever alerts you, it's a sobering experience because it may signify that your network has been breached. If investigation proves this, the compromised host should be reassigned to a new IP address (number).

Router Management

Firewalls allow you to install rule-based security policies on two types of enforcement points: computer-based servers and routers. As is the case with computer-based servers, routers can be controlled and adminis-

Figure 8-11
Central management
of router-based
enforcement.

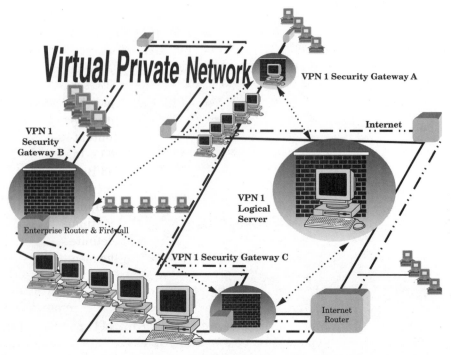

tered from a centralized point. (See Figure 8-11.) The firewall security
modules run directly on certain types of routers; check with the VPN
vendors to clarify the router compatibility of their security solution. Popular router types compatible with VPN-enabled firewalls include Cisco,
Bay Networks, and 3Com.

Third-Party Support and Interoperability

Interoperability among competitive vendor offerings is a critical issue
for the long-term acceptance and viability of VPN solutions in supporting mainstream, enterprisewide communications. The next year or two
will be a crucial time frame in the role and maturation of key standards
such as IPSec and L2TP, as well as, perhaps, supporting standards such
as X.509 and RADIUS. In the meantime, VPN vendors have taken matters into their own hands by providing a working model for managing
the interoperability of third-party security products. Check Point Technologies' Open Platform for Secure Enterprise Connectivity (OPSEC) is

such a framework for achieving seamless integration among competitive security products.

OPSEC provides a centralized management feature, published APIs for interfacing with open protocols, and out-of-the-box compatibility with third-party security products. OPSEC's centralized management feature supports enterprises' ability to deploy and manage a variety of security products from Check Point and other vendors. The API, among other things, can support third-party content-screening applications. As for out-of-the-box compatibility, VPN-1's Inspection Module is installable directly to routers such as Cisco and Bay Networks types. After installation, the resulting security component can be plugged into an OPSEC framework with other third-party applications for centralized control and management. As standards continue to mature, proprietary solutions such as OPSEC will find a definite niche in the networking community for enterprise security deployment.

Basic Services and Protocols Supported

The basic application-level services supported by firewalls are discussed in detail in this section. In support of application layer services such as SMTP and HTTP, a practice of firewall vendors involves providing dedicated security modules called security "servers" or "proxies." Overall, security servers or proxies take into account the inherent attributes of an application, so when security services are delivered, the most appropriate security measures are being administered. For example, one of the primary features of email is its ability to transmit attachments. Security servers strip certain types of attachments that are known for causing security problems.

Security Proxy Concepts

Security proxies force all connection attempts to the firewall for processing. In this scenario, if the firewall approves the connection, then the original source address is replaced by the firewall's address as the new "source" address. In other words, security proxies automatically perform address hiding operations. (See Figure 8-9 above.) However, security prox-

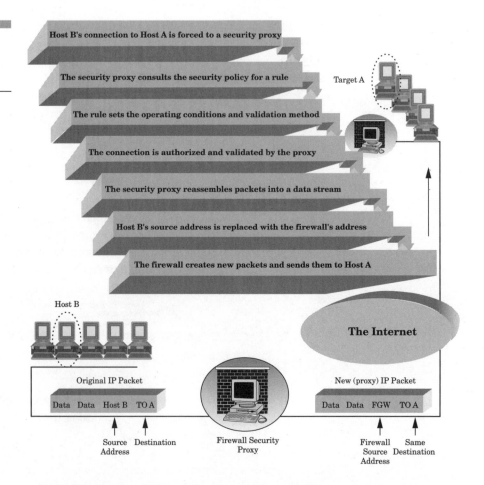

Figure 8-12
Security proxy connection validation process.

ies also conduct some additional steps to authorize and authenticate the connection. After receiving a connection attempt, the security proxy checks with the firewall's security policy to determine if there is a rule that authorizes the connection. If there is, then the rule sets the conditions under which the connection will operate and the type of user authentication method to expect for user validation. For a complete picture on how security proxies handle connection attempts, see Figure 8-12.

Key Service Offerings

Security proxies are the firewall's version of distributed processing. The firewall performs efficiently because the security services and the associated rule processing set are compartmentalized around a particular service. For instance, when a network user attempts a connection to browse a certain Web site, the HTTP security proxy automatically receives the connection attempt on behalf of the firewall. To authorize and authenticate the connection, the HTTP security server will consult with the rule set in the firewall's security policy database concerned only with governing its connections. In this section, an overview of the standard set of security proxies and related services is covered in detail.

Secure Web Browsing: HTTP Security   Security proxies are the security patrols that police the network for secure connections. They ensure that connection attempts are processed by the rule-base set comprising the security policy that relates specifically to their services. In general, the routine collaboration between the security proxy and the firewall delivers security services to network users on an ongoing basis. However, security proxies also convey specialized services that are *exclusive* to their particular type of services.

In addition to regular proxy duties, HTTP security servers may provide a special pass-through for HTTP packets. Also, some HTTP security proxies can be configured to channel all outbound Web or HTTP accesses to a Web-caching server. This capability is transparent to the end user and can significantly reduce the volume of Internet accesses attempted by internal users. Other specialized services that HTTP security servers offer include support for encrypted HTTP or HTTPs, file transfer with FTP, and access to Gopher URLs. This specialized capability enables you to accomplish granular control over browser traffic in and out of the secure network. The HTTP security proxy of the Raptor Firewall supports these features.

Secure Email: SMTP Security   The SMTP security server or proxy concentrates on securing your email connections and related activity. The SMTP security module supports transparent, bidirectional email communications through the firewall. In transparent connectivity, the security server performs procedures normally performed by users.

Like the HTTP proxy, the SMTP also performs duties that are indicative of the service area. For example, the SMTP scans email for structural integrity and email-based hacker attacks such as backdoor command raids and buffer overrun gambits. It also strips specific attachment types that may be a potential "silo" for launching email-based attacks and drops messages that are over a certain size and conspicuously large. Moreover, some security proxies do not store email. So if any attacks slip through security measures, storage will not provide an opportunity to initiate any offensive operations.

Secure Domain Name System (DNS) Server   One of the most challenging stages in firewall installation is getting the network's Domain Name System (DNS) installed correctly. The DNS makes it possible to send and receive electronic mail, browse Web sites, and use other Internet services requiring data exchange. The DNS functions like a global directory that maps domain names like "your.business.com" to specific IP addresses like "111.22.33.4." A DNS security server is set up to maintain separate public and private (internal) listing of DNS entries on certain firewalls. In this format, the firewall does not pass any information on internal hosts or networks to the public networking community. This, of course, fortifies the internal network against intruder attacks. This straightforward structure simplifies the DNS setup process and ongoing management of the security server.

File Transfer Protocol Server   The FTP server is devoted to the file transfer protocol that services the Internet. You can't have enough security services in effect when information travels the mean streets of the information superhighway. An FTP security server can provide authentication services and security for application-level content based on FTP commands such as PUT/GET and filename attributes. An FTP server will also perform antivirus functions directly or provide interfaces to a third-party antivirus server. In this situation, the FTP server will operate as a client to the antivirus server.

Stateless Protocols Security Server   Most firewalls will support the big-three applications—FTP, HTTP, and SMTP—right off the shelf. In addition, firewalls furnish a generic security proxy to custom-fit stateless protocols such as UDP and TCP and other application layer services without a great deal of effort. When additional services are defined and put into service, they will function exactly like the application proxies that are ready to go out-of-the-box.

URL Screening and Selective Blocking Server   URL (Uniform Resource Locator) screening is an important feature that facilitates how enterprises control users' time spent on the Internet at undesirable Web sites. Every individual document and file on the Internet possesses its own unique URL, which facilitates linking to other Internet documents and sites. The typical format for a URL is the "www," such as those provided in this book. The full URL for the NTBugtraq server is http://www.ntbugtraq.com. The HTTP is considered a URL type; FTP and Gopher are other URL types. The "www" portion is the Web site address. Some URLs also include the name of the document in the format of "*xxxx*.html."

URL screening servers typically provide granular control over Web site access down to the Web page level. For example, access can be provided to a particular Web site. Yet access to Web pages on that very same site may be blocked. URL Filtering Protocol (UFP) servers are also offered through third parties that equip their products with the appropriate interfaces to firewall systems. UFP servers provide lists of undesirable Web sites categorized by subject area, such as violence/profanity, drugs/drug culture, and full nudity.

9

Innovative Firewall Implementations

A firewall is a firewall is a firewall. No matter how innovative manufacturers are with their firewall implementations, a firewall is designed to deliver access control by managing network access from remote dial-in and network users. Access control boils down to this: Connections that are not explicitly permitted by the security policy are denied. Consequently, it should be stated up front that the firewall systems covered in this chapter are no different than any other firewall with regard to inherent functionality.

However, the firewalls covered here differ in the manner in which they are implemented and operate while handling network traffic. One featured firewall operates within the network's infrastructure instead of on its perimeter as firewalls normally do. Because of this operational difference, the firewall must work as a bridge instead of as a router, which is the normal operational characteristic of firewalls. Another featured implementation operates in a switch as a hardware implementation complete with VPN capability built in. These new innovative implementations are not coming into being because firewall makers want to be fancy or offer a smorgasbord-like variety. Instead, they are being driven by an evolution of enterprise needs that are not being met by standard firewall implementations.

Firewall Innovation Drivers

Firewall vendors are listening to their clients, and the innovative new products are a commitment to their support. Firewall makers acknowledge that the threat from internal sources or employees is growing faster than from external sources. As a result, the firewall's perimeter is increasingly becoming a departmental boundary instead of an enterprise one. (See Figure 9-1.) Consequently, enterprises need more firewalls. Although firewall setup and management interfaces are GUI-driven, and creating a rule-based security policy essentially involves responding to a series of dialog boxes, the network administrator has to be fairly familiar with key network terminology such as DNS conventions, TCP/IP functionality, and network deployment strategies. However, experienced security administrators may be hard to come by for enterprises that are looking to do it themselves. In fact, it is a well-known fact that there is a chronic shortage of experienced security administrators. Moreover, when enterprises decide to add more firewalls at the department level, the resulting firewall implementation can become expensive and hard to manage, especially if the network security staff lacks experience. Therefore, to address these shortcomings, vendors are responding with the following innovations:

1. Compatibility with non-UNIX operating systems such as NT

2. New physical deployment strategies such as security appliances

3. Integration with more comprehensive VPN components

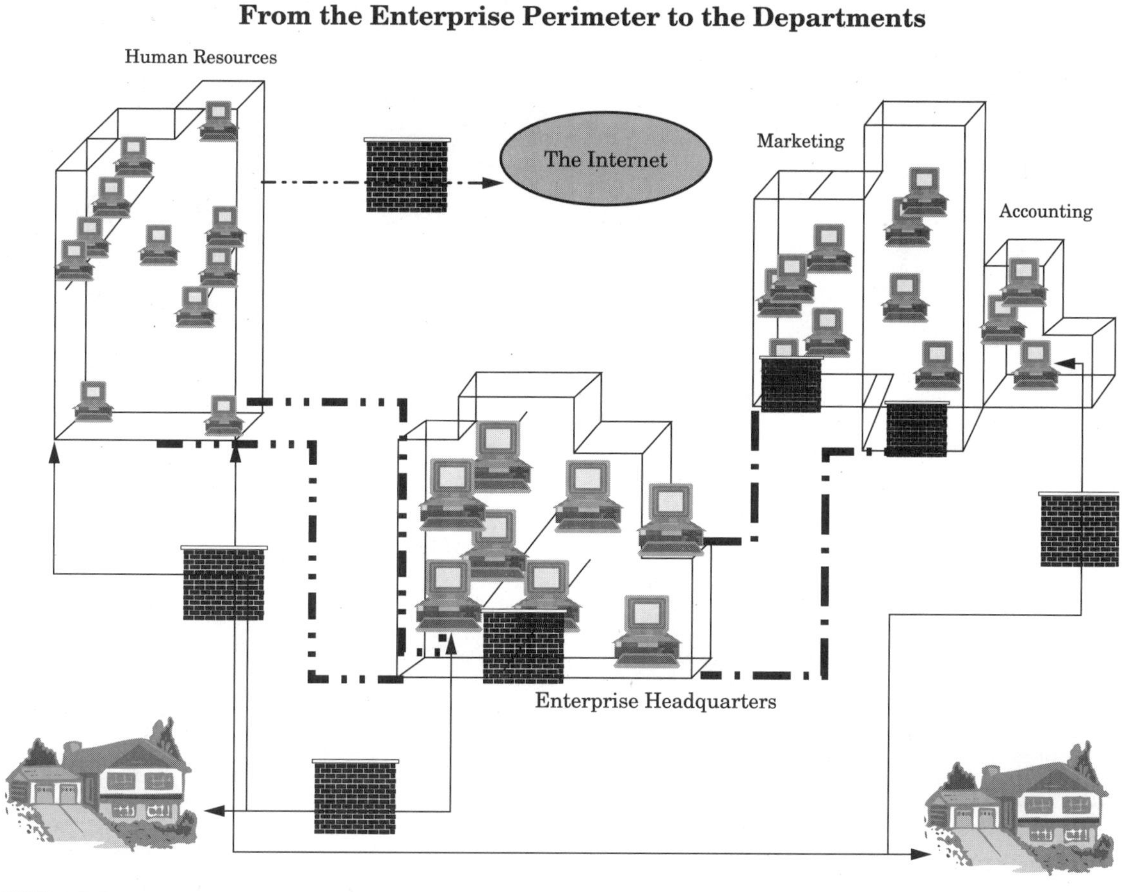

From the Enterprise Perimeter to the Departments

Figure 9-1 A new firewall trend.

In this chapter, we'll review these innovations closely to determine their fitness as a viable component in the overall support of enterprisewide communications. This chapter also answers the question of whether or not the new firewall innovations are a fad or new marketing gimmick, or whether they have mainstream applicability.

The Lucent "Brick"

Lucent recently released a product called the Lucent Managed Firewall appliance, or "the Brick." The Brick operates under the company's pro-

A Security Appliance Deployment

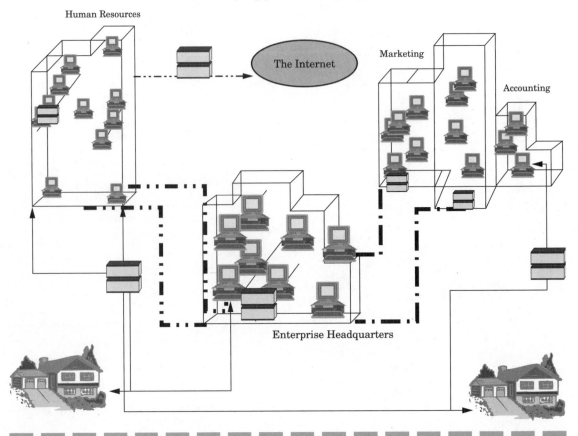

Figure 9-2 Example of a firewall security appliance.

prietary operating system yet possesses no file systems, administrator logins, or even a keyboard or pointing device (mouse). The Brick falls under a new class of firewalls known as *security appliances*. It is the first firewall product to be designed from the ground up to be a network infrastructure component instead of just a mechanism on the perimeter of a network. Lucent released the Brick to provide enterprises with the means to easily insert a firewall anywhere in the infrastructure of an intranet, extranet, or VPN. (See Figure 9-2.) Lucent's firewall Brick actually operates as a bridge rather than a router, the manner in which a firewall usually operates.

Lucent's motivation was to provide a firewall that was easily installable within an enterprise on the departmental or other suborganizational level, which is potentially at as much risk from internal security problems as external. With the Brick you forgo the need to configure subnetworks or partition your network to install them. The company is also motivated to provide a firewall that could support multiple security policies in diverse organizations or organizations that work online with many business entities.

Since Bricks can be deployed as network infrastructure components, they can also be managed as such from a central management point. The management system can be configured and controlled through an NT workstation to define access controls in terms of security zones. The huge advantage of security zones is that each can have a separate security policy and separate management. For these reasons, the Brick is ideal for organizations with many business partner connections and suborganizations with diverse security requirements.

Optical Data Systems' Screaming Demon Firewall

An ongoing challenge of firewall systems has been and will always be performance, especially in packet-filtering systems. In general, firewall security gateways should be installed on high-performance servers because, in heavily trafficked networks, inspecting each packet can easily bog a system down or, worse, create a bottleneck. Also, networks are constantly being upgraded to faster processing hubs. Switched networks can transmit data up to speeds of 100 mbps. If you have packets coming into a firewall at super speeds, even a CPU operating at 300 MHz may have a lot of difficulty figuring out what to do with packets screaming in with afterburners. There simply aren't enough CPU cycles at 300 MHz. Since current firewall implementations protect the network's perimeter, in addition to using a high-performance server, two network interface cards should be installed in the system. One connects to the router, and the other links to the network that it is protecting. This configuration ensures that all incoming network traffic is channeled through the firewall at a reasonable level of performance, especially in medium to large networks.

Figure 9-3
An evolution: firewall
in a switch.

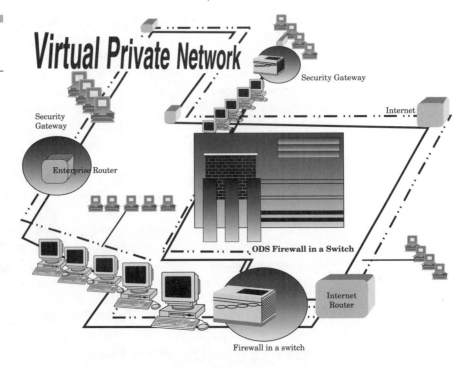

Optical Data Systems (ODS) is taking firewalls to a new plateau of high performance by building them into high-speed switches. (See Figure 9-3.) Since the trend in networking is to deploy faster and faster networks, ODS is betting that integrating security into high-performance devices is a natural evolution of firewalls that should pay off big. With this screaming demon firewall, ODS intends to be on the "bleeding edge" of firewall technology.

The company also includes an add-in card that handles decision processes that are off loaded by the switch. The card usually contains an Intel processor, which runs under a dedicated operating system. However, it could also work with other "security" processors as well. ISS's RealSecure intrusion detection engine, for example, can also operate on the card. The switch's internal architecture forwards packets to the detection engine for analysis, security decisions, and authorization for entry into the network.

WatchGuard's Fancy Firewall Solution

WatchGuard Technologies' current firewall implementation is a second-generation security appliance called Firebox II. WatchGuard's first-generation firewall appliance was called the Firebox Firewall. In fact, Firebox I was one of the first firewall appliances of its kind. Released in 1996, it also was one of the first, if not *the* first, to offer a firewall appliance/VPN combination. The Firebox quickly earned a reputation for having a simplistic but well-behaved firewall system. One of the reasons for the initial success was that it operated under a hardened firewall. Although it operated under an operating system called "Linux," the operating system was "hardened" by being stripped down to its bare essentials, and any supplemental application programs that posed potential security risks were either patched or removed.

Firebox II, introduced in May 1998, is basically designed for large-scale firewall deployment in enterprise WANs. It was the first firewall of any type to issue a private key within the confines of the appliance hardware. With this move, WatchGuard was acknowledging both the growth and critical importance of certificate authorities (CAs). (See Chapter 3 for a review of the certificate authority process.) The resulting public key that is generated is, of course, used for authenticating and encrypting the sessions for remote setup and initialization of the enterprise security policy. The resulting cryptosystem is also used to provide authentication and privacy for subsequent management activities and system upgrades.

With Firebox II's remote setup and initialization procedures, administrators can configure Firebox II appliances after they have been drop-shipped and installed by local WatchGuard representatives. Once in place, administrators can set up the DNS ID and IP address and load the enterprise security policy on all Fireboxes in the field. (See Figure 9-4 for a summary of the installation process.) An advanced yet unique deployment model will support the development of security policy templates and the configuration and management of fireboxes as a single object. This process is attractive to multilocation companies because the cost of setup and administration can be kept within acceptable limits. Future releases will have the ability to aggregate and control Firebox logs so that the resulting reports do not become unwieldy as the firewall appliances proliferate.

Figure 9-4
Security appliance
installation example.

Figure 9-4
Security appliance
installation example.

Firebox II
Instillation and
Management
Procedure

WatchGuard (WG) receives private key from CA

Private key installed to Firebox II at WG factory

Enterprise obtains Firebox II and Public key from WG

Firebox II is installed to the network and readied for setup

Firebox management systems installed, encryption keys created

LAN, IP addresses and routing info entered to management system

Setup info is encrypted with Firebox public key and downloaded

Administration generates shared secret with Firebox II to complete install

Outsourcing Firewall/VPN Management

After firewalls are in operation for a period of time, it is easy to forget about them, especially if the job is being done. Network security people are hired away or assigned to different projects. The consultant who originally installed the firewall was not retained after the system went live, and the staff on hand lacks experience. Or simply no one relishes the responsibility. Telltale signs that firewall management is growing cobwebs include unread logs piling up, new releases for system upgrades remaining in the shrink-wrap, and regular security meetings giving way to a general addendum item in a network status meeting. (See the "Apathy" section in Chapter 6.)

Thus, organizations are choosing to outsource the management of their security systems/firewalls to ISPs or security services companies.

These service bureaus are for enterprises that are convinced of the importance of security and require it 24 hours a day, 7 days a week, but do not want to make the investment in the infrastructure. Some ISPs may be able to deliver management services at a reasonable price; however, if you add VPN capabilities to your network, the added responsibility of supporting your VPN may start to become expensive. In this situation, you are better off building your own network security staff to manage your system.

If you decide to build a viable network security staff and infrastructure, the potential complexity of administering and managing your own system should never be taken for granted. Although experienced security analysts are not a dime a dozen, a comprehensive training program should be set up that works in conjunction with companies that market firewall/VPN systems. VPN vendors are eager to work with you to help you close the knowledge gap for inexperienced staff. They have excellent courses available on their products and will gladly work with your MIS department, for modest fees, to train and assist in establishing an effective internal organization.

Epilogue: Firewalls that Include Everything but the Kitchen Sink

In this and the previous chapters, you have seen that firewalls have evolved into a central processing hub for add-ins, third-party applications, and extended security technology. These components work together to provide a robust network security system for your organizations. No doubt, manufacturers of firewall appliances will be collaborating with vendors of third-party add-ins and security applications to improve or achieve integration between their products. As more and more innovative firewall implementations are introduced, look for these new systems to come up to speed with features such as the firewalls of previous generations.

Although URL blocking plug-ins, security application servers, and other features are nice to have, the big question remains: What is the impact on overall performance? Undoubtedly, extended features slow things down in relation to a standard firewall implementation, if there is such a thing. Rest assured that vendors are aware of performance requirements of enterprises and are building offerings to maximize network performance and providing the supporting research and testing to prove their claims. Over the next few years, performance will be a key issue, so make certain you challenge your firewall/VPN providers to provide performance information on their respective products. This issue will be explored in full in Chapter 12.

10

Other Key VPN Concepts and Technologies

This chapter is a review of an eclectic assortment of other important VPN and related concepts and technologies. The items discussed in this chapter are not in the mainstream of VPN terminology. However, you may encounter any one of them as you conduct your research into this subject area. As the VPN area continues to grow, solution providers borrow technology and concepts from a variety of technical areas to ensure that the most comprehensive technology suite is available to fulfill the promise of the Internet. If the Internet is to truly challenge leased lines and other private communications mediums, then expect strategic technology adaptations to be the main driver in positioning VPNs as a preferred communications backbone for enterprise WANs.

Content Vectoring Protocol

One of the most interesting trends in the VPN game is the commitment of key players to third-party interoperability. The goal of the IETF is to achieve interoperability through development of the standards under its charter. In addition to achieving this often elusive goal through industry-sanctioned standards, certain VPN solution providers have developed proprietary methods for achieving seamless integration with third-party offerings. Content Vectoring Protocol (CVP), developed by Check Point Software Technologies, is such a mechanism and has been designed to handshake with third-party products. VPN-1, Check Point's firewall solution, works in concert with CVP to incorporate *content inspection* servers, such as URL blocking or antivirus applications, that are developed by third-party solution providers. Typically, URL and Java blocking are standard features of firewalls. When implemented as part of a standard feature set, the services tend to be fairly basic. In contrast, however, third-party implementations of such features are usually more comprehensive due to their specialization in the subject area.

CVP is a straightforward process that begins when a VPN user originates a request for a file transfer using FTP services. (This scenario assumes that the FTP connection request is allowed by the firewall.) Next, the destination server responds by sending the requested file. Upon arrival at the firewall's port, the firewall diverts the incoming FTP traffic via CVP to a content inspection server for antivirus checking. The server gives the incoming file a thorough once-over for known viruses. (New viruses are discovered on the Internet at the rate of over 200 per month.) If none are found, VPN-1 allows the connection to proceed. (See Figure 10-1.) Check Point also provides an open API through OPSEC, a third-party integration and management framework, to define custom transactions between CVP-enabled servers and VPN-1. (See the discussion on OPSEC in Chapter 8.)

Applying Digital Signatures to Diffie-Hellman with RSA

One of the most powerful and attractive attributes of VPN solutions is the ability to administer authentication and privacy for each of the operational VPN stages from certificate authority (CA) key distribution to

Figure 10-1
Example of a Content
Vectoring Protocol
operation.

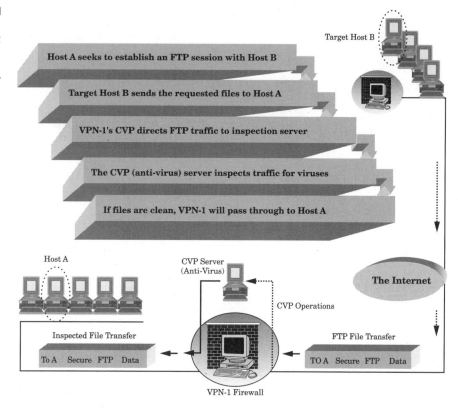

the critical payoff itself: the actual ongoing VPN sessions. (See Figure 10-2.) With a well-implemented VPN solution, either user authentication or data validation procedures utilizing encryption, hash function, and digital signature procedures are administered every step of the way. For all intents and purposes, VPNs should be synonymous with encryption, user authentication, data validation, and tunneling. The key exchange stage is no exception to the general VPN functional rule, which is delivery of privacy and data integrity.

In Chapter 3, it was demonstrated how the digital signature process could be used to authenticate data or key exchange within the RSA cryptosystem itself. The best definition of data authentication is that information is confirmed as being from the sender and not having been modified in transit. However, the RSA process can also be used to validate key exchange with a Diffie-Hellman cryptosystem.

In this scenario, when the Diffie-Hellman private/public key pair is deployed at each of the VPN endpoints, the public keys of each party

Figure 10-2
VPN operational services deployment.

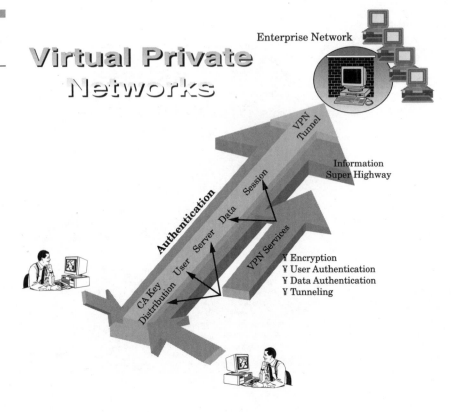

must be exchanged to establish the shared secrets, which in turn produces the two-way trust model for encrypted data exchange. The shared secret between two parties is created when the private key of one party and the public key of the other party are generated through a Diffie-Hellman calculation to produce the shared secret. (Refer to discussion on this subject in Chapter 3.) To ensure that the shared secret is in fact between intended parties, the public keys should be validated using the RSA digital signature process. (See Figure 10-3.) In effect, each party initializes the public key, submits it through the digital signature process, then forwards it on to the other party involved in the intended communications. Upon receipt, the digital signature process is completed when the public key's digital signatures are compared. A match proves that the digital signatures were created by each party's private key and that the key was not tampered with during transit. At this point, both parties can be certain that when the shared secret is generated, it was not compromised by a man-in-the-middle attack along the

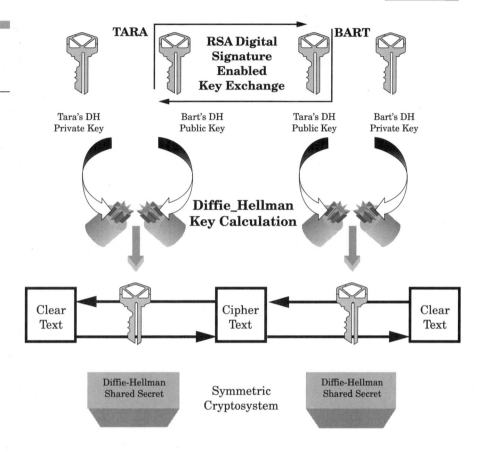

Figure 10-3
RSA Secure key
exchange of DH
public keys.

way. Note that when a shared secret is used to encrypt and decrypt a session, the *same* encryption key is used for both operations. When this happens, the resulting cryptosystem is a *symmetric* key system, even though the encryption keys and digital signature procedures are executed through an *asymmetric* cryptosystem.

Key Exchange Properties according to ISAKMP

ISAKMP defines key exchange properties in terms of key establishment methodology. ISAKMP prefers two types of key establishment methods: key generation and key transport. Both methods are based on public key cryptosystems. Actually, the ISAKMP key transport property definition borrows from the features of the RSA public-key cryptography system. In *key transport mode,* the establishment of a randomly generated session key reflects the *one-way* trust model association incorporated by RSA cryptosystems. When party A wants to establish a key for encrypting subsequent sessions with party B, party B's public key is used to encrypt a randomly generated session key. ISAKMP enables the encrypted session key to be sent to party B, the public key owner, who decrypts the randomly generated session key with his or her private key. Afterwards, both parties have the same session key; however, it was derived based on input from only one side of the VPN channel. The big advantage of the key transport method is that less computational overhead is involved so that key exchange is executed very efficiently.

As with the key transport mode, the *key generation mode* is based upon a public key cryptosystem. However, key generation properties resemble those of the Diffie-Hellman cryptography system. Thus, the establishment of key exchange for randomly generated session keys reflects a *two-way* trust model. The shared secret keys are generated after the VPN endpoints exchange their public keys. The resulting shared secrets can be used to generate a session or encrypt another encryption key that may be used for a randomly generated session. The major benefit of the key generation method is the ability to achieve perfect forward secrecy. As mentioned, perfect forward secrecy reduces the potential risk of compromising an encryption key by limiting the amount of time it is used for encrypting VPN sessions on an ongoing basis.

Keep in mind that ISAKMP's key transport and key generation properties are not specifications, but are essentially recommendations of key exchange attributes that it is capable of handling. Thus, any key exchange protocol, such as IKE and SKIP, that possesses these attributes can take full advantage of ISAKMP's key management services. Understanding the properties of the key exchange protocol that your VPN ultimately uses will greatly enhance your ability to manage the encryption keys employed by your network users.

Smart Cards

Smart cards are actually an emerging standard for two-factor or strong user authentication and are enormously popular in European countries. (See the discussion on two-factor user authentication in Chapter 3.)

Europeans use them for identification, paying parking tolls, registering at state health care facilities, and for other creative applications. Here in the U.S., they are primarily used for authenticating users to access enterprise networks. Sometimes smart cards and tokens are used synonymously. However, smart cards typically incorporate certain features that are not included with tokens. While tokens and smart cards are both credit card-sized devices that use batteries to power internal memory, only a smart card includes external leads for connecting to a smart-card reader. Adding smart-card readers to network workstations is a no-brainer. Smart cards have also been designed to fit in PCMCIA II slots, which are found in laptop computers.

From the perspective of VPNs, smart cards can be configured with a user's public/private key pair and digital signature that are required for authentication and establishing VPN tunnels. Smart-card deployment brings an added security feature by allowing users to remove the device when not in use. In contrast, public/private key pairs can be compromised or confiscated if they are stored in a file in a user's PC directory. Smart-card acceptance has been slowed due to smart-card vendors' inability to export them with strong encryption deployed. As more vendors decide to include government access to keys (GAK) through a back door or key escrow, expect more smart-card solutions on the horizon.

TACACS+: Yet Another System for User Authentication

TACACS+ is the enhanced successor of TACACS, which stands for Terminal Access Controller Access Control System. TACACS was created by the ISP BBN Planet Corporation and initially adapted by Cisco systems in their router products. TACACS was actually the first commercial product of a new generation of *three-tiered* user authentication systems. (RADIUS is another example of a three-tiered authentication system.) The three-tiered user authentication process begins when a user initiates a connection request to a remote access server. In response, the access server becomes a client when it connects with a user authentication server to validate the user. If the user is authorized on the validation server, the connection attempt is allowed through the access server or security gateway. (See Figure 3-6 for a summary of the three-tiered authentication process in RADIUS.)

Unfortunately, TACACS was difficult to implement and encountered operational problems when it was first put in use. Cisco Systems introduced TACACS+ in 1995 to correct the shortcomings of the original version. In addition to authentication, TACACS+ offers access control and accounting much like RADIUS. Also like RADIUS, network administrators can choose from a variety of front-end user authentication mechanisms, such as the typical ID/password access or encrypted submissions through tokens. Although TACACS+ has been submitted to the IETF for standards track attainment, RADIUS is expected to be the standard of choice for remote user authentication.

Lightweight Directory Access Protocol (LDAP)

One of the most daunting and time-consuming challenges for network administrators is managing the user community, especially in large enterprises. The task can become hairy when numerous user groups must be maintained and when individual users belong to more then one group. In light of VPN installations, if multiple-user authentication options are available, this could also contribute to the complexity of management responsibilities. LDAP is a system for managing multiple-user domains or groups within secure networking environments. LDAP not only provides a seamless interface between security gateways, it supports interfaces to popular user authentication methods such as RADIUS, S/KEY, and TACACS+.

In Check Point's VPN-1, for example, LDAP requires three components for operation: the LDAP server, the protocol itself, and an Account Management Client (AMC). The network administrator builds and manages the various user domains in the network through AMC, the GUI front end that manages the system. The multiple-user databases are housed on an LDAP server, and communications between AMC and the server are supported by LDAP. The LDAP server is also referred to as an "Account Unit," and LDAP is used to integrate the Account Unit with VPN-1's available user authentication options. In other words, LDAP supports communication between the firewall and a repository of information profiles on network users residing on an LDAP server. (See Figure 10-4.)

One of the key features of the LDAP system is the support of distinguished name (DN) conventions through the AMC. DN capability facili-

Figure 10-4
The LDAP user management system.

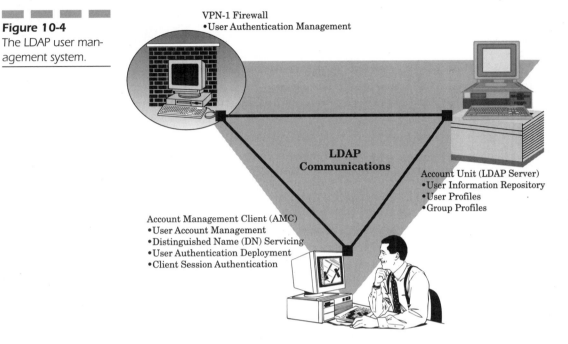

tates the overall process by allowing the administrator to assign a globally unique name for each network user. The structure of the global naming convention is hierarchical so that a user can be identified by the country, organization, and common name (given and surname) identifiers. Therefore, you may have two "Joe Smiths" that work in the U.S., but one works in accounting and the other in marketing. In this situation, the "organization" identifier of the convention affords the uniqueness to each "Joe Smith" network user. If management of a large network user base describes your situation, then a user management system such as LDAP makes a lot of sense.

11

Exploring VPN and Firewall Security Policy Concepts

So far, *Managing Virtual Private Networks* has taken you behind the GUI for a close-up inspection of the operational characteristics of VPN and firewall functionality. This chapter will bring you out in front of the GUI for the purpose of taking you in to explore security policy concepts and management. The security policy is the most important guideline you will formulate for your enterprise network. As the network administrator, you need to understand how and when your users work, what network applications and services they require, the type of environments they work in from a security standpoint, the available network resources, and the number of users and user groups that depend on the enterprise network. The resulting findings become the bricks and mortar of your firewall's security policy.

Other important aspects of security policy include deployment and management. This chapter will also focus on how a security policy is deployed and managed for the entire enterprise. Keep in mind that security policies based on stateful inspection technology process network traffic differently than security policies based on application proxy technology. These functional differences may be key in deciding what VPN solution is best for your organization.

Enterprisewide Security Management

You cannot begin too early in determining how to manage your network's security. Like many organizations, your enterprise may already utilize a certain approach in managing enterprisewide efforts. If your organization traditionally employs a centralized approach, most likely you are inclined to use a centralized approach when implementing a VPN security solution as well. If the management style is decentralized, you would probably use a decentralized approach. Or, your organization may employ a combination of the two. Whatever the case, you should determine the most feasible scenario for your organization, especially when security is the issue.

A key factor in this consideration is resources. If human resources are not a major concern, perhaps management of the enterprise security policy should be decentralized. If resources are limited, this may beg a centralized effort. The centralized-versus-decentralized question should be explored because many firewall-based solutions do not offer true centralized management of an enterprisewide security policy. Some vendor solutions require that a separate security policy be developed and installed wherever a firewall will be physically located. This is an important consideration. If, for example, you are planning a half dozen enforcement points, development and deployment of six separate security policies is required. In this situation, vendors usually provide the means of monitoring the status of all firewall stations from one remote point. Monitoring entails tracking operational status, examining log files, activating/deactivating a firewall, and perhaps killing actual connections. However, *configuring* each firewall with its associated security policy entails a series of separate efforts. From this perspective, preparing the entire contingent in this way may present greater opportunity for errors.

In contrast, true centralized management allows operational status checks as well as centralized construction of the entire security policy. It also includes the ability to disseminate security policy from a remote centralized point and to manage the resulting enforcement capability from that same location. Check Point Software Technologies' VPN-1 is one of the few popular systems that offers true centralized security policy management. In fact, one central security policy controls firewall enforcement points as well as any routers that implement security. The firewall is divided up accordingly and installed to various servers to create the enforcement points or security gateways. The centralized approach signifies that the policy and resulting apportioned pieces need only be constructed, implemented, and installed once. Thus, management and editing of the distributed security policy can then be handled from a centralized point.

The tools for building, implementing, and managing a security policy are accessible through a firewall's management GUI. Figure 11-1 is an example of the security policy GUI for VPN-1.

Rule Base Editor

Firewall security policy is translated to the network by a rule base. A *rule base* is a set of rules that the firewall uses to test each communication attempt that goes in and out of a network that is securely tucked away behind the firewall's perimeter. (See Figure 11-2.) Generally, firewall rules specify the source, destination, services, and action initiated for each communication. Rules may also specify time-of-day and date restrictions, user restrictions, and which events and related information should be logged.

Figure 11-1

Example of security policy graphical user interface.

Figure 11-2
Example of a security policy main management screen.

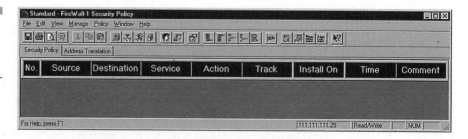

Each rule consists of *rule-based elements,* as indicated by the fourth row of categories in Figure 11-2. Each of the entries in the row is a column heading for the specific element in question. See Table 11-1 for an explanation of these elements.

Rule Base Attributes in Packet-Filtering Systems   In the case of stateful inspection systems, the set of rules that make up the rule base are ordered. VPN-1, for instance, examines packets by comparing them to the rule base, one rule at a time. Therefore, it is necessary to define each rule in a security policy in the appropriate order. The following depicts the order in which VPN-1 applies security policy rules to packets:

1. Application of antispoofing rules.

2. Properties labeled "First" are processed before any "numbered" rules. (See Figure 11-3.) The property labeled "Last" is matched last.

TABLE 11-1

Description of Rule-Based Elements.

Element	Definition
No.	Rule number; defines the order in which FireWall-1 enforces each rule.
Source	The source of the packet.
Destination	Where the packet is going. Source and destination can be any network objects.
Services	TCP, HTTP, SMTP, UDP, RPC, and ICMP.
Action	What to do with a packet.
Track	Log or alert rule.
Install On	Which firewall objects will enforce the rule.
Time	When a rule is effective. Define times as needed.
Comment	User-defined description of the rule.

Figure 11-3
Changing rule base
order through prop-
erties setup menu.

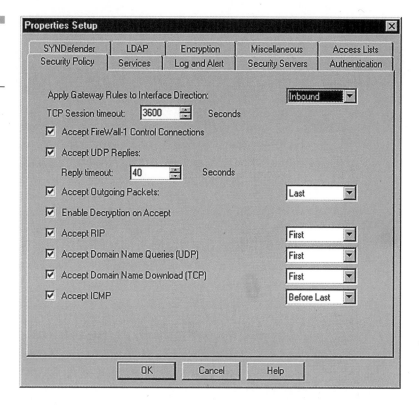

The properties selected with a check mark in the Security Policy tab
of VPN-1's Properties Setup screen and labeled "First" are matched
prior to the numbered rules. In the rule base, properties define overall standards or criteria for communication inspection. The Properties Setup tab eliminates the need to enter repetitive information for
each rule.

3. Rules are matched in accordance to their order in the rule base,
   except for the last rule.

4. Properties with a check mark and labeled "Before Last" are
   matched after every other rule except for the last rule.

5. The last rule in the rule base is matched accordingly.

6. A property checkmarked and labeled "Last" is matched last.

7. Finally, the implicit drop rule is matched. This rule follows the
   principle: That which is not expressly permitted is dropped, period.

Rule Base Attributes in Application Proxy Systems   In general, application proxy-based firewalls do not depend on the order of the rule base to process packets. When rule base setup is non-order-dependent, establishing the "bricks and mortar" of the security policy is easier than building a rule base for a packet-filtering firewall. Application proxies use a two-pronged approach to processing packets against a rule base. First, the proxy requisitions all the potential rules that apply to a connection. For example, it selects all rules that apply to a particular service requested by packets of a given source and destination address. The IP source and destination addresses are given the top priority in determining a match. On the second leg, the application proxy determines which rule provides a *best fit*. This is in contrast to packet-filtering firewalls, which seek a *first-fit* match. The proxy then consults other properties or parameters and qualifies the rule, which best matches the fateful connection. If no rule is found to match the best-fit inspection mode, the proxy disallows the connection attempt.

Object Classes and Management

A crucial step in building an effective rule-based security policy is defining, in rule-based terminology, the various networking entities, such as

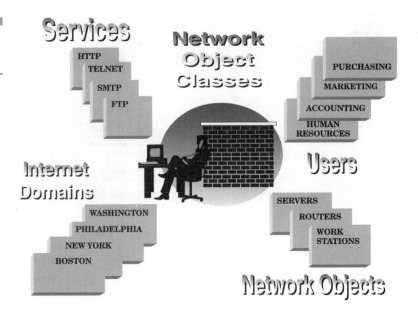

Figure 11-4
Defining security policy object classes.

hosts, servers, gateways, users, services, and resources, and the interrelationships between them. Firewalls enable administrators to define the
network's "playing pieces" as objects in order to facilitate the efficient
rule base dispensation of security. Check Point's VPN-1 takes object definition even further by categorizing similar network entities into object
classes. (See Figure 11-4.)

Defining a network object in VPN-1 is a straightforward process. For
example, to define a Web server host as a network object, the administrator would interface with VPN-1's Workstation Properties dialog. (See
Figure 11-5.) The Web server's name, *www.newyork.com,* is entered in
the Name field of the Properties' dialog. Notice that the Web server is to
be located behind the firewall's defenses. This is accomplished by selecting the Internal field under the Location heading. Also, under the Type
heading this server is designated as a host. In VPN terminology, a host
terminates a connection and a gateway passes on the connection.

Other object classes are defined in a similar manner. In VPN-1, object
classes are defined as follows:

1. *Network objects.*   An entire network or subnetwork can be defined
   as a single object. This category also includes hosts, gateways, and
   servers (firewall or not). In addition, this object class includes
   routers, Internet domains, and Logical Servers.

2. *Users.*   The Users object class is comprised of individuals and
   groups that access and utilize the network. When setting up this

Figure 11-5
Example of a
Network object
definition.

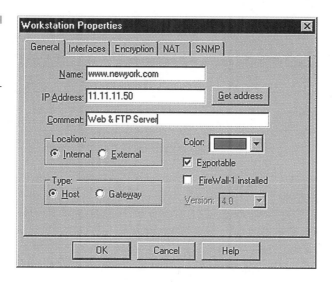

class, administrators can define user access rights, including eligible sources and destinations and user authentication schemes.

3. *Services.*   VPN-1 accommodates a variety of TCP/IP- and Internet-based services available and deployed throughout the network. The ability to define new network services is also a capability of VPN-1 and perhaps other firewalls as well.

4. *Resources.*   This object class defines systems accessed by certain protocols such as HTTP, FTP, and SMTP.

5. *Servers.*   The Servers object class defines specialty servers designated for content screening or user authentication.

6. *Keys.*   Encryption Keys object class enables the definition of keys for third-party interoperability that do not function with automated key management.

7. *Time objects.*   Time periods that certain rules are effective.

Object managers and their related GUIs simplify the process of defining all of the elements of a network in terms of object classes and their properties. Objects can be arranged by families or organized into hierarchies for efficient control. Object properties are also centrally managed.

Every object owns a set of attributes, such as network address and subnet mask. The administrator specifies some of these attributes, while others are extracted by the firewall. Firewalls can retrieve information from network databases, the files of hosts and servers, Network Information Service (or NIS; formerly Yellow Pages), and the Internet domain service.

Characteristics of Centralized Security (Rule Base) Management

Regardless of whether a security policy for the entire enterprise is built once or separately for each enforcement point, when in place, a centralized management capability is beneficial. A comprehensive centralized security management system entails more than the ability to manage the security policy alone. In addition to building and centrally managing the security policy (rule base), an effective centralized management system should also allow you to manage the potentially heterogeneous group of platforms while the security policy may reside out on the network. These platforms include CPU-based servers, routers, switches, and remote access devices. The central management system should also support real-time "suspicious activity" by alerting and monitoring and enterprisewide logging of successful and unsuccessful user login attempts from a single location. Finally, a central management system must support accounting and/or reporting capabilities.

Centralized Management and Control

In general, vendors rely on a client/server model to centrally manage enterprisewide security policy. The administrator engages a GUI-based *client* that connects directly to the firewall gateway *server*. There are basically two incarnations of the client/server model for managing security policy on an enterprisewide basis: a *many-to-many* central management approach or *one-to-many* approach. (See Figure 11-6.)

In a many-to-many central management approach, the difference lies

Figure 11-6
Centralized security management methods.

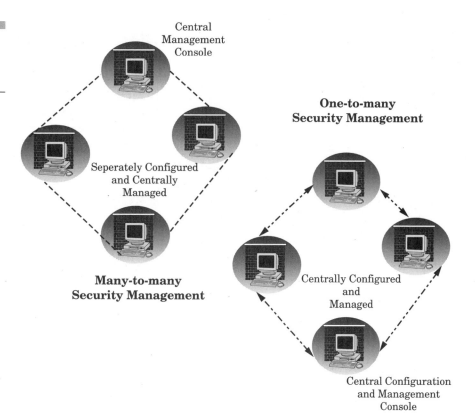

within the strategy for deploying the security policy to the actual network enforcement points. Most vendor solutions mandate that you build a security policy for each security gateway planned. For example, if you are planning six enforcement points, you must configure six security policies. As a result of this strategy, the configuring and subsequent management function requires a dedicated system (client/server capability). In this scenario, configuration activity results in a one-to-one relationship between the security policy and the security policy system platform. When the security system goes into production, vendor solutions will enable a console attached to one enforcement point to also centrally manage the other enforcement points, even though they were separately configured. The administrator engages a GUI, which provides support for other management functions such as real-time login tracking.

In a one-to-many approach, all planned enforcement points can be configured from one client/server system through a single security policy. The security policy components that are common to the separate enforcement points are distributed accordingly. In this scenario, the administrator has only one comprehensive security policy to configure. Once the pieces of the comprehensive policy are in place, all enforcement points can be centrally managed from the same system that was used to configure the security gateways. Check Point's VPN-1 uses the one-to-many central management and configuration approach.

Check Point's VPN-1 centralized security configuration and management system is composed of two main components: the Management Module and the Firewall Module. The two modules are fully integrated and can be distributed into a variety of client/server configurations. (See Figure 11-7.) The Management Module consists of the Administrative GUI, the Management Module itself, and the Management Server. The Administrative GUI on the client workstation accesses the Management Module on the Management Server. Through the GUI, the rule base is defined, security policy administered, network login attempts tracked, firewall status monitored, and real-time alerting activated.

The Management Module controls and manages all firewall enforcement points whether deployed locally or remotely. The Management Server contains all the data and configuration files relating to the firewall system. It also manages the actual firewall database, which consists of the rule base, network objects, servers, users, and user groups. The Client Management GUI and Management Module can reside on the same computer or on two separate computers.

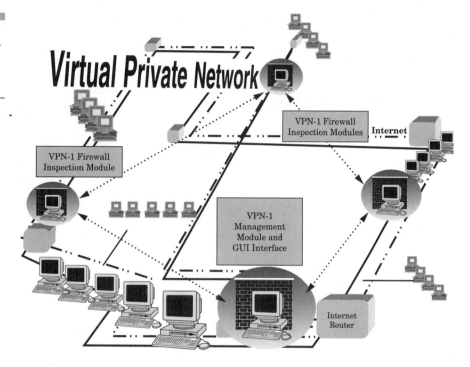

The Firewall Module consists of the Inspection Module and security servers. (See discussion on the Inspection Module in the "Stateful Inspection Technology" section in Chapter 8.) The Firewall Module's major functions include access control and user, client, and session authentication. This module also provides network address translation (NAT). (See "Network Address Translation" in Chapter 8.) NAT hides internal network structures and prevents addressing-scheme conflicts between networks. Other features of the Firewall Module include multiple firewall synchronization, content security, and auditing.

The Inspection Module performs a vital role for the firewall. It is composed of three components: the Inspection Engine, compiled INSPECT code, and dynamic state tables, which contain various state and context information. When rule base construction is completed, the administrator generates security policy and rule-based information into INSPECT code or a script. The script is, in turn, loaded onto all the firewall enforcement points in connection with the Inspection Engine. The INSPECT script compares the information in a data packet to the rules in the rule base.

Optimal Deployment of Security Gateways

When administering a security policy for the entire enterprise network, you should recognize the fact that the security gateways become the gatekeepers for traffic flowing in and out of the network. Depending upon network traffic, it is very important to deploy the right solution architecturally and the optimal number of firewall enforcement points. Firewalls inspect every single packet in and out of the network. The flow can amount to hundreds of thousands per session, especially if you consider FTP information transfers. If you have hundreds or thousands of users, it is easy to understand the workhorse potential of firewalls.

Also important to note is that the firewalls inspect and evaluate each packet in terms of a rule base. When the packet arrives at the firewall's port, it gathers from it source and destination addresses, services being sought, resources required, time and date of the connection attempt, and data from higher-level applications or protocols. The firewall retrieves this information and does conditional comparisons between the gathered information and the individual rules in the rule base. If the results of the comparison authorize the connection, then the firewall triggers all the services that are allowed for that individual connection. If this is the initial phase of a connection attempt, all levels of authentication transpire. If the user is authenticated and related data validated, several other phases takes place. The firewall services come into effect, including address translation, access control, antispoofing, load balancing, and finally the actual session. (See Figure 11-8.) Since a relatively significant amount of activity occurs for each connection attempt, depending on the size of the user base, the number of attempts could be large at any given time. Thus, a feasible number of firewall enforcement points should be deployed to support network operation at peak efficiency.

Network Traffic Logging and Monitoring

The success of your network's security is directly correlated with the effectiveness of the logging capability. How effective the logging mechanism is depends on the robustness of the vendor implementation. In theory, security gateways should log every connection attempt, whether successful or unsuccessful, and the actual sessions resulting from successful connections. Having the option to control the logging function from a centralized or decentralized standpoint is also desirable. Logging

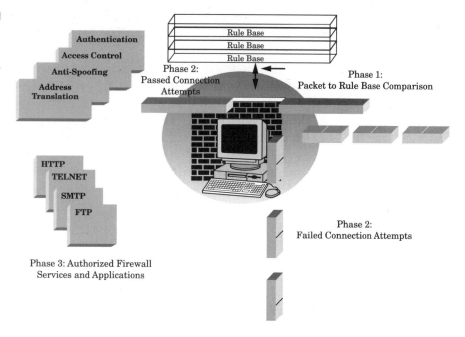

Figure 11-8
Phased process for
connection attempts.

should actually entail two primary real-time activities: generating physical records (logs) and monitoring network activity. In general, security solutions tend to provide both features. Believe it or not, some solutions do not provide session logs, which is totally unacceptable.

In addition to tracking and monitoring connection attempts, security solutions can include a variety of supplemental tracking features. Some systems track bandwidth utilization and the ability to export logs into a third-party reporting management tool. Microsoft's Proxy Server System version 2.0, for example, allows logs to be directly written to a SQL or open database connectivity-compliant system.

An effective monitoring system, especially if centralized, will also enhance the overall security management process. For one thing, it can be utilized to assist in determining how effectively the firewall is interpreting the rule base. In the event of an emergency, such insight may be instrumental in pinpointing a problem. An effective monitoring system also allows the administrative team to customize the information, which is displayed in connection to the real-time operating environment. Since the logging monitoring function is the window into your enterprisewide security system, it is very important that you assess what logging functions are desirable for your needs. In subsequent discussions with potential solution providers, you can assess what they have to offer in this

area. Generally, most solution providers offer an adequate logging function, but some do not. Frankly, the logging function is the one area
where capability is often lacking. However, be prepared to trade off certain desired logging features to gain another benefit that is more critical
to your network's security.

Real-Time Event Alerting and Notification

Another desirable feature of a centralized security management system
is real-time notification of extraordinary or emergency network conditions. Firewall security systems allow all network connection activity to
be classified relative to conditional developments. This classification
includes standard sessions and routine failed attempts as well as critical
and emergency situations. The security policy rule base allows administrators to establish conditions that would trigger a variety of alert mechanisms commensurate with the severity of the condition. Table 11-2 provides a summary of the types of routine, extraordinary, or emergency
conditions that firewalls may be configured to flag.

In the event of an emergency, extraordinary event, or critical situation, rule-based security systems provide specific mechanisms for notify-
ing security staff. These methods include the sounding of audio tones on
a client console, automatically generating an email message to a desig-

TABLE 11-2

Network Security
Alert and Notifica-
tion Classifications.

Category	Description
Emergency	Usually signals a firewall enforcement point failure. As you would expect, all traffic through the gateway has ceased.
Critical	An important critical security function has failed, such as Java stripping.
Alert	A signal that suspicious activity has been encountered per the rule base.
Error	Implicates routine security gateway operations that cannot be executed. Typically, this feature is automatically in effect.
Warning	Potential error condition in the making. Error states are normally recoverable.
Notice	Instrumental in flagging events having potential for concern, such as a denied connection attempt.
Informational	Routine tracking of pedestrian connections and sessions.

nated recipient, paging, and special-notification dialogs to the GUI interface. For example, a security manager can be paged on the weekend in the event of an emergency such as a firewall failure. The comprehensive functionality built into these two features can be the difference between having an adequate centralized security system and a highly effective one. Do your homework in this area, as the payoff will be well worth the effort.

Special Features

Solution providers that are interested in establishing their offerings as viable state-of-the-art security solutions tend to offer special features in current releases and consistently plan new enhancements for future releases. Examples of two special features are *synchronization of firewall modules* and *suspicious activity monitoring*.

Synchronization of Firewall Modules   In the section on load balancing in Chapter 8, we discussed how this feature coordinates equal sharing of connection processing among multiple points. To distinguish between this and the synchronization of firewall modules, the latter is concerned with sharing *state* information of active sessions among multiple security gateways. When activated, firewalls mutually update each other's inspection tables with real-time connection activity. If one security gateway fails and completely shuts down, a second security gateway takes over for the failed unit without so much as a hiccup from network performance. The consistent reciprocal updating of each other's inspection tables allows this seamless substitution to occur.

This feature also allows for an activity called *asymmetric routing* of connections between participating hosts. As noted in Chapter 5, IP source routing capability allows return responses from a target destination host to return to the source, or originating, host along a different path than the source host utilized, hence, asymmetric routing. As a result of synchronization of firewall modules or the ability to share state information, asymmetric routing is possible.

Suspicious Activity Monitoring   One of the slickest firewall capabilities is suspicious activity monitoring (SAM). SAM will sound a system alert for any connection attempt that exceeds the specific limits anticipated for a given rule. For example, you may have a rule that specifies that an HTTP session be allowed in the afternoon hours for a given user.

If that user uncharacteristically logs on after the limits set forth in the security policy rule, say, in the evening, this may suggest suspicious activity.

SAM capability works by initializing the rule thresholds such that when they are surpassed, an alert registers at the central control system. This condition also generates a written alert message in a log file and initiates an audit trail to the user host that triggered the alert. A rule modified for SAM may also be configured to issue more than one alert, depending upon the potential gravity of the suspicious activity. Note that SAM capability by default does not prohibit the connection; it only issues alerts if the connection suddenly operates outside of anticipated parameters.

Exploring the Logic of Rule Base Editors

In this section, we explore the exacting world of firewall rule base logic. The rule base is the electronic manifestation of the enterprise's security policy in the firewall. This discussion is designed to familiarize you with the somewhat procedure-oriented process and the nomenclature necessary to translate security policy statements to an ordered rule set. In other words, this section reviews the process of implementing a security policy by developing a rule base and installing it to firewall-based enforcement points throughout the network.

The first stage in writing a security policy is defining the network components such as LANs, gateways, servers, and objects that will be governed by the rule base. The next step involves defining the services. In Check Point's VPN-1, for example, commonly used services such as FTP, HTTP, or SMTP are defined to the Firewall Module by default. After the definition stage, the actual rules are formulated, then installed. In VPN-1, security policy implementation consists of the following steps:

1. Define the network objects by the object manager in the Security Policy main menu. (See Figure 11-9.) In this step, only the network objects planned for use in the rule base are defined to the system.

2. Define the services that are specified by the enterprise security policy. As noted above, certain commonly used services are already defined to VPN-1. Therefore, this step should be utilized to define

Figure 11-9

Rule base network object definition mode.

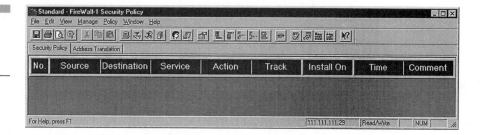

uncommonly used services identified in the enterprise security policy. To facilitate these two steps, the firewall only requires the name of the network component/object. The system is smart enough to retrieve other vital object properties' data from databanks provided by the DNS or host system files.

3. Define the actual rules that will make up the rule base.

4. Install the rule base. In VPN-1, this involves installing the INSPECT code on the security gateways.

The network object, services, and user-definition mode is the most critical aspect of the rule-base definition process. Depending on the size of your network, this could involve a considerable amount of effort. However, care should be taken to ensure that the rule base covers the particular network activity for which it was intended. When all the network objects are defined, the rule base editor is engaged next to define the relationships between the objects.

External Users Send Emails to Local Users

To begin building the rule base, assume that the following security policy was established:

1. *External* networks may access the local (internal) network to send email to local computers only.

2. Local computers can access all networks, which consists of the immediate local network and the Internet.

In this example, the challenge involves expressing the simple security policy into rules that explicitly represent its intent, or *directive*. The first policy item must be translated to capture the directive "external or nonlocal networks may send email to local computers only." For the first step in making the translation, the policy must be expressed in terms of the roles specific network components must play to execute the directive. This includes factoring in security gateway operations. Consequently, in this policy statement, when any external user sends email to local or internal network users, the email must traverse the security gateway before reaching any users. (There is actually an interim step in terms of what the network actually does before email reaches network users. In networks, email is usually received and serviced by an email server, which users interface with transparently to work with a given email system.)

To review, the operational components of the network that are involved in performing this policy statement are external network users, internal network users, the security gateway, and the email server. For the benefit of this discussion, the network components that are required for performing rule base operations will be referred to as *required network performance components*. There is also an implied factor in this policy statement, namely the use of the SMTP protocol that email requires in traversing the Internet. (Remember, we are working with a VPN that is supporting communications for Internet/intranet network and applications protocols.)

Now you have all the elements needed to construct a rule for the policy statement. If the rule base editor for VPN-1 is utilized, this security policy statement can be expressed by the rule format in the following table:

Source	Destination	Services	Action	Track	Install On
Any	mailsvr	SMTP	Accept	Short log	Gateways

Thus, the first security policy statement rule tells the firewall, "Accept on all security gateways, any email messages supported by the SMTP service (protocol) from any external users (Source) clearing the gateway to mailsvr (Destination; the ultimate destination is internal network users). Log these connections on the 'short' version of the system logs."

Local Users Access Entire Network

The second security policy element states: "Local computers may access the entire network. This includes the immediate LAN, enterprise WAN, and the Internet." What are the required network performance components needed to support this statement? The components consist of all internal network users; all external users, or users outside the enterprise network; and the security gateways. The implied required network performance component for this policy statement is all network services. In the case of VPN-1, all common network services, such as FTP, SMTP and HTTP, are by default defined to the network. In VPN-1, the rule statement in the following table expresses the second policy item:

Source	Destination	Services	Action	Track	Install On
localnet	Any	Any	Accept	Short log	Gateways

In rule base, this statement says to the firewall: "Allow all security gateways to accept connections from all internal (local) users to external or outside users for the purpose of engaging in sessions related to any allowable network services. Log all connections on the short version of system logs."

Implicit Communication Drop on Login

In general, firewalls come out of the box primed to drop all communications that pass through their security gates unless the communication is expressly permitted by a rule. This is called the *implicit drop rule*. In the case of VPN-1, this rule is automatically added to the end of the rule base. The effect is that any communication attempt not expressly covered in the rule base is automatically denied passage through network enforcement points. The implicit drop rule is captured in the following table. Note that the Track field, which designates how a connection should be logged, is blank.

Source	Destination	Services	Action	Track	Install On
Any	Any	Any	Drop	None	Gateways

Recall that VPN-1 is a packet-filtering or stateful inspection system. Stateful inspection systems inherently process rules in a specific order. Therefore, all connections will be evaluated first with regard to the two rules above. Any connections that are not covered are routinely dropped.

In the interest of security, however, it may be helpful if the firewall logs such denials in its system logs. The information could provide useful insight into whether or not the denials should be cause for concern or merely incidental. In order to log all connections rejected by the implicit drop rule, the command `long log` should be entered into the Track rule statement field. The adjustment is shown in the following table.

Source	Destination	Services	Action	Track	Install On
Any	Any	Any	Drop	Long log	Gateways

In summary, this rule says drop all communications coming in and out of the network not expressly permitted by a rule. However, log all denials in the long version of the system logs.

"Stealthing" the Gateway

The following table summarizes the rule base for the basic security policy example:

Source	Destination	Services	Action	Track	Install On
Any	mailsvr	SMTP	Accept	Short log	Gateways
localnet	Any	Any	Accept	Short log	Gateways
Any	Any	Any	Drop	Long log	Gateways

Implicit though it may be, the rule base has a glaring shortcoming. If an internal user is somehow able to obtain the user ID and password of another person, the internal network user can gain entry to the security gateway. This creates an unacceptable risk to the network's security, especially since the incidence of internal hacking is on the rise. To prevent any computers either inside or outside of the network from gaining access to the security gateway, a specialized rule must be added to the rule base. This rule is illustrated in the following table:

Source	Destination	Services	Action	Track	Install On
Any	Securit	Any	Reject	Long log	Gateways

In the destination field, the security gateway in question is named "Securit." It is assumed that the security gateway was defined to the firewall in the network object phase. The rule reads: "For any access originating from outside or inside the network, and any connection attempts in support of any service (protocol) that tries to access the security gateway called 'Securit,' those attempts should be routinely rejected. Log any attempt regarding this rule to the long version of the system logs." Protecting the gateway in this manner makes it inaccessible to all network users except for the firewall administrator. For all intents and purposes, the firewall is invisible. From that point forward, the security gateway operates by stealth.

We're not done yet, however. Another not-so-obvious situation that poses a risk to the network is possible. This rule does not prevent someone from physically sitting at the security gateway's console to gain access to the network. To eliminate this possibility, the rule listed in the next table should be added to the rule base:

Source	Destination	Services	Action	Track	Install On
Securit	Any	Any	Reject	Alert	Source

This rule eliminates the ability to physically originate communications going out of the network from the security gateway's console. Notice that the variables in the Source, Track, and Install On fields do not contain your usual responses. Construction of this rule does two things. It demonstrates the flexibility of the type of security mechanisms you can institute with rule base logic, and it also underscores the level of knowledge one should possess concerning security issues that are often overlooked.

The reason that `Source` is entered in the Install On field is that by default, security gateways enforce rules on *incoming* traffic only. In order for this rule to work, it must be enforced on the Securit gateway only, not any other gateway. When the Securit gateway is specified as Source, the rule is enforced only on the communications actually originating at Securit's console—in other words, on packets that both originate and would leave Securit. If `Gateways` remained in the Install On field, the rule would apply only to packets *entering* Securit and also *originating from* Securit, a situation that is physically impossible. As a result, the firewall would interpret this situation to mean no packets at all. In effect, this rule locks out an individual from using the security gateway Securit as a workstation. It would also trigger an alert condition at the management console.

The stealthing and lockout rules should be indicated at the beginning of the rule base because these two conditions must always be met first. In ordered rule set, conditions that should be met first should be listed first in the rule base unless exceptions are encountered. The following table is the complete rule base of our basic security policy example:

Source	Destination	Services	Action	Track	Install On
Any	Securit	Any	Reject	Long log	Gateways
Securit	Any	Any	Reject	Alert	Source
Any	mailsvr	SMTP	Accept	Short log	Gateways
localnet	Any	Any	Accept	Short log	Gateways
Any	Any	Any	Drop	Long log	Gateways

Translating More-Complex Policy into Rules

In this section, the logic of rule base editors is extended to accommodate more complex or real-world situations. Suppose, for example, that you would like to provide general business information and a Web site to external clients and business partners. (See Figure 11-10 for a look at the required network configuration.) Notice that the Web server called DMZ is located outside the internal network but attached to the security gateway (Securit). Although this situation could constitute a major business strategy change, covering business transactions with external clients by the rule base is a straightforward process. In this situation, the only preparation needed to generate a rule is to define the DMZ server to the rule base. Using the security policy GUIs indicated in Figure 11-9, the DMZ server would be defined as a network object. No services need be defined because the services in question, FTP and HTTP, are defined to VPN-1 out of the box.

Thus, to maintain the current security status of the network in the previous section, only one rule should be added to the rule base. This rule is represented in the following table:

Source	Destination	Services	Action	Track	Install On
Any	DMZ	FTP, HTTP	Accept	Short log	Gateways

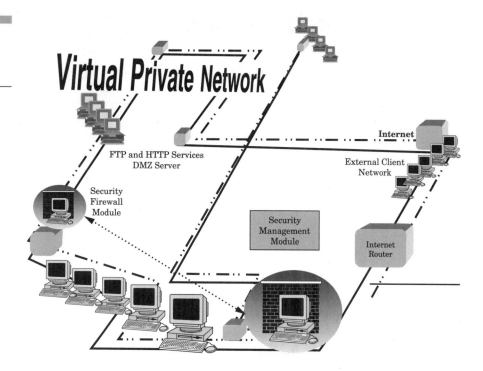

Figure 11-10
A configuration
for the rule base
exercise.

This rule states that "for any communications originating from any
source (external clients and internal users), allow connections to pass
through the security gateway (Securit) to the FTP and HTTP server
for information exchange and Web browsing." The rule would be
added to the bottom of the completed rule base developed in the previous section.

Select User Access to Select Services at Specific Time

For the next scenario, you receive a request from two project managers
who must go on assignment in the field. In order for them to perform
their job assignments, they need access from several field locations to
the network at headquarters. The field locations usually access headquarters' information databanks via Telnet. In preparation for adding a
new rule to accommodate the two project mangers, they must be defined
to the firewall as a "user group" object. The new group object is defined
as "Outside_Users." Assume that the project managers were individu-

Figure 11-11
User group object
definition.

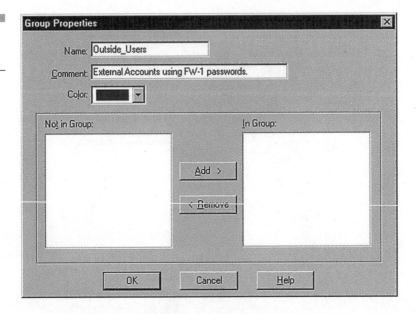

ally defined as users to the firewall. This scenario also assumes that the
Telnet resource was defined as a "Service." To define the user group in
VPN-1, the administrator would engage the GUI screen indicated in
Figure 11-11.

After the user group Outside_Users is defined, the rule can be written
in rule base logic. The rule that supports this effort is as follows:

Source	Destination	Services	Action	Track	Install On
Outside_Users @ Any	FTP Server	Telnet	User authentication	Short log	Gateways

The rule states: "For the outside user group (project managers), allow
communications to pass, regardless of location, through the gateway to
engage information exchange via Telnet. Accept communications only
after successful user authentication and log all activity on short version
of system logs." Notice that the Action field contains User authentication. In this case, acceptance of the connection is implicit. The firewall accepts the connection only after successful user authentication.
The user authentication requirement is set up in the User Properties
dialog screen. (See Figure 11-12.)

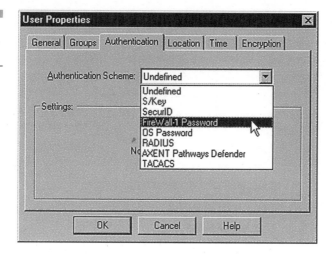

Figure 11-12
Firewall user authentication dialog.

Once the enterprise security policy has been converted, the resulting rule base elements are downloaded to their respective enforcement points. Firewalls verify that the rule base is logical and consistent, and the administrator runs system tests to assess operational readiness.

12

VPN Performance Considerations and Review

In a 1998 survey by TeleChoice, Inc., an independent industry consultant, respondents indicated that the number one concern for VPN solutions was performance. The second-greatest concern was security. Just 2 years ago, security was the primary concern in VPN considerations. What a difference a few years makes. One of the reasons why security took a backseat to performance was due to the strides that the IETF made in cultivating IPSec. The security services provided by IPSec were the cool waters that quenched everyone's thirst for a secure interoperable tunneling standard. The read on the industry is that everyone appears to be content with the new security advancements afforded by IPSec. At least for now. Thus, the new buzz around town is performance.

There are a number of factors that impact VPN performance, including latency and the underlying architecture of a VPN's technology suite. Latency is the time delay imposed on throughput as VPN operating components process information in response to operations. The inherent characteristics of the underlying architecture may also induce performance penalties in a VPN. Furthermore, the network medium itself, in this case the Internet, also poses performance barriers in terms of available bandwidth for VPN connections. In this chapter, these factors and their interrelationships are identified and discussed in terms of their effects on VPN performance. This chapter also divulges where current and future challenges for VPN performance lie and what the industry is doing to address them in VPN solutions.

Performance in the Real World

Now that IPSec seems to be allaying everyone's concerns about VPN security, performance has taken center stage. Big business is ready for that crucial leap, being right on the precipice of total acceptance of VPNs as a true enterprisewide communications backbone. The trends, industry research, and, above all, the demands of a global economy are strong drivers for the ubiquitous access, scalability, and cost-effectiveness of the Internet. Research has shown that the Internet can deliver savings of 30 to 70 percent over traditional remote access solutions such as frame relay or ATM. Now that "acceptable security" can be factored into the equation, enterprises are poised to reap the fabled promise of the Internet.

The Internet's time is near for other reasons as well, including, ironically, both the success and inherent shortcomings of public/private networks. Public data networks (distinguished from the public Internet) such as UUNET, MCI Communications, CompuServe, and other frame relay-based networks are the real-world model of what an enterprise communication backbone should be. (See Figure 12-1.) In these services, transmissions occur at close to wire speeds, including T3 rates and beyond. These public networks also guarantee reliability and quality of service from end to end, along with the ability to control bandwidth allocation relative to priority of transmissions.

The vendors mentioned above are also ISPs because they are major carriers of Internet traffic. In 1998, a standard called Resource Reservation Protocol (RSVP) was introduced to address quality of service (QoS)

Figure 12-1
Real-world model of
a high-performance
network.

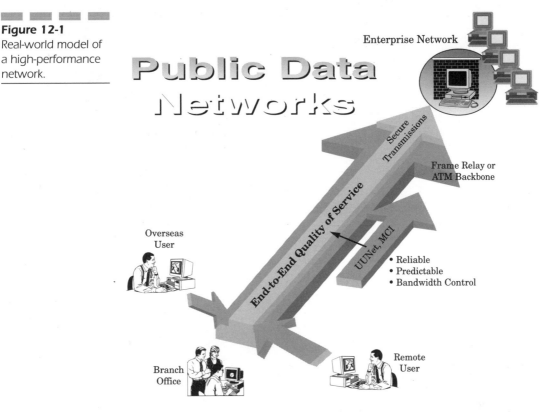

issues within the confines of ISP networks. RSVP was designed to provide QoS levels that approach the QoS provided by frame relay or ATM networks by enabling ISPs to guarantee bandwidth on the Internet according to the priority level of the traffic. (See Figure 12-2.) RSVP is primarily a scheduling and management system with intelligence for establishing acceptable limits of delay/latency of network communications gear and associated error rates. However, many ISPs cannot handle RSVP, and for those that can, RSVP only formally requests service. Delivery of the *actual* service levels is the responsibility of the service provider. In other words, RSVP is just the reservation clerk. It can only request what is there. It's up to the ISP to have the quality infrastructure in place. Thus, if the service is poor, it doesn't matter how good the reservation clerk is.

Although service providers such as MCI and UUNET have credible reach, it pales in comparison to the reach of the Internet. Furthermore, the typical service provider does not have the geographical coverage of an MCI. What happens if you are working with a service provider that

does not support a geographical area required by your business endeavors? In this situation, you have no other choice but to employ a second service provider that supports your network's protocols for remote coverage. If two or more separate service providers are utilized, how is a consistent quality/level of service ensured across multiple providers?

Until the advent of switched virtual circuits (SVCs), a consistent quality of service delivery between service providers could not be achieved. SVCs and "smart" permanent virtual circuits (PVCs) are designed to connect frame relay networks between different common carriers. This joint collaboration between service providers requires multicarrier coordination and service agreements. So far, this technology has not been widely available and does not consistently work between common carriers that may have tested them. Even if they are able to pull it off, the cost may be prohibitive. To cover the cost of acquisition, installation, configuration, and management, common carriers must charge various rates for all the possible levels of service. They would also need to put in an infrastructure for an intercarrier management team, adding further costs. Furthermore, the resulting intercarrier service still may not have the ubiquitous coverage of the Internet. In the final analysis, this solution may be too expensive for many enterprises, as with private networks.

All things considered, VPNs are emerging as the reasonable choice for enterprises that are faced with the pressures of establishing a global presence but cannot afford public data networks. For these embattled organizations, the achievements in security have positioned VPNs with the capability to deliver high-speed global connectivity at reasonable prices. For the cost of Internet access, whether through a 56K dial-up modem, fractional T1, T3, or beyond, VPNs leverage the price advantages that IP-based intranets offer over traditional networks and telecommunication systems. QoS issues are soon to be adequately addressed. When this happens, all major barriers preventing the Internet from becoming a legitimate communications backbone for business-to-business transactions will be lifted.

The VPN Performance Challenge

The IETF and other Internet concerns are currently reviewing discussions and proposals for a standard to address QoS and performance issues of VPNs and IP-based networks. The proposal that is currently receiving the most attention is the one describing the Differentiated Services (DiffServ) protocol. DiffServ is a specification for providing end-to-end QoS on ISPs' service offerings. It will also offer a means for prioritizing traffic so that different levels of service can be offered on IP networks such as the Internet. DiffServ is the IETF's way of acknowledging the industry's demand for performance assurances in VPN solutions. Users want assurances that VPN solutions will in fact deliver reliable and predictable communications.

Yet the IETF's understanding goes beyond this. The security functions performed by VPNs involve delivering encryption and key management services. By default, these functions are inherently CPU- and memory-intensive. Early vendor VPN implementations caused bottlenecks at VPN gateways as these nodes struggled to negotiate and apply strong encryption algorithms and authentication to traffic flows. Thus,

Figure 12-3
The Internet (DiffServ)
QoS and perfor-
mance management.

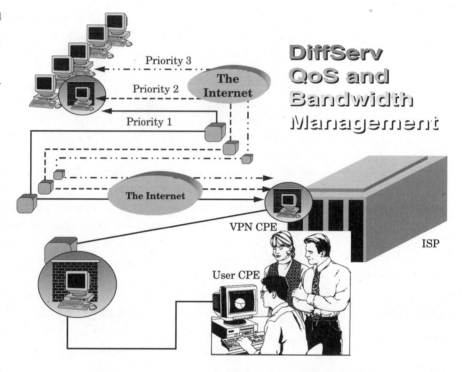

any standard that the IETF would sanction must be able to accommodate the CPU-intensive processes of encryption and key management
functionality, as well as reliability and predictability issues. Since Diff-
Serv provides QoS for IP networks, it will accommodate network-level or
layer 3 protocols such as IPSec.

In a DiffServ application, a user's customer premise equipment (CPE)
would tag network-bound traffic according to some predetermined priority service level supported by the network's infrastructure. The ISP's
VPN CPE would receive the DiffServ "priority tag," reserve the
requested bandwidth, and send the transmission over the Internet. (See
Figure 12-3.)

Multi-Protocol Label Switching (MPLS) is a QoS capability directed
towards data-link or layer 2 protocols such as L2TP. MPLS adds a special label to layer 2 traffic that directs how it should be switched
through a layer 2-compatible network. Many vendors are already ship-
ping VPN solutions enhanced to support DiffServ and MPLS QoS and
performance management for IP-based networks.

Inherent Performance Factors of VPNs

The ability to prioritize IP traffic over the Internet is a major performance advancement. As the Internet Bandwidth and Priority Service Management protocols begin to emerge, you will see them implemented in an increasing number of VPN solutions. These latest developments seem to be light-years away from the first generation of VPN solutions that routinely caused bottlenecks at the security gateways as strong encryption was administered to transmissions. However, since the advent of VPN solutions, solution providers have been generally performance-conscious to the extent of being innovative in providing those extra rpms to boost VPN performance. Solution providers have turned to traditional areas such as the operating system and memory-management techniques to obtain desired performance enhancements. In some cases, attempts at QoS and bandwidth management features were implemented. It is not surprising that there is a direct correlation between performance innovations and market leadership. Products like Cisco's PIX Firewall and Check Point Technologies' VPN-1 are market leaders and also performance leaders when compared to competing products.

When either vendors or independent testing laboratories test performance, it is usually measured in *throughput*. Throughput is the result users see on their screens after data is processed by application commands and is usually measured in megabits per second (mbps), where the upper limit on speed is usually the maximum speed of the cable in a LAN or telephone lines that connect LANs to form WANs. Typical LAN speeds are 10 mbps or 100 mbps. Typical telephone line speeds are 1.5 mbps (T1) and 45 mbps (T3).

When a vendor indicates that their VPN performs at rated LAN speeds, this is virtually impossible. There are just too many factors that come into play for a vendor to get a reading of this type. Let's face it. Encryption and data validation operations are CPU-intensive; consequently, there are performance penalties to pay in throughput. Companies that add performance innovations like memory caching and data compression techniques can offset the effects to a considerable degree. Further, you need to clarify whether they are referring to a VPN node or a workstation that is connected through a VPN security gateway. This makes all the difference in the world. After encrypted data is decrypted back into cleartext and passes through a VPN security gateway, when the information hits the LAN, it should be traveling to the client workstation at close to the rated cable speed (10 mbps or 100 mbps). However, if a VPN endpoint is the workstation and any encryption processes occur, the throughput should be considerably less, relatively speaking, than the rated speed of the LAN.

In general, the top firewalls operating without VPN functions tend to operate close to rated LAN speeds. Most operate on the average of 50 to 60 percent of rated speed for LAN throughput. However, when VPN operations are introduced, throughput can decrease on the average as much as a factor of three compared to rated LAN speeds. Keep in mind when we measure performance in mbps, we are still speaking of speeds that are incomprehensible to the senses. For the most part, even VPNs that are rated at the bottom of the performance curve still operate at fairly fast speeds and acceptable response times. However, in medium to large installations that support hundreds, perhaps thousands, of users, the VPNs at the low end of the performance curve could produce bottlenecks and noticeable delays in response time. For VPNs on the top of the curve, however, overall performance should be exceptional and delays in response time are rarely noticeable.

Other Performance Considerations

The great debate in the VPN industry is whether VPNs based on stateful inspection firewalls or VPNs based on proxy firewalls perform best. Those in the proxy firewall camp maintain that stateful firewalls are slower due to table lookup functions required by the firewall. In contrast, the stateful inspection/packet filters camp insists that proxies are inherently slower because each connection through the firewall must be replicated as an application to be inspected. The truth of the matter is that independent research has shown proxy-based firewalls are inherently slower due to how proxies reproduce applications for inspection. As for security, the proxy camp maintains that their wares offer better security because connections are inspected at the application layer. In theory, this should be true. However, in reality stateful inspection systems that add security proxies are slightly more secure than proxy firewalls.

Again, these are general guidelines. The main thing is to decide which firewall architecture best serves your needs. Then look for the system with the best fit for your organization. It may very well be that you may be willing to trade off speed and performance for security, and vice versa.

PART

4

VPN Implementations and Business Assessment, Just for the Record

Y ou are the expert in managing your business. No one knows it better than you do. And, if you are in management or performing management duties, you certainly know about or have been exposed to various techniques for evaluating your business needs. Thus, this section will not regurgitate the steps involved for any specific methodology but will provide a different spin on assessing business needs.

There are various options available to provide the functionality of a given VPN solution. In Chapter 13, we identify and explore a logical set of criteria that you may find useful in pinpointing your own specific requirements. An implementation checklist of VPN considerations is built to assist you in the evaluation. For each consideration, the related operational or functional choices become the actual evaluation tools of the assessment. For example, an important consideration in an enterprisewide deployment is determining the best overall deployment strategy. VPNs can be deployed in LAN-to-LAN, client-to-LAN, or client-to-client configurations, or a combination of the three. Using these choices as the criteria, the one that best fits your organization is determined after an in-depth consideration of the enterprise's specific business needs, culture, user expertise, geographical limits, financial availability, and ISP support. To complete the chapter, a review of several scenarios is presented to challenge your critical thinking and general adroitness in applying VPN terminology to potential real-world situations.

Chapters 14 and 15 focus on the business case of VPNs. These chapters explore the business case for VPN solutions from the viewpoints of small to multinational enterprises. Certain VPN requirements are common to enterprises regardless of size. These common areas will be pointed out but not discussed in great detail. The purpose of these chapters is to focus on the requirements that are more indicative of or unique to the given size of an organization. In completing this part, you will possess the necessary tools to assess and specifically identify your potential fitness for a VPN communications backbone.

13

VPN Implementations: Evaluating Your Business Needs

A VPN is the collaboration of a complementary set of technological components that are integrated to harness the power of the Internet for an enterprise communications backbone. For each technological or functional component, solution providers afford potential VPN users a variety of options. This chapter looks closely at these functional components by building a checklist that you may utilize as criteria for evaluating your specific needs. The intent is to familiarize you with the breadth of VPN functional capability while providing insight into your potential fitness for a VPN solution.

Configuring Your Organization's VPN Checklist

This discussion assumes that you are considering the expansion of your WAN to a VPN-based communications backbone. If your WAN is an IP-based intranet, the discussion should be more applicable to your situation. If, on the other hand, your WAN is based on other wide area communications' protocols such as frame relay, ATM, or LAN-based protocols (for example, IPX or NetBEUI), the discussion will still be interesting, but perhaps not as applicable to your situation. That's because the VPN standards that support non-IP based protocols, such as L2TP and PPTP, are still maturing in key areas and as such, the richness in available options may not apply. PPTP's encryption algorithms have been breached and strong encryption options are limited. (See discussion in Chapter 2.) L2TP will eventually support IPSec's security services, and it will be a momentous occasion for the networking world when commercial implementations become readily available. And when PPTP-based VPN solutions prove that they are just as viable as IPSec-based solutions, PPTP will probably find a stronger following as well.

This section recommends that you begin this process by answering key questions about your network from several critical perspectives. For example, what is the general purpose of your network? What types of applications are supported and what functions do they provide? What is the application mix and what is the breakdown of user demographics for each application? Are your users a mobile workforce or do they work in remote locations? Are they power users, or do you have a high concentration of either professional or administrative users or a balanced mixture? As these and other related questions are answered, you will begin to understand your current situation in terms of what VPNs can do for you.

General Implementation Considerations

Vendors incorporate three deployment strategies to implement VPN solutions: LAN-to-LAN, client-to-LAN, or client-to-client—or a combination of the three implementations. Many VPN solution providers do not support client-to-client VPNs. In a LAN-to-LAN communication link, the two VPN nodes, or endpoints, are security servers. In this deployment scheme, the server-to-server link usually involves one encrypted

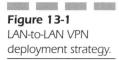

Figure 13-1
LAN-to-LAN VPN
deployment strategy.

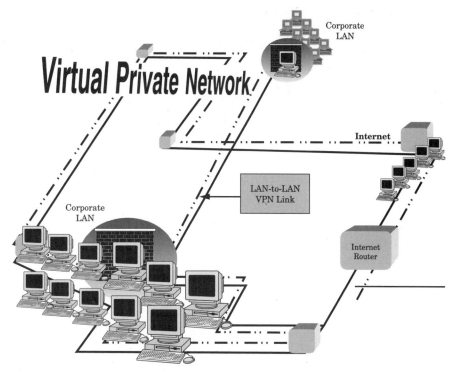

tunnel to handle the communications between users connected to either end of the LAN. (See Figure 13-1.) LAN-to-LAN VPNs hide functions like data integrity and encryption from the end users. The devices at either end of the VPN link operate as part of one homogeneous network to all network users regardless of what end of the link they are on. Ultimately, VPN functions are transparent to the user.

A client-to-LAN VPN deployment is designed to accommodate data links between remote or mobile users and the enterprise LAN. In a client-to-LAN link, there is a one-to-one relationship between clients and VPN tunnels into the security gateway of the enterprise WAN. Thus, if you have 14 remote VPN users dialing in on an ISP service, the resulting number of tunnels will be 14. (See Figure 13-2.)

The third VPN implementation option is a client-to-client deployment. In this situation, communications are between two VPN endpoints that are client hosts, distinguished from server hosts or security gateways. In a client-to-client link, the client host or workstation is fitted with VPN software. The software goes into action when a client wants to talk to another client that has also been equipped with VPN

Figure 13-2
Client-to-LAN VPN
deployment strategy.

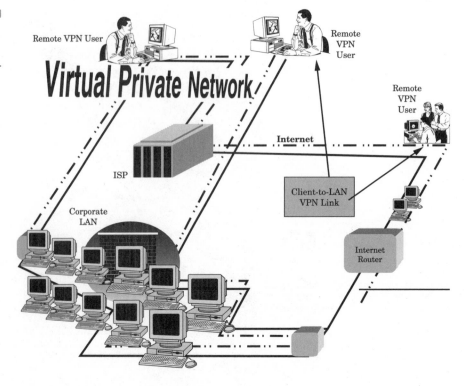

software. This type of link allows secure communications with the VPN host and does not interfere with communications with non-VPN hosts. Client-to-client links allow remote users to communicate directly with each other without having to go through a VPN security gateway or enterprise WAN.

If your challenge involves connecting a series of geographically dispersed networks, and each network supports a number of users, a LAN-to-LAN connection is your ideal scenario. This would also be an appropriate strategy if remote or mobile users were not dialing in. However, because of the demands of a global economy, many organizations sustain a mobile workforce in addition to the normal in-office network users. Or, some organizations accommodate a staff working in remote customer offices or in branch offices that support an enclave of customers in a specific geographical area. Thus, if your staff's modus operandi consists of mobile, remote, and in-office users, your planned VPN would require both a client-to-LAN and LAN-to-LAN deployment strategies. Furthermore, remote or mobile users may require direct connection to other remote or mobile users. If so, client-to-client VPN support is required.

In deployment strategies involving client support, the network administrator/decision maker must be concerned with two issues in particular. First, VPN client functions are not transparent to the client users. Therefore, you must be concerned with whether or not mobile or remote users have the aptitude to work with VPN software. In general, solution providers provide intuitive, object-oriented GUI front ends. However, client users still must possess a general understanding of how VPNs work and what the technology can do for them to transition to an effective VPN client. Consequently, a learning curve is required, and the duration of the curve depends upon the enterprise culture and their general experience in working with such systems.

The second issue is that most VPN solutions afford client users the ability to turn VPN functionality, such as encryption and data validation processes, on and off. As a network administrator, this may provide cause for concern, especially if the wily hacker has visited your network. Furthermore, if the link is a client-to-client connection, there is less concern for the internal network. However, if clients turn off VPN functionality and in the process pick up a virus or Trojan horse, unwanted risks could be created when these clients dial in to the internal network. While this may be a critical concern, you may have to choose a system that does not allow turning client VPN security on and off. In the interest of security, find out if your VPN solution provider includes this feature in client software. Since most tend to offer it, however, your choices may be limited. In order to avoid this one feature you may have to trade off other features that are more desirable. If you find yourself in this situation, it may be helpful to adopt an appropriate policy, specifically that remote clients cannot deactivate VPN functionality under any circumstances when dialing in to the internal network or especially when involved in client-to-client connections.

A final thought: If subnets deployed in a LAN-to-LAN implementation support a large user base and you plan to utilize one of the gateways supporting the LAN-to-LAN configuration for remote users, the resulting network traffic could be overwhelming, especially if the mobile or remote workforce is large. Due to the sheer number of tunnels that would need VPN accommodations, a separate security server should be set up to handle client-to-LAN or remote traffic into a particular subnet. The cost of high-performance servers makes this option very feasible. However, if this option isn't available, performance boosters, such as server load balancing, memory caching, and directory hashing, should be employed to optimize VPN performance. Some solution providers offer add-in cards for the security gateway to handle CPU-intensive encryption, data validation, and key exchange functionality.

User Access Considerations

One of the most critical challenges facing network managers involves controlling access to the network's information assets and resources. Very rarely will one homogeneous access policy apply to all users or cover the various access scenarios created by their information requirements. User access would probably fall into one or more of the following categories depending on information needs: open, somewhat restricted, restricted, and very restricted.

Senior-level managers are typically afforded full and open access to all network resources. Some may have the added responsibility of guarding a "piece" of the organization's private key in lieu of an external escrow agent. Organizations, however, are at risk from the backlash from an unpleasant senior-manager separation, which occurs more often than one may think. In these circumstances, the network may be at risk of some type of sabotage if these individuals plan to retaliate. In the interest of network security, executive managers should not be given carte blanche for network access, nor should access be limited to that of a typical user. However, the level of access should be carefully considered, and the more access an individual is granted, the more checks and balances should be implemented as a countermeasure.

For any given user, access privileges will be assigned according to one of the three remaining classifications. Managing access control will be one of the greatest challenges because of all the information requirement combinations possible by VPN users. In addition, managing the resulting keys will intensify the management effort, especially if manual key management is used (in large installations this would be equivalent to masochism or suicide). As you know, user information requests constantly change, creating a situation that could potentially get out of control if a tight ship is not run. Fortunately, VPNs provide centralized management functions that allow user setup, assignment of access rights, and subsequent management efforts using a fairly straightforward process. Many systems might also support import of requisite user information from corporate databanks through standard features or published APIs. Be sure to ascertain if import functions are available. Otherwise, each user would have to be set up one at a time.

Firewall-based VPNs streamline the process of assigning users access to specific network services. That's because access control is an inherent capability of firewalls. Thus, when it comes to building users' access rights in access profiles in a rule base, no other network technology is as adept as firewalls in enabling access to network services and resources. Non-firewall VPNs may provide access control also. However, access tends to be based on addressing operations at the IP packet level. If IP-based access control is your best option, this is still better than not having this feature at all.

Security Requirements

It goes without saying that network managers desire the most appropriate security measures available for the enterprise's network communications. A network that has global coverage presents a potentially infinite amount of opportunities for intruders. The security dispensed by the VPN must be granular and effective down to the packet or transmission level and flexible enough to secure a variety of network services and resources at the application level. Before IPSec and security servers, this would have been a tall order. However, if you have an IP-based network, the maturation and component integration of critical VPN standards and related technology make attaining the highest level of network security as accessible as obtaining a Big Mac and fries.

When you are enabling encryption functions for network sessions, foremost you must decide what encryption strengths to initialize and make available for the network community. Remember, for encrypted overseas transmissions, the law does not permit use of key lengths greater than 56 bits. For domestic transmissions and the practice of perfect forward secrecy procedures, 40-bit keys may be sufficient for network communications. More sensitive communications can be fitted for use with stronger encryption algorithms through your VPN system.

User Authentication Desired

A variety of user authentication methodologies are available to VPN users. User authentication techniques can be classified as weak authentication, such as user password and ID, or strong authentication. Some of the strong authentication techniques include two-factor authentication, one-time-use password systems, and three-tier authentication systems such as RADIUS, TACACS+, and S/KEY. Digital certificates are also part of the user authentication process because they commission the encryption keys required for validation procedures.

There is no rhyme or reason as to which type of user authentication system to deploy. If your workforce is fairly mobile, a two-factor system such as a token may be the most feasible solution. In this scenario, the ability to keep strong encryption on one's person may be more appropriate. On the other hand, a three-tiered system such as RADIUS works in concert with VPN security gateways to validate users. If you are supporting a large user base, incorporating a system such as RADIUS facilitates management of the user authentication process for the entire VPN system.

On the horizon, technology exists that would allow validation of a user by that user's "thought print." Imagine the absolute level of authentication such a system would provide. Also, Check Point Software Technologies released a PKI system called VPN-1's Certificate Management (CM). CM combines user authentication management, key management through PKI, LDAP directories for user information management, and a GUI management interface. As VPN solutions continue to grow, user authentication will continue to present one of the most exciting areas for innovation.

Client/Server Considerations

In general, VPN products and services are compatible with mainstream platforms such as UNIX and Windows NT. Until the advent of NT, UNIX was the platform of choice for firewalls. VPN UNIX compatibility spans several platforms, including AIX, DEC UNIX, HP-UX, Solaris, and Sun OS. Other Windows platforms include Windows 95 and Mac OS. Compatibility issues should not be of major concern for VPN users. Vendors have done a good job of producing products that are compatible with popular client/server information system platforms. The only caveat: Make certain the version of the VPN solution and the version or level of the operating platform that you select for your organization are compatible. Sometimes more then one version may exist for a given VPN solution on a given system platform.

Let's Test Your Mettle

In this section, several potential scenarios are presented to reinforce your knowledge of VPN functionality. Take a few moments and decide what VPN functional deployment strategy you would implement to satisfy the scenario in question. Remember, no peeking.

Typical Scenario A LAN-to-LAN VPN implementation with user administration from remote site, basic security for the session, and application level.

1. VPN system:

2. User authentication:

3. IP session authentication:

4. Data integrity check:

5. Remote system administration:

Solution

1. VPN-based firewall, supporting IPSec for tunneling; 2. RADIUS; 3. For all services including HTTP, SNTP, and FTP; 4. Using MD5 or SHA-1 for authentication and integrity; 5. Centralized user management

Typical Scenario B Remote client-to-LAN implementation, with strong point-to-point security and restricted access into various departments located in the Midwest region.

1. VPN System:

2. User authentication:

3. Host and session authentication:

4. Data integrity check:

5. Remote system administration:

Solution

1. VPN security gateway supporting multiple tunnels from clients, or a firewall with VPN features also supporting multiple client tunnels; 2. Firewall with two-factor authentication or digital certificates (X.509); 3. Using VPN-based firewall compatible with RADIUS; 4. Using MD5 or SHA-1; 5. Centralized management system

Typical Scenario C Mobile client-to-LAN implementation with extensive, point-to-point security requirements. Access to applications and sessions for various services are restricted to a variety of departments on the East Coast.

1. VPN System:

2. User authentication:

3. Encryption and session authentication:

4. Data integrity check:

5. Remote system administration:

Solution

1. VPN Security gateway supporting multiple tunnels from East Coast clients, or a firewall with VPN features supporting multiple client tunnels; 2. Firewall or VPN with certificate authentication, digital certificates (X.509), or smart cards; 3. Using VPN or firewall with IPSec for various intranet services; 4. MD5 or SHA-1; 5. Centralized management system

14

VPN Business Assessment:

MULTINATIONAL AND LARGE ENTERPRISES

The purpose of the previous chapter was to put VPN functionality in the context of general business requirements while providing insight into your own potential fitness for a VPN solution. Since you are now familiar with the technical and functional aspects of VPNs and their potential for application, the next two chapters build the business case. (In a sense, this entire book builds the business case.) This chapter focuses on the specific business case for multinational and large enterprises/companies. Chapter 15 focuses on the business case for small- and medium-sized enterprises/companies. As a result of the emergence and subsequent maturation of IPSec and the general strategy of implementing performance boosters, the timing is ripe for VPNs to become a strong candidate for an enterprisewide communications backbone. VPNs can now go head-to-head with private networking technologies to challenge for security supremacy or toe-to-toe with frame relay public data networks for supremacy in performance. When it comes to its ability to harness the ubiquitous Internet in a cost-effective manner, VPNs know no challengers. After the business case is built, you will have everything you need to justify bringing in a VPN solution as your enterprise's communication backbone.

Multinational Enterprises/ Corporations

In consideration of multinational enterprises, size is not the only qualifier. The key qualifier is that they operate on foreign and domestic soil. Notwithstanding size, there are more multinational enterprises today then ever. Due to the convergence and saturation of traditional domestic markets, enterprises of today are compelled to turn to a global economy for opportunities. The lure of international markets is strong and exciting, and the prospects for business are unlimited. Domestic enterprises that are building strong infrastructures today, including information systems, are being strategically positioned to perform well in the global arena of the twenty-first century.

To prosper in a global marketplace, an organization must possess all the right elements, including an agile workforce, a learning-organization motif, a diversity of ideas, a spirit of innovation, a receptiveness to change, and a cost-effective, flexible information system. The critical success factor in this recipe is the information system. To support international operations, the information system must be secure, scalable, have acceptable performance, and be readily accessible. VPNs possess all the characteristics that matter to a multinational concern. In the pages to follow, critical factors in assessing multinational enterprises will be closely reviewed. At the end of the discussion, you will have the tools you need to justify a VPN for international operations. (See Figure 14-1.)

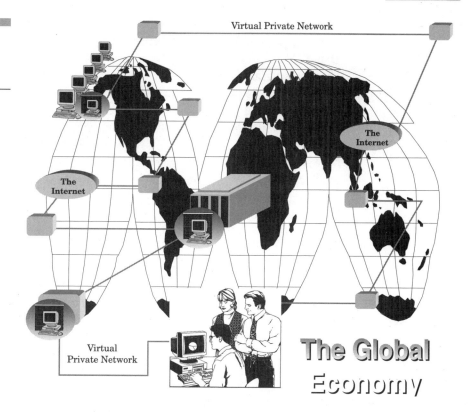

Figure 14-1
VPNs: The global marketplace connection.

Business Goals

Operating on foreign shores creates certain new business conditions. The impact of operating in a new culture and the costs associated with gearing your sales and marketing efforts to that end is one matter; succeeding at it is another. In today's global economy, you must constantly assess your progress in foreign markets to justify your continued presence. If progress is in synch with business goals, you stay. If it's not on track, you make adjustments. If sound new strategies don't work, you take down your shingle and you move on. The overall decision-making process is not that cut-and-dried, however. Before moving into foreign markets, enterprises undergo a thoughtful process of analysis. However, no matter how much thought goes into a decision, if the venture is not profitable, few enterprises would hang on. International forces are too dynamic and uncertain to expend resources where the payoff is jeopardized by increased risk. Establishing the enterprise in the global market place is important for long-term survival. A failure in one country does not necessarily portend a failure in another international business arena.

The uncertainty and the complexity of change agents in the global marketplace suggest that the information system must be flexible, scalable, dynamic, readily accessible, secure, and cost-effective. For organizations to meet their goals in the global economy, harnessing the ubiquitous Internet offers the best prospect for success. Access only requires a call to your local ISP. Connecting your information system only requires a VPN. Bringing another location online, albeit an international one, is a straightforward, relatively simple process. Define the network objects, required services, resources, users, and user groups to the rule base of the security policy, and *voilà,* you are online. Considering the speed and agility with which enterprises must move in international markets, the ultimate impact of VPNs is a positive effect on the enterprise's bottom line.

Organization Considerations

When a multinational organization sets up shop in a foreign country, the workforce pool is drawn from the host country. If a client-to-LAN VPN is established to support remote users in one country, the learning curve needed to become an effective VPN client in that country versus another may be as different as night and day. The difference may lie in cultural diversity or the level of experience with computer-based technology. The other problem you may encounter is that the indigenous personnel may not see the urgency in conducting secure transmissions every time they connect into either the local or headquarters' network in the U.S. Hackers overseas are just as skillful and diabolical as those found in the U.S. That one time a remote professional in the hinterlands of that country decides to conduct a session without VPN safeguards may be the very time the network is successfully breached. LAN-to-LAN deployment between international and domestic offices may be the most feasible option because more control can be exercised over the network. Client-to-LAN connections should only be authorized if that remote client dialing into the local office is capable of adhering to the enterprise security safeguards and directives without compromise.

Pinpointing Worldwide Communications Requirements

Determining where you need information system support in the world is a fairly demanding but straightforward process. If you are growing fast or trying to preempt the competition by moving into a particular market, how do you deliver your domestic information resources to accommodate expansion of international operations? What applications or services are needed to support the new international office? How soon can they be made available? Will new applications or network services be required? And if so, will they be built by the staff of the new international office or headquarters staff? Will the new international office require direct collaboration with either local or U.S. business partners or suppliers, or both? If direct collaboration with business partners is preferred, how soon could they be equipped with a network interface and host?

Implicit in addressing these requirements is an information system with a *flexible response* capability—in other words, a system that is readily accessible, scalable, easily deployed, application-ready, secure, and cost-effective. Not too long ago and on a lesser basis today, this would have entailed developing and deploying some client/server DBMS application utilizing an object-oriented engine such as Oracle or Informix and a GUI front end developed with either PowerBuilder or Visual Basic. Communications would be supplied by either leased lines or an ATM or frame relay public data network. This particular client/server information system was the state-of-the-art, bleeding edge of distributed processing applications. Such solutions were thought to be scalable, and they were, compared to legacy systems. However, their top billing was that they were cost-effective, easily deployed, comprehensive, and easy to use. While these client/server applications are still in full-scale use today, change is under way.

When the Internet-based protocols and applications emerged and enterprises begin to build Web sites and use email to send visually exciting attachments and transfer massive information files handily, those new, visually exciting, and expedient information tools were adopted for more-serious applications. Internet-based protocols have become and are still becoming the new client/server model and the foundation for enterprise intranets. And developing networks based on Internet protocols and technologies is the fastest-growing client/server segment of today. Businesses are finding intranets even more scalable then client/server systems based on object-oriented DBMS systems. They are also finding them easier to use because users access network applications through browser interfaces. Everyone would agree that Internet browsers are simple to use.

The only thing missing from the original equation was security. With security measures in tow, enterprises can now harness IP-based wide area networks such as the public Internet. And, if they can utilize the Internet for applications and communications, then they could benefit anywhere in the world. Because of the advancements and developments achieved with VPNs, VPN solutions have emerged as perhaps the most cost-effective alternative for a viable information system for multinational organizations. VPNs are also secure and scalable, and Internet-based applications are easily leveraged to support the operations of new international offices. Most importantly, VPNs afford multinational enterprises the ubiquitous reach of the Internet. As a result, wherever a multinational concern decides to set up shop, access to a strong information system is only a phone call away into the local ISP.

Private Networks vs. VPNs

Private networks are proven commodities. VPNs are emerging. If a multinational concern is already utilizing a private network based on a distributed processing information system such as an object-oriented DBMS application, a GUI-based front end, and a communications backbone supported by leased lines, it may be more cost-effective to leverage the current private network. However, if anyone on the private network wants to access an IP-based network such as the public Internet, the entire network becomes at risk to intruders. Even the addition of firewalls may not be enough to thwart attacks. (See the section on private networking in Chapter 1.)

Bringing the international office online may require coordinating the purchase of dial-up capabilities based on digital telephone lines using overseas rates and network routers. It also may entail expanding the network access server or perhaps adding another at the central office. Assuming that you have a network administrator, additional overseas tariffs, rates, and management activities must be included in overall management responsibilities. Or you can install a VPN, call up the local ISP, and access a central office anywhere in the world in a cost-effective manner.

Attack of the 56 K Monsters

Migrating over to an IP-based network or establishing an enterprise intranet is a definite process. Adding a VPN for a secure communications backbone extends the process. Though it may appear to be more cost-effective to expand your current private networking capability, this might be a good opportunity to plan for a phased implementation of a WAN that leverages Internet protocols and technologies such as HTTP, SNTP, UDC, and FTP, along with a VPN backbone. If you plan to stay and grow in the international arena, migrating to an IP-based network and VPN may be more advantageous in the long run. The opportunity to use Internet development suites such as HTML and Java to develop multimedia Web sites with vivid graphics, full-motion animation, video and GUIs, news group applications, and email may provide the competitive advantage required in a global marketplace. With the maturation of VPN technologies and their ability to provide the reach of the Internet, it might be frugal to start now and transition to the most cost-effective WAN solution available.

Perhaps as an incentive to go forward, determine if your current private network has ever been breached. If the answer is yes, what sorts of intrusions were they? Viruses, sabotage, or confiscated information? Were the breaches initiated from the outside or from within the enterprise? If you determine you were not breached, does the potential for a breach exists? If yes, how does that impact your current thinking? If analysis proves that hacker or virus problems do not exist in your private network, this may be the confirmation you need to stay with the private network. However, if long-term viability and competitive advantage is what you seek in the global economy, migrating to an IP-based WAN with a VPN implementation as the communication backbone might be the optimal system for your enterprise.

Large Corporations

There are not many so-called large enterprises that do not conduct business overseas. For the sake of discussion, a large enterprise is one that realizes $100+ million in annual revenues or operates with a budget of $100 million. Organizations at this revenue or operating level typically employ 750 to 1000 individuals. To facilitate this discussion, assume that the assessment takes into account only domestic factors that would impact large organizations. If you are a large company planning to expand into the international arena, the previous section should also be reviewed.

In today's global marketplace, healthy enterprises at this revenue level tend to be candidates for acquisition by larger enterprises. They also have a firm footing in certain markets and have succeeded in distinguishing themselves as market leaders. The information system is client/server based and usually anchored by a DBMS application with a GUI front end. Communications tend to be supported by leased lines and/or public data networks such as UUNET or MCI Communications. Companies at this revenue level have been in operation from 12 to 15 years or spun off from a larger business entity at some point. They have also been operating at least as long as the Internet has been popular. Thus, being very familiar with Internet protocols and technologies, they may be more inclined to implement an intranet or, at a minimum, have an external Web site in operation.

Business Goals

The goals of enterprises depend in large part on the level of success incurred as of a given period of time. They also depend on the run of success experienced in years immediately preceding the current year. If growth rates are strong, growth must be managed accordingly, or the organization may falter in meeting demand for its products or services, or in other areas. However, if growth is well managed, enterprises are capable of sustaining consecutive years of desirable performance. A key ingredient for sustaining a run of success is a robust information system.

Client/server distributed processing systems that operate on the department level typically anchor information systems of large enterprises. A GUI front end to a DBMS application is the heart of the information system and may support hundreds of users in a given department. Realization of corporate goals depends in large part on the vitality of the information system. In fact, the information that spews forth from the information system platform must be in direct support of the desired direction of corporate strategy. The strategy, in turn, must drive the organization toward corporate goals. The information system should always map inextricably to the strategy and goals of the enterprise in order for the enterprise to realize its mission. (See Figure 14-2.) Theoretically, in dynamic, ever-changing business environments, the goals of the enterprise should be modified whenever business conditions change. Depending on the business environment, goal modification could transpire every 6 to 9 months. Consequently, when organizational goals change, the strategy, and ultimately, the information system, should also change to reflect the new corporate direction. This suggests that the information system should be scalable, flexible, and timely.

MIS managers turned to distributed-processing client/server systems

Figure 14-2
Mapping information
systems to business
goals.

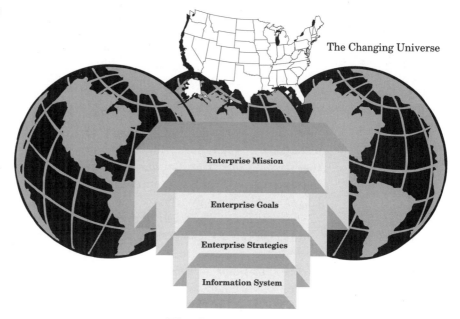

The Changing Universe

Enterprise Mission

Enterprise Goals

Enterprise Strategies

Information System

The Strategic Mapping

because of these three attributes. For the most part they performed to
satisfaction. However, if DBMS-based client/server applications are compared to intranets or TCP/IP-based client/server systems, the latter systems are believed to be more scalable, flexible, and timely. Developing a
business application (Web site) with HTML and Java requires less time
than developing one with an object-oriented DBMS system with a GUI
front end. The resulting application is as effective and potentially more
exciting than a one-dimensional GUI-based DBMS system.

From that standpoint, Internet-based applications are more scalable.
They are also easier to use. Users interface to Web applications with a
browser that is almost single-handedly credited for the popularity of
the Internet. Computer users in every field of endeavor are familiar
with browsing the Internet's multimedia Web domains. That's its
attraction. It is also the attraction of intranets. VPNs afford enterprises
the ability to leverage intranets over the ubiquitous Internet and
accommodate access from any enterprise location in the U.S. in a cost-
effective manner.

The bottom line is that intranets that leverage the Internet through
VPNs' are arguably the most scalable, flexible, and timely information
systems to fuel strategy and business goals in a dynamic, ever-changing
business environment. If you sprinkle in security and ubiquitous access,

you have created the recipe for successfully fulfilling corporate goals in the new millennium.

Organization

In today's business environment, we are witnessing the effects of the "learning organization" culture at work. (See Table 1-1 and the related discussion in Chapter 1.) Acknowledging the persistent forces of change, the learning organization works consistently "outside the box" with an innovative spirit and an unprecedented willingness to tackle new challenges with new approaches. Under the right circumstances, they chance to reinvent themselves with the precision and accuracy of a surgical procedure. Ultimately, the demands that the learning culture exerts on the information system are a never-ending story. Thus, the challenge is to ensure that the most responsive system "plugs and plays" with the information requirements of a culture that is on a mission. This equates to a system that is flexible, secure, timely, scalable, and easily accessed.

Until the emergence of strong VPN solutions, the information system companion of the learning organization was the departmental DBMS application with the GUI front end. For the most part, it still is. In the days when the learning organization was in transition and learning how to cope with the dynamic forces of change, this distributed processing system was there like a trusted friend. The DBMS-driven client/server model delivered information for critical thought processes and decisions at the point of need. Notwithstanding the virtue of distributed processing DBMS systems, somewhere along the way, the learning culture discovered the potential of intranets, especially for the future. The learning culture discovered that the Internet is revolutionizing the way enterprises communicate and do business. Publicized case studies and industry articles reveal that intranets, extended through VPNs, increase business and enhance customer service. In a 1997 study, the Gartner Group predicted that 60 percent of large firms implementing an intranet through the year 2003 will require extended secure networks. Strong VPN solutions could not have come at a better time.

Pinpointing Enterprisewide Communications Requirements

If you are in a growth mode, you are probably expanding into new offices or perhaps planning to upgrade existing offices. Also, if you are currently implementing an intranet and looking to connect remote users, suppliers, contractors, or top clients to the enterprise network, this might be the opportune time for implementing a VPN. If you decide to proceed with a VPN, the next phase involves coordinating the effort with all the internal and external business entities you are planning to bring online. First, analysis should be initiated to determine the VPN solution that provides the best match for the planned network. Next, the ISP question should be explored.

If different ISPs are being utilized, you may be able to negotiate a group rate for all of the locations you are planning to connect with a particular ISP. However, be prepared for external organizations you are planning to network with to stay with a certain provider. That's fine. After all, no matter what ISP is employed, all wide area communications will be handled by the Internet. When the ISP question is settled, the next phase involves building your VPN to extend your present intranet.

Let's revisit those organizations that utilize a standard distributed processing system with leased-line support or a public data network. If you are planning to migrate to an intranet, your migration process requires you to first establish Internet-based applications, like an internal Web site, for starters. (Most organizations probably have an external Web site for business purposes.) Unless you have staff that is proficient in HTML or Java, or someone who is willing to learn, hiring a contract programmer for the job is the most likely path. When the base network is established, the next phases include deciding on the ISP and VPN.

Private Networks vs. VPNs

If you are still on the fence about whether you should migrate to an intranet, the decision to go forward may depend on several factors. For one thing, if you are satisfied with your present client/server distributed system—it's safe and it does the job for your enterprise—there may not be enough incentive to make the transition from a business perspective. On the other hand, there are not too many organizations where users do not browse the Internet for either business purposes or on their own time. As a result, the familiarity level with the Internet runs high in most organizations. Even if you aren't using an intranet internally, most likely you have a Web site set up for external information dissemination. So, it is a certainty that internal users frequent the site. If they frequent the site, guess what? Your network is at risk to the wily hacker, even if a firewall is in place.

Furthermore, if you can somehow justify building an intranet for later expansion with a VPN, and you are still not convinced that the resulting intranet would be the mission-critical network, then why bother? However, if your organization is expanding domestically and perhaps internationally, and since most people find browsing the multi-media Internet world to be enjoyable and fun, wouldn't it be advantageous, perhaps even competitive, if the exciting Internet environment could benefit business expansion? Most prospective clients would prefer to see an animated video describing your services online than a static one-dimensional product brochure. Though your present indicators may not suggest migrating to an intranet and extending it with a VPN at some point, take another look at your situation. You might be glad you revisited the decision.

Last-Minute Considerations

In summary, distributed-processing client/server-based systems have provided the support needed for the learning culture. However, are these systems able to keep pace with the speed of the business world, or is it time for the promise of the Internet to finally be realized? Ubiquitous access is certainly one critical advantage, but all the other benefits afforded by VPNs make the combination difficult to pass up. The Internet is definitely exciting, and since technology exists to provide this exciting world safely for business-to-business transactions, the payoff is definitely greater than the risk. However, it's ultimately your choice. Before closing, here are a few last-minute considerations. Have there been any external or internal breaches of the enterprise network? Is business leveling off or not meeting expectations? Would there be any benefit to bringing partners, suppliers, or prime customers online? Would the Internet fulfill some other purpose for your enterprise that is not discussed here? If the answer is yes to one or more of these questions, your learning culture will be glad you reconsidered your position.

15

VPN Business Assessment:

SMALL/MEDIUM COMPANIES

It is said that timing is everything, especially in the business world. The advancements and cost of VPNs make them a very attractive networking solution for small businesses. Some VPN solutions can be obtained for as little as $10,000. Being a small company sometimes has its advantages, especially if you are in a growth mode. The decision to migrate to a VPN may be easier for a small company than for a large company, which has made a significant investment in a particular client/server technology suite. Having 25 to 50 employees, with revenues of $2 to $5 million a year, typically means the company depends on a basic LAN information system. The applications usually entail some productivity or workgroup software suite such as Corel's PerfectOffice or Lotus Smart Suite. The accounting system is probably a basic double-entry system with a human resource module attached to it. In this section, a VPN acquisition strategy is laid out for small businesses. If you are in a growth mode and planning to open offices in another geographic location (whether in another part of town, state, region, or country), this chapter is the blueprint for expanding with a VPN.

For the sake of discussion, enterprises that range in revenue from $20 to $150 million are classified as medium-sized enterprises. However, depending on the industry, a $20 million enterprise could be considered a large organization. For example, a men's clothing store chain at this revenue level could be considered a large-size enterprise compared to the revenue of a typical clothing store. On the other hand, in the software manufacturing industry, a $20 million enterprise is considered a small company. In comparison, Oracle Corporation is a megasoftware enterprise, realizing over $5 billion in annual revenues.

From another perspective, it is hard to envision that AOL and UUNET were at one point in their existence considered medium-sized enterprises. If your company is on a fast growth track, and you anticipate reaching the $200 to $300 million range by 2003, you should factor into your planning considerations for a multinational operation.

Business Goals

As a small company this could be a momentous time. You have overcome some critical barriers and clearly positioned your organization as a viable entity. You have landed some strategic accounts and arranged a line of credit, and cash flow is adequate. To make it to the next level, however, you must expand operations to support the expected growth. One of the critical components in this expansion is the information system. Currently, you have a LAN with workgroup software, email capability, and a Web site for external information dissemination. The only security measure you've installed to date is comprehensive virus-detection software. There have been no visible signs of intruders.

One other development should be factored in with your planning. You are working as a subcontractor to a business partner in another region. In addition to assigning several staff members to support the effort, you are also considering connecting your business partner to your internal network so that they can access information in real time. And to maintain a competitive edge, you want the new Web site to disseminate a rich complement of multimedia information. Also, if cost-feasible, you would like all enterprise marketing staff and business partners to place orders and check order status. Finally, you would like to provide staff members that are out on contract with the ability to access the internal network from mobile laptops and remote workstations.

The preceding example has painted a pretty clear picture for a VPN solution with access control (firewall). While there are literally thousands of scenarios where VPNs would work for a small company, this is one possibility.

As a medium-sized company, the strong annual growth rate that your enterprise is experiencing is fueled by a strong market demand for your product or service. Since you have found a healthy market niche for your flagship product, perhaps diversifying into other areas is appropriate. This could be the most critical time for your enterprise as you decide which direction the enterprise should take. It's like a sailboat that is trying to catch that main head wind to propel it to its destination. When you find it, you know that it is true as you settle in for the journey. As with any expansion activity, the critical assessment involves the information system.

What does the information system do for the enterprise? Will the current applications support diversification or expansion efforts? Will they support achievement of corporate goals? If yes, how scalable are applications? Can they be tweaked with a reasonable level of effort? Is there a better information system approach that if transitioned will provide a greater payoff later? If the scalability findings suggest that the current information system is not easily scaled or achieving long-term results is at risk, you may need to consider another solution. However, with the relative ease of application development and scalability, security, and reliability, VPNs and related applications might be the "head wind" your enterprise needs on its next journey.

Organization

At the heart of the small business that has firmly entrenched itself as a viable business entity is an entrepreneurial spirit. The more successful a small enterprise is, the greater the sense of entrepreneurship that permeates the organization. In general, the organizations of such enterprises are akin to the learning organization culture of enterprises 100 times their size. As a small enterprise, organizational decisions will be one of the key decisions you will be required to make on an ongoing basis. Typically, small business staffs tend to wear a variety of hats to accomplish daily tasks. The more responsibility, the more hats you wear. However, if there is an area where there should be a one-for-one relationship between employee and responsibility, it is the information system area, especially if you are planning to develop a small intranet to leverage into a VPN. You don't want the subsequent network manager also having the responsibility of developing the intranet applications for the enterprise. Each job in itself entails a lot of responsibility. If your former office manager has expressed interest in becoming the network manager, it should be understood that the network manager must possess a strong working knowledge and vision of translating business requirements into information systems requirements. Thus, you may need to bring in an individual who has a strong networking background. While that person may not wear as many hats, the one or two that he or she does wear is pretty impressive.

A medium-sized organization that is in a growth mode may possibly present the best opportunities for professional occupations. Individuals in midsized enterprises don't wear as many hats as individuals in a small business. However, the operating budget of a department manager can be larger then the revenue of a small company. A manager's responsibilities can be as glamorous as they are critical. Managers who achieve can be handsomely rewarded with an executive-level appointment or other incentives that are harder to attain in larger enterprises.

Like the learning culture of larger organizations, subordinates approach their responsibilities with innovation and determination. The more visible the achievement, the greater the recognition and subsequent reward. Organizations that are driven by a strong sense of purpose or whose corridors are teeming with a constant flow of fresh ideas and willingness to try new approaches require a comprehensive distributed processing system such as an intranet that is leveraged by a VPN.

Growth companies in this category have considerable latitude for making business decisions. For example, should expansion entail opening more offices in the current region, or would another geographic region be more feasible? What about international expansion? Should you take the typical expansion routes into London or Japan to test international waters or should you start with something closer to home, such as Canada? Can international managers be chosen from the current in-house management pool or should you go outside? Companies at this revenue level may also have the ability to employ a variety of approaches to achieve a particular end. As a result, it would not be unusual to find a standard DBMS-driven client/server implementation and an intranet working in tandem.

Pinpointing Communications Requirements

As a small organization, extending the reach of your network beyond the walls of the enterprise may be a new experience, especially when determining the optimal communications backbone to use. How will communications be handled? Should an ISP be used, or should you install a communications server and modem bank with a complement of leased lines? Perhaps digital telephone lines such ISDN lines would be more reliable and cost-effective. If you decide to go with a private network setup, do you have in-house experience with someone who could work as liaison with the telephone companies in the various areas where business is planned? Is there someone currently on staff capable of becoming a full-time network manager, or should someone with a strong networking background be hired? Could initial requirements be handled by a consultant, followed by the hiring of a full-time person at some point in the future? What about a VPN for network communications? Maybe the business would be better served if you transitioned to a network solution that could take full advantage of a VPN. Does this idea map to your company's short- and long-term goals better than any other strategy? An in-depth review is a very critical process. It should be used whenever you decide to extend your network beyond the confines of the central location or the boundaries of the current network.

As a midsized growth company, your primary determination is deciding the extent of expansion possibilities. Should the organization expand within the region or into another geographic area? Should expansion include going international on a limited basis, perhaps to Canada or Mexico? What communications system should be used to connect the new domestic and international locations? If VPNs are truly matured to the level where they can support business-to-business transactions for a mission-critical application, maybe VPNs should be brought in on a limited or trial basis. If the trial run is successful, a full-scale VPN rollout will follow.

Private Networks vs. VPNs

A small enterprise that is deciding to extend its network is used to a certain level of privacy. Naturally, when the network is expanded, users expect the highest level of security. However, regardless of the size of the company, computer users are familiar with the Internet and its potential dangers. Companies that access the Internet on a consistent basis have antivirus software installed at a minimum. For a small company to consider a solution that includes the use of the Internet, the idea is sure to create a certain level of anxiety. But if you have read the information in this book, some or perhaps much of your concern has been alleviated. If you decide to go with a private networking solution, be prepared to spend considerably more than you would for a VPN. This is a well-known industry fact also expressed in this book. Before making the decision to go with a VPN, make certain that you express your concerns to your prospective VPN solution provider.

Though midsized enterprises have more resources at their disposal, present and future information processing needs should be thoroughly ascertained before you make a decision. Only after such a review will you be able to choose the appropriate system that matches the direction of the enterprise. If a VPN does not provide the best fit, perhaps the corporate direction should be reassessed.

A Few Additional Considerations

For a small business, ascertaining whether your current network has been breached is an important consideration. No doubt, your current LAN has antivirus software in place. And most likely, a security policy at some level has been instituted to provide guidelines for internal users. Extending the network to accommodate remote or mobile users or a business partner on a critical job creates certain new circumstances. How much security would your company be afforded by implementing a private network in support of the remote office, mobile users, or business partner? If a private network is implemented, what is the cost associated with expanding to another remote location and what effect will that have on security? What other alternatives do you have? Should you explore the "make vs. buy" scenario? What if you outsourced the entire effort to an ISP? How does this compare to "making" the application yourself? What security advantages does an ISP offer? How much would it cost if a VPN were supported through an ISP? How much would a VPN cost if implemented and managed in-house? The answers to these questions and the others in this assessment will provide the optimal direction for your organization. One last caution: Make certain to factor in future business plans as well. This could make all the difference in the solution you ultimately select.

The only real concern for a medium-sized company is how fast the organization is growing. An assessment concerning security issues should be explored and findings factored into the evaluation. As with small companies, make sure future plans are considered as well.

PART 5

Solutions of VPN Providers

In a sense, this section is anticlimactic. You were exposed to the individual technology building blocks that compose the revolutionary networking phenomena called VPNs. You know the scope of the full collaboration of authentication, tunneling, and encryption for VPN applications. You were also provided with some tips for evaluating your potential requirements for VPNs. More importantly, however, you know what's possible for your business endeavors in harnessing the ubiquitous Internet. In this final section of *Managing Virtual Private Networks,* we take a close look at how individual vendors blend the technology building blocks of encryption, authentication, and tunneling to forge individual solutions for a prime marketplace.

In Chapter 16, the VPN implementations of eight prominent solution providers are compared and contrasted in feature comparison tables that facilitate the review process. There's no magical reason for the number eight, except for the fact that all of the companies in this group have been providing VPN solutions for several years. Their solutions are refined and comprehensive, and their resulting popularity is understandable. This vendor VPN review consists of the categories of VPN architecture, security services, authentication, management, administration, and performance management. The security services section covers VPN products in relation to tunneling protocols, encryption schemes, and the status of IPSec certification.

In Chapters 17 and 18, a firewall and VPN of the market share leader are configured to demonstrate the relative ease of this activity. The GUIs of VPN products streamline the entire process of defining network components to administering user authentication and encryption schemes for VPN session support.

CHAPTER **16**

The Playing Field

The eight vendors that are the subject of the discussion have received industry recognition at one time or another for product excellence. This recognition has come in a variety of forms, including published customer testimony, testimony from industry watchdogs such as market research firms, and trade journal articles. The recognition that tends to count the most is usually bestowed by the top industry newspapers and magazines such as *PC Magazine, PC World, Data-Comm, Infoworld,* and *Network World,* to name a few. As you know, these publications conduct independent research and product comparisons periodically against some arbitrary but elaborate performance benchmarks to determine how one vendor's product compares with another.

The vendors that fare the best are bestowed king-for-a-day-type recognition by the magazine or newspaper that sponsored the roundup. Usually, the recipient of such recognition features the publication's official commendation in trade literature, presentations, and magazine article reprints that have been glossed over for individual handouts. For example, TimeStep's PERMIT Enterprise VPN Solution won 1998 Product of the Year honors when it received *InfoWorld*'s Golden Guardian Award. Among other things, this honor was heralded in a formal press release and the company's Web site. Such recognition is very prestigious, to say the least, and is therefore highly coveted. Where appropriate, specific vendor citations will be provided during the course of this review.

The vendors that are featured in this chapter and their respective VPN solutions are listed in Table 16-1. Note that all the companies provide a flagship firewall product that delivers the security gateway functionality in conjunction with the VPN solutions. It should also be pointed out that TimeStep licensed Check Point Technologies' FireWall-1 technology for its PERMIT firewall system. Also note that Cisco's VPN solution is router-based and WatchGuard's firewall is a security appliance.

TABLE 16-1   *Generic Feature Comparison of Selected VPN Vendors*

Company	VPN Solution	Firewall Solution	Platform	VPN Family
Digital Equipment Corporation	AltaVista Tunnel 98	AltaVista Firewall 98	*Servers:* ■ Digital UNIX v. 4.0A or higher ■ Windows NT 4.0 *Clients:* ■ Windows 95, NT ■ Mac OS v. 1.1.1 and 1.1.2, and v. 1.2 or 1.3	■ AVT 98 Client ■ AVT 98 Telecommuter Server ■ AVT 98 Extranet Server
Cisco Systems Inc.	Cisco VPN (Cisco IOS software provides encryption and tunneling)	■ PIX Firewall 4.1 (firewall appliance) ■ Cisco IOS firewall software	■ VPN-enabled routers ■ VPN-optimized routers	*Client Access:* ■ Cisco 800 series ■ 1700 series *LAN-to-LAN:* ■ 1700 series ■ 2600, 3600, 7200 series
NetGuard Inc.	Guardian VPN	Guardian Firewall 3.0	*Server(s):* ■ Windows NT 4.0 *Clients:* ■ Windows NT 4.0	*Client Access:* ■ Guardian authentication client *LAN-to-LAN:* ■ Guardian Agent

TABLE 16-1 Continued

Company	VPN Solution	Firewall Solution	Platform	VPN Family
TimeStep Inc.	PERMIT Enterprise	PERMIT Firewall Appliance (Check Point Technologies OEM)	*Server(s):* ■ Windows NT 4.0 *Client(s):* ■ Windows 95, 98, NT ■ Mac OS 7.1 or later	■ PERMIT/Client ■ PERMIT/Gate ■ PERMIT/Director Suite
AXENT Technologies, Inc.	PowerVPN	Raptor Firewall 5.0	*Servers(s):* ■ Windows NT ■ Solaris, HP/UX, Linux, BSDI *Client(s):* ■ Windows 3.x, 95, NT	*VPN Clients:* ■ RaptorMobile VPN ■ Power VPN *VPN Gateways:* ■ Raptor Firewall ■ Power VPN
CyberGuard Corporation	Stoplock Connect-IP	CyberGuard Firewall Release 4	*Server(s):* *Client(s):* ■ Windows 3.x, 95, NT	■ Connect-IP *Mobile Client:* ■ Connect-IP Remote *Client:* Connect-IP Gateway
Check Point Software Technologies LTD.	VPN-1 v. 4.0	FireWall-1 v. 4.0	*Server(s):* ■ HP/UX 10.10, 20 ■ IBM AIX 4.21, 4.3 ■ Solaris 2.5, 2.6 ■ Windows NT *Client(s):* ■ Windows NT, 95 ■ X11R5	■ VPN-1 SecuRemote ■ VPN-1 RemoteLink ■ VPN-1 Gateway
WatchGuard Technologies Inc.	WatchGuard VPN	WatchGuard Firewall	*Server(s):* ■ Firebox Firewall Appliance (security gateway) *Client(s):* ■ Windows 95, NT	■ Remote User VPN ■ Branch Office VPN Firebox II, Firebox 100 *Gateway:*

Security appliances are a new generation of firewalls that are revolutionizing firewall functionality. Firewall security appliances are self-contained enforcement units (black boxes) that operate within the network's infrastructure, as opposed to the network's perimeter as they normally do. Thus, they perform a bridging or pass-through function versus a gateway or routing function. A security appliance is configured and managed by a remote management system. When deployed, the appliances establish and protect network *security zones*.

VPN Architecture Implementation

One of the main premises of VPNs is to provide a cost-effective communications backbone alternative to other, more-expensive backbone options, such as frame relay and public IP networks (as distinguished from the Internet). A recent VPN cost study conducted by *Data Communications* magazine revealed that a VPN could save enterprises more than 50 percent in connectivity costs over a comparable frame relay-based network. In addition to cost-effectiveness, the Internet offers other salient advantages and disadvantages as well. Figure 16-1 provides a comparative summary of the Internet versus other WAN backbone alternatives.

As you may expect, the Internet receives a "Low" score for "Inherent Security." However, when VPNs are factored in, security is equal to or

Figure 16-1
Comparison of WAN communications backbones.

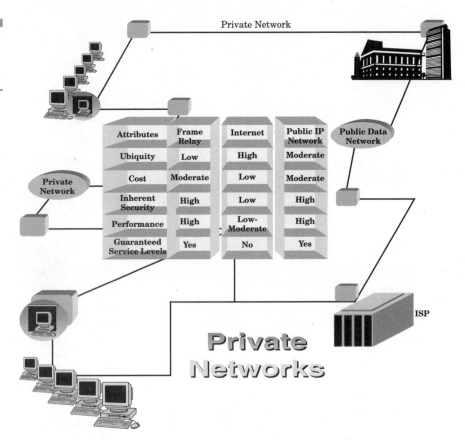

Attributes	Frame Relay	Internet	Public IP Network
Ubiquity	Low	High	Moderate
Cost	Moderate	Low	Moderate
Inherent Security	High	Low	High
Performance	High	Low-Moderate	High
Guaranteed Service Levels	Yes	No	Yes

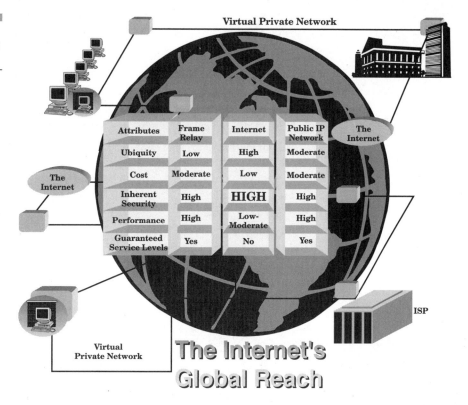

Attributes	Frame Relay	Internet	Public IP Network
Ubiquity	Low	High	Moderate
Cost	Moderate	Low	Moderate
Inherent Security	High	HIGH	High
Performance	High	Low-Moderate	High
Guaranteed Service Levels	Yes	No	Yes

The Internet's Global Reach

greater than the other two methods. (See Figure 16-2.) If and when the
IETF's Differentiated Services (DiffServ) QoS standard initiative is commercially accepted and implemented, the benefits of VPNs will be
unsurpassed.

Since communications backbones that support private networks also
provide dial-up and leased-line access among remote users and corporate LANs, VPNs must also provide such capability in order to be a
viable option. Therefore, to play in the VPN game, vendor solutions
should offer dial-up access for telecommuter/mobile users, remote satel-
lite/branch offices, and secure network-to-network WAN connections via
the Internet. All of the featured VPN solutions in this review support
remote access for telecommuters and remote offices (i.e., client-to-LAN
connections) and LAN-to-LAN connections for enterprise business. In
the sections to follow, we look closely at the architectural characteristics
of client-to-LAN and LAN-to-LAN implementations.

Client-to-LAN Implementation Review

The term *client-to-LAN* can conjure up a variety of thoughts, such as from small to big, the client/server relationship, remote or long-distance access, and dial-up connectivity. However, in the context of VPNs, it should mean secure remote access for a mobile or remote user. The operative word here is *secure*. Security of long-distance dial-up connections can only be achieved with encrypted tunnels because the transmission medium is the Internet. All VPN vendors understand this, and most include encrypted tunneling in their respective remote access dial-in implementations. Some, however, do not. Therefore, an important caveat: Do not assume that encrypted tunneling capability is always included in vendor remote access or client-to-LAN implementations.

Table 16-2 is a comparison of the "Big Eight's" client-to-LAN solutions. Surprisingly, Guardian does not offer encrypted sessions for its client-to-LAN offering. Instead, the only security measure for mobile

TABLE 16-2   Comparison of Client-to-LAN Implementations

Product	Remote Access		Encrypted Tunnels?	Type
	Mobile User	Office		
AltaVista Tunnel 98	■ AVT 98 Client ■ AVT 98 Telecom- muter Server	AVT 98 Client	Yes	Proprietary
Cisco VPN	800 series VPN- optimized routers	1700 Series, VPN- optimized routers	Yes	■ IPSec* ■ GRE**
Guardian VPN	Authentication Client	Guardian Agent	Only with Guardian Agent. *Not for mobile users.*	IPSec used with Guardian Agent only.
PERMIT Enterprise	PERMIT/Client	Same	Yes	IPSec
Power VPN	RaptorMobile VPN	PowerVPN	Yes	IPSec
Stoplock Connect-IP	SC-IP Secure Mobile	SC-IP Remote Access	Yes	IPSec***
VPN-1	VPN-1 SecuRemote	VPN-1 RemoteLink	Yes	IPSec
WatchGuard VPN	Remote User VPN (Uses PPTP only)	Branch Office VPN (Uses IPSec and proprietary)	Yes	PPTP, IPSec, and proprietary

*In Cisco's VPN-optimized 802 and 803 series routers, tunneling and encryption through IPSec and GRE are enabled with Cisco's IOS software.

**GRE, for Generic Routing Encryption, is a proprietary encryption and tunneling standard developed by Cisco.

***Although CyberGuard's Firewall Release 4 supports IPSec, it is unclear how the Stoplock VPN solution incorporates IPSec for tunneling. If you are interested in this solution, clarification is in order.

user access is user authentication utilizing a one-time password-generating system. Technically, since no encryption occurs, data privacy is not achieved. Thus, what Guardian offers in its remote access for mobile users is a virtual LAN capability, not a VPN solution.

Given the fact that most remote users rely upon 28.8K modems to dial into the ISP's local POP, some solution providers incorporate performance boosters for roaming mobile users. For example, AltaVista Tunneling 98 employs a data compression algorithm to compress data before it is encrypted for transmission. This improves transmission performance over the inherently low-bandwidth Internet.

Other vendors such as AXENT's PowerVPN, Cisco's VPN-1, and AltaVista Tunnel 98 also support remote-access dial-in through ISDN connections. ISDN provides bandwidth connections of up to 128K. Since ISDN lines could run anywhere from $35 to $150 per month, they are used more for branch offices rather than home offices.

Much like a private network, remote access VPNs extend the enterprise network to telecommuters, mobile employees, and remote offices. By employing the Internet for remote access instead of traditional dial-up access solutions, client-to-LAN VPN offers the following specific benefits:

- *Reduction of long-distance telecommunications costs.* Mobile and remote users can enjoy the ability to use local numbers to dial into the ISP point of presence (POP).

- *Reduction of related staff costs. VPNs allow reduction of costs associated with managing and maintaining a staff and dial-up network facilities.* In fact, the need for such facilities might be eliminated entirely.

- *Scalability.* VPNs allow enterprises to either connect or disconnect remote offices, international locations, mobile users, and external business concerns as business needs demand.

- *Accelerated payoff period.* Due to the economies of scale of remote access VPNs, payback periods can be measured in months instead of years.

LAN-to-LAN Implementations

It is a given that 99 percent of all VPN vendors offer a LAN-to-LAN implementation. Just for the record, the VPN solutions featured in this review offer LAN-to-LAN connections. According to a recent study by Infonetics, a networking management consulting firm, LAN-to-LAN connections are 20 to 40 percent less costly than domestic leased-lines.

Early implementations of VPN capability concentrated on LAN-to-LAN connectivity. This included establishing connections between central and remote offices and between branch offices. At one point, when solution providers discussed tunneling capability, they primarily referred to LAN-to-LAN connections; in fact, IPSec's primary focus was LAN-to-LAN implementations. Eventually, however, vendors offered IPSec-compliant client-to-LAN links. In contrast, PPTP and L2TP functionality was geared toward dial-up VPNs. Typically, LAN-to-LAN connections provide one VPN connection that is shared by users on either end of the connection. Although one channel is established, the security gateway at the end of each connection can employ as many servers as needed to process VPN and access control operations. The ability to employ as many "load-balancing" servers as needed is an excellent example of the inherent scalability features of VPNs.

Security Services

VPNs are synonymous with security. More exciting, however, is the fact that VPNs are synonymous with security on the Internet. VPNs achieve security in transmissions with encryption, authentication, and tunneling protocols. Encryption is the most important element in VPN functionality because it scrambles header and payload data at the packet level during tunneling, encrypts the message digest produced in digital signature or data integrity operations, and encrypts passwords in the user authentication process. In other words, encryption puts the "private" in VPN and, consequently, is key to the tunneling protocols, user authentication, and data security measures that drive VPN solutions.

In this section, we take a close look at what makes VPNs what they are—security agents. We compare how the featured vendors deployed tunneling protocols, authentication, and encryption to provide their respective brand of security services. This section also provides information on the vendors that were IPSec-certified, along with tips on how to assess key management capability in VPN solutions.

Tunneling Protocols Supported

IPSec is the granddaddy of them all. Every vendor in this review supports IPSec, with the exception of AltaVista Tunnel 98. Like AVT 98,

Cisco also provides a proprietary tunnel capability in GRE. Cisco also supports L2TP and L2F for tunneling layer 2 or link-layer protocols such as frame relay and ATF. WatchGuard's Remote User client-to-LAN implementation achieves tunneling through PPTP. See Table 16-3 for a comparison summary of vendor security features.

Table 16-3 Comparison of Vendor Tunneling and Encryption Features.

Product	Tunneling Protocols	Hash Algorithms	Encryption Algorithms	Key Length
AltaVista Tunnel 98	Proprietary	Message Digest 5 (MD5); generates 128-bit checksums	RSA Domestic RSA International RSA RC4 Domestic RSA RC4 Overseas	1024-bit 512-bit 128-bit 40-, 56-bit
Cisco VPN	■ IPSec ■ GRE ■ L2TP, L2F	■ MD5 ■ Secure Hash Algorithm (SHA)	Data Encryption Standard (DES) Triple DES	56-bit 112-bit
Guardian VPN	IPSec	None	RSA RC2 RSA RC4	42- to 48 bit 128-bit
PERMIT Enterprise VPN	IPSec	■ MD5 ■ SHA-1 (Generates 160-bit checksums)	DES Triple DES Blowfish IDEA (International Data Encryption Algorithm)	56-bit 112-bit 160-bit 128-bit
Power VPN	IPSec	MD5	RSA RC2 DES Triple DES	42- to 48-bit 56-bit 112-bit
Stoplock Connect-IP	IPSec	MD5	DES Triple DES	56-bit 168-bit
VPN-1	IPSec	■ CBC-DES-MAC ■ MD5 ■ SHA-1	Symmetric RSA RC4 CAST-40 FWZ-1 DES-40 CAST Triple DES Asymmetric RSA Diffie-Hellman	Keys 40-bit 40-bit 48-bit 40-bit 128-bit 168-bit Keys 512/1024 bit 512/1024-bit
WatchGuard VPN	■ PPTP ■ IPSec ■ Proprietary	MD5	DES Triple DES RSA RC4 RSA RC4	56-bit 168-bit 56-bit 128-bit

IPSec is the IETF standard designed to provide tunneling interoperability among third-party offerings. IPSec security services deliver security to the packet level of layer-3 protocols such as IP through AH and ESP security headers. (See the discussion on IPSec security services in Chapters 3 and 10.) Although most of the vendors in this roundup support IPSec, do not assume that a client-to-LAN solution of one will be compatible with a LAN-to-LAN solution of another. There are just too many variables, given the differences in the operating environments, programming techniques, utilities employed, and the manner in which IPSec is programmed into the solution to expect seamless interoperability between competing systems. This is not to say that true interoperability does not exist now between certain solutions or will not exist on a larger scale in the future. However, because of the different variables prevalent, development systems used, and potentially different application interfaces deployed, it's safer and less of a hassle to stay with one vendor's implementation.

Certain vendors have been able to achieve a level of third-party integration with proprietary solutions. For instance, Check Point Software Technologies provides a utility called OPSEC (Open Platform for Secure Enterprise Connectivity). OPSEC is an application framework for providing management and integration of third-party security applications with FireWall-1 and related security applications.

One final point: When implementing IPSec, a given vendor may choose to implement either Authentication Header (AH), Encapsulating Security Payload (ESP), or both. In IPSec, implementing both security headers provides the strongest security. (See discussion in Chapter 10.) When AH is encapsulating ESP, the entire IP packet is authenticated and encrypted, and the outer IPSec header is authenticated as well. This presents the highest condition of security for the resulting tunnel. In early implementations of IPSec, vendors such as Cisco implemented the ESP header only, thereby affording only the security services provided by this particular header. Before you make your selection, ascertain to what extent IPSec is implemented in the VPN solution in question. If AH encapsulating ESP or the full security measures of IPSec are not implemented, perhaps this will not impact your requirements. In any event, it is better to know these things up front before they surprise you later.

IPSec Certification

With the announcement of the completion of the first round of IPSec certification testing, the International Computer Security Association

TABLE 16-4

IPSec-certified
Products as of May
1998

VPN Company	VPN Product	Platform
AXENT Technologies Inc.	PowerVPN (Raptor Firewall) Server/version 6.0	Windows NT 4.0
Check Point Software Technologies, Ltd.	FireWall-1 version 4.0 (b 4013)	Solaris
Check Point Software Technologies, Ltd.	FireWall-1 version 4.0 (b 4013)	Windows NT 4.0
Cisco Systems (proprietary)	Cisco IOS version 11.3.3	IOS platform
TimeStep Corporation	PERMIT/Gate 2500/4500 version 1.1	Proprietary hardware
TimeStep Corporation	PERMIT/Client version 1.1	Windows 95, 98, and NT 4.0

(ICSA) laid the foundation for achieving interoperability among VPN offerings of different vendors. ICSA is the worldwide security assurance company that has been designated by the security industry to design, develop, and administer comprehensive certification programs for Internet-based products. (See the discussion in Chapter 5.) ICSA's certification programs have successfully led the security industry in the development of high-quality security products.

In May 1998, ICSA formally announced the results of the initial IPSec Certification Program Version 1.0. The products of four of the vendors featured in this section were certified for meeting certain IPSec specifications. (See Table 16-4 for a list of IPSec-compliant vendor products.) In general, certification signifies that the products meet the minimum set of required elements to prove *baseline interoperability* among *similarly certified* products of different vendors. Certified products also were tested for compliance with ICSA's Cryptography Product Certification.

The goal of the IPSec certification program is to enable multivendor interoperability among VPN products down to the security function level, which includes authentication, data integrity, and privacy. Consequently, certification under the ICSA IPSec Version 1.0 program indicates that:

1. The products meet the minimum set of required elements for IPSec.

2. The products meet numerous detailed clarification criteria to prove baseline interoperability among products of different vendors.

3. The products meet all of the requirements of ICSA cryptography certification.

Specifically, ICSA will analyze and evaluate either software or hardware that is submitted through requisite channels for IPSec certification. The initial IPSec Certification Program Version 1.0 sort verification has the following capability:

1. Proven interoperability with other version 1.0 ICSA-certified products.

2. The Internet Key Exchange (IKE) for security association and cryptographic key establishment functions using preshared keys.

3. IP ESP to provide for interoperable data integrity, source authentication, and confidentiality in "tunnel" mode only. (See the discussion in Chapter 3.)

4. Compliance with ICSA, a Cryptography Product Certification Criteria.

As you may guess, future ICSA IPSec certification will include examination for AH authentication and provide the following:

1. Proven interoperability with other version 1.xx ICSA-certified products

2. Interactions with certificate authorities

3. ISAKMP/IKE functions with dynamic exchanges

4. IP AH to provide for interoperable data integrity and source authentication

Encryption and Data Authentication

In Table 16-3, notice that RSA algorithms are the dominant encryption algorithms used, followed by DES algorithms. The dominant hash algorithm employed is the de facto standard Message Digest 5 followed by Secure Hash Algorithm. Check Point's VPN-1 provides the largest selection of encryption and hashing algorithm choices, including a proprietary encryption scheme known as FWZ-1. As you know, encryption scrambles plaintext into ciphertext to privatize data transmissions across the Internet. Encryption, working in conjunction with hashing functions, provides digital signatures for data validation and integrity operations. (See the discussion in Chapter 3.) As confirmed by the table, encryption for privacy and digital signing for data integrity are

generally expected, because they are two of the four functional requirements of VPNs. (The other two, of course, are tunneling and user
authentication.)

Key Management Considerations

Encryption is encryption is encryption. However, the key aspect of
encryption in terms of VPNs is key management functions. How are
keys commissioned into use and exchanged for encrypted transmissions
over the Internet? And what procedures and techniques do the companies featured in this section use? Generally, there are two aspects to key
management: key exchange and public key infrastructure (PKI). Key
exchange, in connection with VPNs, means negotiation, key exchange,
and key replenishment. PKI is concerned with issuing keys for use by
specific users, applications, or hosts and with providing an active repository for *certified* user encryption keys. PKI is also involved with revocation of keys and publishing the revocation lists. The main function that
a PKI provides, however, is certifying the identity of users and validating their identities for use with particular keys. (See the discussion in
Chapter 3.)

There are several emerging standards for both key exchange and
PKI. Internet Key Exchange (IKE), formally OAKLEY, and Simple Key
Management for Internet Protocol (SKIP) are the important standards
for key exchange. VeriSign, Entrust, and X.509 are the emerging standards for PKI systems. In a PKI system, VeriSign (or Entrust) functions
as the certificate authority that issues digital certificates, such as the
X.509 type. The digital certificate contains the encryption keys that
have been assigned for use by the validated users. The CA's digital signature verifies the authenticity of the certificate. X.509 specifies a standard format for both digital certificates and associated revocation lists
used within the PKI. VPN solutions use either IKE or SKIP for key
negotiation and exchange and either VeriSign or Entrust as the CA.
Some VPN solutions provide the X.509 digital certificates only. Their
customers are free to establish their own PKI or choose either an
Entrust or VeriSign system if they don't supply their own. (See Table
16-5 for a summary of key exchange and PKI systems offered through
the featured products.)

One of the most potentially demanding aspects of VPN administration is key management. Network administrators are faced with the
challenge of maintaining many pairs of shared secrets, or keys. Network

TABLE 16-5

Comparison of Key
Exchange and PKI
Implementations

VPN Product	Key Exchange	PKI	Other
AltaVista Tunnel 98	RSA Asymmetric transport	Open	Customer choice for PKI. Session keys are refreshed at 30-min intervals.
Cisco VPN	IKE	Open	Same as previous.
Guardian VPN	IKE	Open	Same as previous.
PERMIT Enterprise VPN	IKE	Entrust/ Manager, X.509	Entrust/Directory: LDAP for digital certificate repository.
Power VPN	IKE	Open	
Stoplock Connect-IP	IKE	X.509	
VPN-1	IKE, SKIP, Manual IPSec, FWZ	Entrust, X.509	Uses LDAP to manage end-user security information.
WatchGuard VPN	IKE	X.509	Planned deployment (X.509).

managers are also responsible for coordinating "perfect forward secrecy" by ensuring that keys are changed frequently to maintain the overall security of tunneling operations. IKE, SKIP, and other key management schemes are central in the key management process. Manual IPSec key exchange is acceptable for small installations. However, as you approach hundreds of users, the resulting number of key pairs can total in the thousands.

Key management schemes negotiate or determine the availability of keys at the receiving end of a VPN tunnel. If the negotiation finds a key that matches the key of the initiating end of the tunnel, the tunnel is established for ensuing sessions. In the case of IKE, keys are exchanged in a one-way trust model association via the RSA asymmetric scheme, or a two-way trust association via a Diffie-Hellman scheme. In other words, IKE encrypts the session keys with its own RSA or Diffie-Hellman encryption procedures before the key is transmitted over the Internet. (See the discussion of key exchange properties in Chapter 10.) IKE decrypts the session key at the receiving VPN node, and the exchanged key can be used for tunneling in the current session and in subsequent sessions as well.

IKE also allows keys to be exchanged or replenished after certain intervals. For example, AVT 98 has a feature that refreshes keys every

30 minutes. Enterprises that institute a program of routine replacement of keys reduce the risk of them being compromised. If keys are suspected of being compromised, the VPN solution should enable you to revoke them through the VPN administrative management system.

Determining how keys are revoked brings up another important consideration. Although VPN solutions allow keys to be cancelled or revoked, *how* this task is handled from vendor to vendor may vary widely. In some VPN solutions, such as Check Point's VPN-1 and TimeStep's PERMIT/Enterprise VPN, revoking keys is a snap. It only requires selecting the user in question to deactivate a key and assign a new one. Other products such as AltaVista's system require a little more work. An administrator has to go into the Tunnel Server management system's key management module to revoke or assign a new key. Some VPN systems may require you to work with a command-line interface to revoke and assign new keys. This is one of the procedures you want to see demonstrated before selecting a particular VPN solution. While you are determining the ease of use in revoking and assigning keys, you should also verify what is entailed in revoking keys remotely.

VPN solutions have remote cancellation features. Again, how this is implemented may vary across the board. For example, in earlier Cisco VPN solutions, a separate Telnet session was required to revoke keys. In contrast, earlier versions of Check Point's VPN solution received high marks for remote cancellation. Furthermore, when canceling keys remotely, VPN solutions may handle recognition of canceled keys in one of the following ways:

1. *Detect a canceled key immediately.* Some solutions such as VPN-1 can detect a canceled key immediately. If a user tries to conduct a session with a canceled key, solutions with this capability can drop the session immediately and log the failed attempt.

2. *Detect a canceled key only after keys are refreshed.* This is acceptable if keys are all refreshed after one or some are immediately canceled. However, if refreshing of keys is delayed, this can create a security risk.

3. *Detect a canceled key only after all related sessions are completed.* This presents the greatest risk because, if an intruder uses the key, valuable information could still be compromised, even after key cancellation.

Thus, ascertain how a prospective VPN vendor handles canceled session keys. It may be a good idea to see this feature in action before making your decision. If a potential solution does not handle canceled keys per Item 1 above, you may have to trade this feature off to get another feature that your enterprise requires more.

User Authentication Implementations

Because you are never 100 percent certain who is accessing the internal system from the far corners of cyberspace, user ID/password authentication provides too weak a link in the VPN security chain. The situations in which user ID and passwords will suffice for strong VPN security are limited. Hackers have too many devices at their disposal to confiscate well-intended passwords. For this reason, complementary strong authentication methods came to fruition relatively quickly. Some systems, such as smart cards and TACACS, have been around for some time. Others, such as tokens and S/KEY, are relatively new. Tweaking these methods to work with VPN solutions was as natural and strategic as the institution of encryption for data privacy. In fact, this is the one area where solution providers across the board recognized that weak authentication or user ID and passwords would not do the job by itself. This section reviews strong user authentication implementations typically utilized with VPN solutions.

Two-Factor User Authentication

Two-factor user authentication systems consist of something you possess, such as a credit-card-sized token, and something you know, such as a PIN code. In fact, the use of handheld tokens is fast becoming the de facto standard for two-factor user authentication systems. AXENT Technologies' PowerVPN offers a choice of handheld tokens or software tokens. Guardian's VPN offers a software token-like implementation.

Software tokens are a derivative of regular or handheld tokens. Software tokens are just as secure as handheld tokens and eliminate the need of toting them about. Software tokens, when installed on PCs and laptops, are just as easy to use as handheld tokens but less expensive. Software tokens are also transparent to the user, are not easily lost or stolen, and are only half as expensive as handheld tokens. Software

TABLE 16-6 Comparison of Strong User-Authentication Systems

VPN Product	Two-Factor	Three-Tier	Comment
AltaVista Tunnel 98	*Security Dynamics ID Tokens:* ■ SecurID, KeyFob, PinPad	N/A	AVT 98 Tunnel Server performs as an ACE/Client
Cisco VPN	N/A	■ RADIUS ■ TACACS+	
Guardian VPN	Client Authentication software token (technically not a two-factor system)	N/A	One-time password (considered a strong authentication system)
PERMIT Enterprise VPN	Open	Entrust/Manager, X.509	Use digital certificates to authenticate users
Power VPN	Software token Handheld token	■ RADIUS ■ TACACS+	Both supported by Defender Security Server
Stoplock Connect-IP	Open	Open	X.509
VPN-1	■ S/KEY (not a two-factor system) ■ Yes, token-based	■ RADIUS ■ TACACS+	Uses LDAP to manage end-user security information
WatchGuard VPN	N/A	N/A	Uses strong authentication system MS-CHAP

tokens are ideal for users who use a single device or workstation to log on to a network. On the other hand, handheld tokens are best utilized by users who frequently log on from many different computer workstations. Software tokens generate a one-time password user-authentication scenario. The bottom line is that such systems qualify as strong authentication. Providing strong user authentication is the goal of VPN security.

Table 16-6 provides a comparison of various strong user-authentication products.

Three-Tier Strong User Authentication

TACACS+ and RADIUS are three-tier user authentication system standards for VPN solution providers. In this group, Cisco VPN, PowerVPN, and VPN-1 offer three-tier systems. Three-tier authentication systems can provide three levels of user verification functionality. Typically, however, they provide just two levels of capability. On one level, user authentication is accomplished through a "challenge-response" system. (See the discussion on RADIUS and TACACS+ in Chapters 3 and 10.) Performing as a user authentication proxy server in connection with security gateways is another level of functionality. A third level of user validation functionality is achieved when RADIUS or TACACS+ is configured with handheld tokens or any other two-factor devices, hence, the three-tier system. This capability provides flexibility in networking environments to support regular network users and mobile users that log in from multiple network stations.

One additional note: Although a solution provider may not bundle a certain strong authentication system with their respective solution, that does not mean the desired system can't be added after the fact. VPN solutions may be RADIUS- or token-ready, even if they are not bundled with the VPN solution mix. In any event, ascertain what may be involved in adding a particular user authentication system if the VPN solution does not bundle in the one you desire. The answer may be the difference between going with one system versus another.

Management and Administration

Managing the VPN entails building the enterprise security policy in terms of a rule base, controlling access to the network's information assets, logging the daily activity, and triggering the necessary alerts by intruders. Managing the VPN also entails configuring and maintaining remote enforcement points. Virtually all VPN solutions provide these management capabilities, including the VPN solutions featured in this chapter. Table 16-7 lists a summary of these features.

At a minimum, VPN solutions allow the corporatewide security policy to be translated into a rule-base system designed to reside on network access points. Network access points may consist of a variety of client/server platforms, including UNIX, Windows NT, Windows 95, and Mac OS. Access or enforcement points also include routers, switches, and appliances. AXENT's PowerVPN supports the widest selection of client/server platforms for its security management solution, including Digital OSF/1, Silicon Graphics, Motorola SVR3.2/4.0, Novell NetWare/IntraNetWare, and Open VMS. Check Point Software's VPN-1

TABLE 16-7 Comparison of VPN Administrative Management Systems

VPN Products	Security Policy Management	Remote Functions		Comment
		Configuration	Management	
AltaVista Tunnel 98	Tunnel 98 Server and Firewall 98	Open	Yes	Automatic system fail-over
Cisco VPN	Cisco Firewall or Cisco Works2000	Yes	Yes	■ CiscoWorks2000 released 4Q/98 ■ Heterogeneous security policy support
Guardian VPN	Guardian Manager and ZoneGuard	Yes	Yes	Manage security through single strategy?
PERMIT Enterprise VPN	■ PERMIT/Director ■ PERMIT/Config ■ Firewall Appliance	Yes	Yes	Introduced CheckPoint Software's Management Console with Appliance
Power VPN	Enterprise Security Manager	Yes	Yes	Supported by a broad number of platforms
Stoplock Connect-IP	CyberGuard Firewall	Open	Yes	Manage security through single strategy?
VPN-1	Management Server	Yes	Yes	Configures multiple enforcement point through single security policy
WatchGuard VPN	■ Security Management System ■ Global Console	Yes	Yes	Security management links are encrypted

and Cisco's VPN offer the widest heterogeneous platform support, which includes client/server, routers, network switches, and appliances for security gateways.

VPN-1, specifically, enables all security devices to be remotely configured and managed through a single security policy. This is an excellent feature in VPN management software. Typically, VPN management software allows remote configuration of enforcement points but through multiple security policies or partitions. If a vendor indicates that they offer remote configuration options, verify whether the configuration is accomplished through a single security policy or through multiple security policies or partitions. Administering through a single security policy minimizes errors, requires less time, and reduces hassle.

Guardian's VPN also claims that multiple configuration of enforcement points can be achieved through a proprietary security management system called ZoneGuard. ZoneGuard works in conjunction with adapters on the security server. Each adapter supports a particular security zone. All security zones can be managed by a single security policy. The number of security zone adapters supported is limited by the capacity of the server.

After configuration activities, the network is ready to be managed. VPN solutions generally provide the same management capability: centralized remote management, network monitoring, disabling of access functions, operational status check, and login activity. Many VPN solutions, such as VPN-1 and WatchGuard VPN, also utilize encrypted links when communicating between the main management system and remote enforcement points. For obvious reasons, this is a nice feature to have.

Intruder Alert

Typically, VPN management systems provide special intruder alert mechanisms, from color coding to the sounding of musical chimes. The features that count, however, include automatic email notification, paging, and automatic logging of spoof attempts. These functions, including the featured VPN solutions, are standard features. This is the one area where you should really determine what specific features are offered. The most important objective of intrusion alert functions is to ward off potential threats to the network. Some solutions, such as PowerVPN, use the intrusion detection function as an extension of the firewall by concentrating on systems such as the operating system or devices such as routers. PowerVPN's system, Intruder Alert, focuses on defending attacks against operating environments including UNIX, NT, and Novell's NetWare, as well as on device-level attacks on routers, the firewalls themselves, and Web servers. AltaVista Tunnel 98 and CyberGuard's VPN provide extended intruder alert capability. However, PowerVPN's is more robust.

VPN Performance

There are basically two aspects of VPN performance. One is concerned with how security gateways distribute the processing load among themselves, especially in response to a failed enforcement point. The other aspect of performance is bandwidth management. Currently, there are no protocols that manage QoS (reservation of bandwidth based on transmission priority) for the Internet. (Review the latest developments outlined in Chapter 12.) IETF is championing the Differentiated Services (DiffServ) protocol, which should offer some tools for managing bandwidth over the Internet through VPNs. Until then, management of Internet bandwidth will remain an ambitious dream. Most VPN solutions, including the products in this roundup, offer redundancy or fail-safe features that prevent a security breakdown in a particular network domain. Such features are transparent to network users and enable networks to operate without any interruption in service. Believe it or not, some VPN solutions may not have a fail-safe procedure per se, so don't assume that the VPN solution of interest provides this feature.

One of the most innovative attempts at bandwidth management is provided by VPN-1's FloodGate-1 solution for VPN traffic management. FloodGate-1 defines and implements bandwidth policies that allocate resources for entire classes of traffic, such as mission-critical applications. Essentially, FloodGate-1 eliminates the burst and delay effect inherent in most Internet traffic. It also prioritizes bidirectional network traffic using weighted priorities, limits, and guarantees. Other VPN solutions such as Cisco also offer performance boosters that impact Internet bandwidth. If you are interested in such bandwidth-management features, make certain that the performance gains are substantial and that they therefore justify any added expense.

17

Let's Configure a Firewall

It should not come as a surprise that the featured firewall system in this section is Check Point Technologies' FireWall-1. FireWall-1 is the industry-leading firewall solution and owns the largest share of the marketplace for software-based solutions. Almost since its inception, FireWall-1 has received numerous awards from industry watchdogs and other concerns. A few of the most prestigious include *DataComm Magazine* Tester's Choice (September 1997), *PC Magazine* Editor's Choice (November 1997), *Network World's* Blue Ribbon, and *Network Magazine* Product of the Year 1998. The list could go on, but you get the idea: Check Point's FireWall-1 takes no prisoners.

In this chapter, a firewall is built according to the exact specifications of Check Point Technologies. If you have been in the MIS area long enough, you'll know that the GUI interface of today is a considerable improvement over the command-line installs of yesteryear. FireWall-1 has been cited time and again for its ease of configuration, a feature that helped catapult it into market leadership. Also, the GUI of the current version FireWall-1 (v. 4.0), featured in this chapter, received a face-lift to streamline the menu choices. One caveat: This chapter is for exposition only. Do not attempt to install the product based upon the information contained in the following two chapters.

Setting the Stage

Getting down to business, there are basically five stages involved in configuring FireWall-1:

1. Define the network objects using a GUI-based network objects manager. Objects, which are required to build the security policy, include network objects, services, resources, servers, users, and time.
2. With the user manager, define user ID/passwords or authentication scheme with FireWall-1.
3. Using the rule-base editor, create the rule base to reflect the security policy.
4. Install the rule base on a FireWall-1 gateway.
5. Test the configuration.

Defining the Network Objects

Defining the enterprise's network objects is perhaps the most critical stage in building the rule base, which implements the security policy. In FireWall-1, only the network objects that are connected to the internal network need defining. When defined, the object becomes an integral component of the security policy. To configure a network object (i.e., define its properties) in FireWall-1 requires the use of one or more of the following management tools: Network Objects Manager, Services Manager, Resources Manager, Servers Manager, Users Manager, and Time

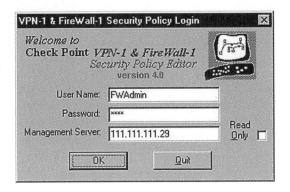

Figure 17-1
Security Policy dialog
box.

Objects Manager. The subsequent illustration assumes that FireWall-1
is installed, the administrator has been selected, and associated rights
have been assigned. Installation includes providing the IP addresses of
all firewall security gateways to the program.

To get started in creating the basic network objects, the admin user
must log in to the Security Policy dialog shown in Figure 17-1. Notice
that the IP address of the Management Server is also entered. This IP
address is the host where a FireWall-1 inspection module is located.

After login, the main management screen appears, as shown in Figure 17-2. From this interface, you are able to create, modify, install, and
monitor security policies installed on local and remote firewalls, as well
as on routers.

In order to facilitate building the firewall, the following network
objects will be created:

1. Internal Web server and FTP client—Host name (alias):
   www.newyork.com (*pc.newyork.com*), IP address: 11.11.11.50 (subnet mask 255,0.0.0)

2. External Web server and FTP client—Host name (alias):
   pc.losangeles.com (*www.losangeles.com*), IP address: 111.111.111.60
   (subnet mask 255.255.0.0)

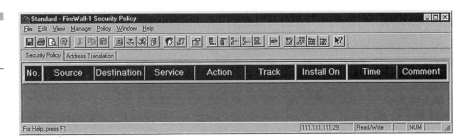

Figure 17-2
Main management
screen.

3. The internal network

4. Users and user groups

5. FireWall-1 hosts

In the next step, the new security policy to be defined must be given a name. In the main management screen, go into File, select `New Secu-rity Policy`, and provide a name. The first network object to be created is a workstation object for the Web/FTP host *www.newyork.com*. This is accomplished by the dialog in Figure 17-3.

Notice in our example that the fully qualified domain name (FQDN) *www.newyork.com* is entered in the Name field. Also, FireWall-1 is told that this Web/FTP server is `Internal` and a `Host` and will therefore be behind the firewall. Next, the internal network is defined to FireWall-1 as a network object using the Network Properties dialog box, indicated in Figure 17-4.

The entire internal network is provided with the name `local_net` and entered accordingly. Note that the IP address and subnet mask are also inserted in the appropriate fields. The previous step must be repeated for the *external* network as well. In this case, the name is `external_net`, and the appropriate IP address and subnet mask data are also entered. After the basic network object properties have been defined, the next phase involves defining user properties.

Figure 17-3
Workstations Properties dialog box.

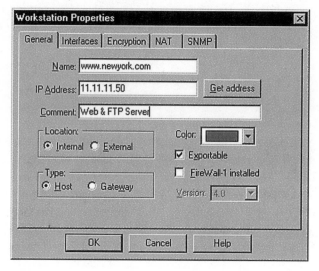

Figure 17-4
Network Properties
dialog box.

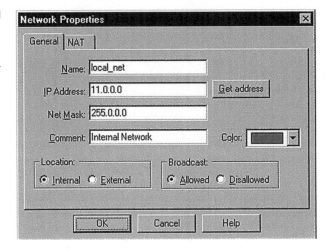

Defining User and Group Objects

To continue, user and group network objects are defined. This is accomplished by FireWall-1's Group Properties dialog. To initialize, the Manage menu is selected from the main management screen (Figure 17-2). From the Manage menu, Users is selected, followed by New Group. The dialog, represented by Figure 17-5, is used to define two user groups for

Figure 17-5
Group Properties
dialog box.

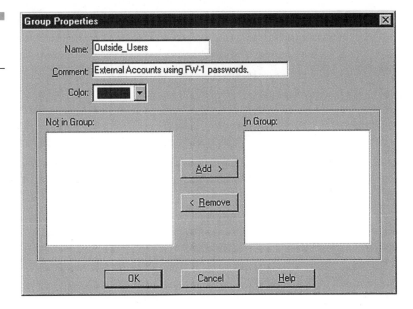

Figure 17-6
User Properties dialog box.

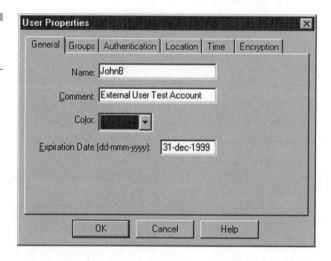

the outside and inside network users. Note that Outside_Users are color-coded for ease of distinction in log files and monitoring. After the outside user group is defined, the internal user group is defined.

The individual users for both groups are defined next. The dialog in Figure 17-6 is followed to create users. As in the previous example, New under the Users menu is selected, and the properties for the user JohnB are created, followed by the other external users.

Notice that this step defines all outside users that will be accessing the *internal* Web/FTP server: *www.newyork.com*. After all users are defined to FireWall-1, the Groups tab is selected, and each user is added to the group Outside_Users. Notice that there is an Authentication tab

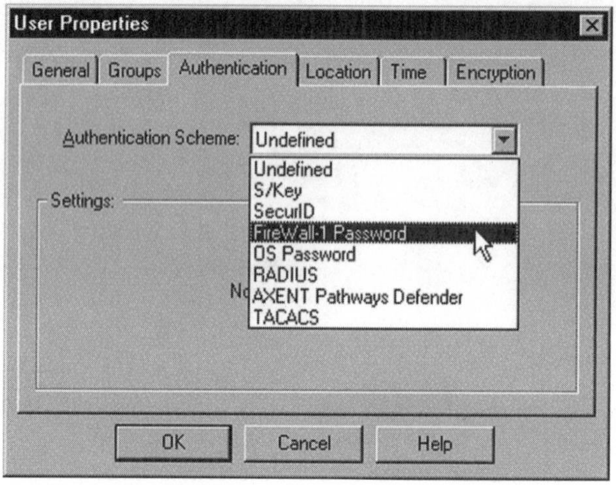

Figure 17-7
Applying user
authentication.

in the Users Properties dialog featured in Figure 17-6. The Authentication tab is used next to assign user authentication to each of the outside contingent.

Figure 17-7 captures the dialog utilized for user authentication. As you can see, the administrator can choose from a variety of authentication systems, including AXENT Technologies' Defender. Besides user authentication, FireWall-1 also incorporates two other authentication types: client and session authentication. (See Chapter 7 for a discussion on this subject.) When the Outside_User group is defined for access to the internal Web/FTP server, the same procedures should be followed to define internal users for the external Web/FTP host: *www.losangeles.com*. All internal users are added to the user group Inside_Users. Upon completion of user definition, the Users dialog (Figure 17-8) is engaged to install the user database with the Install button on the dialog.

Defining the Firewall Object

The preceding steps defined all the network, user, and group objects that will be governed by the rule base that represents the enterprise's security policy. In FireWall-1, the next logical operation involves defining the firewall object. From the Manage menu, select `Network Objects`. Then select `New`, then `Workstation`, as shown in Figure 17-9.

Figure 17-8
Users dialog box.

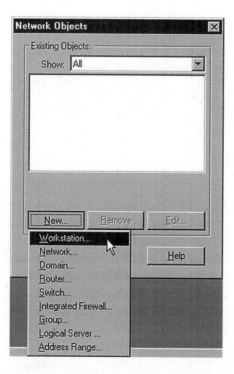

When Workstation Properties dialog appears, the firewall object is
configured. (See Figure 17-10.) Note that the firewall name,
fw1east.newyork.com, is entered along with its IP address.

Assuming that the firewall's host machine was configured properly,
FireWall-1, through the Get Address button, is able to retrieve the IP

Workstation Properties

General | Interfaces | Encryption | NAT | SNMP | Authentication

Name: fw1east.newyork.com

IP Address: 111.111.111.29   Get address

Comment: New York Firewall

Location:
◉ Internal ○ External

Color: ▮ ▾
☐ Exportable

Type:
○ Host ◉ Gateway

☑ FireWall-1 installed

Version: 4.0 ▾

OK   Cancel   Help

Figure 17-11
Defining access for
valid IP addresses.

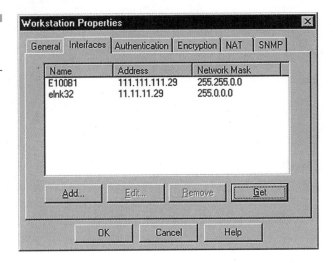

address assigned to the network interface card (NIC) of the host. Also, this is the firewall that will dispense security for the internal network users in New York's internal network. Therefore, `Internal` is selected for the location, `Gateway` is selected for the type of host, and Fire-Wall-1 `installed` is also checked off to complete the process.

The next step is critical. This is where you indicate to FireWall-1 what IP addresses are allowed on internal and external interfaces. Initializing antispoofing safeguards is an important consideration at this stage. Note the Interfaces tab in Figure 17-10. When this tab is selected, the dialog in Figure 17-11 appears.

Again, going through the Get button brings up the IP addresses for the installed NIC cards of the two FireWall-1 enforcement points. The first entry, which is the interface for the internal network, is selected. A double-click on this selection brings up the dialog in Figure 17-12. Selecting the variable `This Net` under the Internal Addresses field authorizes all internal network users on the firewall for the internal network. (Note that the dialog in Figure 17-12 reflects the operation for authorizing *external user access* to the internal network.)

The settings reflected in Figure 17-12 authorize external users access to the internal network and at the same time guard against internal host spoofing. (See the discussion on host spoofing in Chapter 5.) Selecting the option `Others` under Valid Addresses allows external users to cross the firewall inspection point successfully. *Note:* All spoof attempts are logged.

The last step in configuring the firewall object is setting the authentication type. The same authentication options available for network

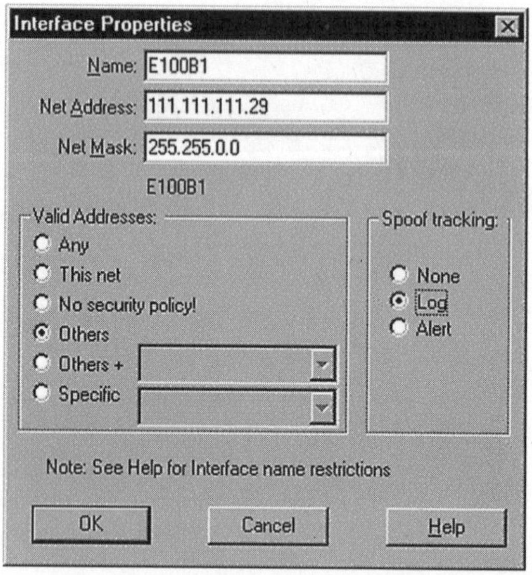

Figure 17-12
Validating access for
external user (IP
addresses).

Figure 17-12
Validating access for
external user (IP
addresses).

users are also available and ultimately controlled by the firewall enforcement points. Figure 17-13 captures the dialog that is used to select the matching authentication type chosen for the users. FireWall-1 is smart enough to properly administer the user authentication process as designated by the system chosen. For example, to gain access to the network, the user merely enters the assigned FireWall-1 password after being prompted. In contrast, if the RADIUS authorization method were selected, the RADIUS server would transmit the prompt for the user's

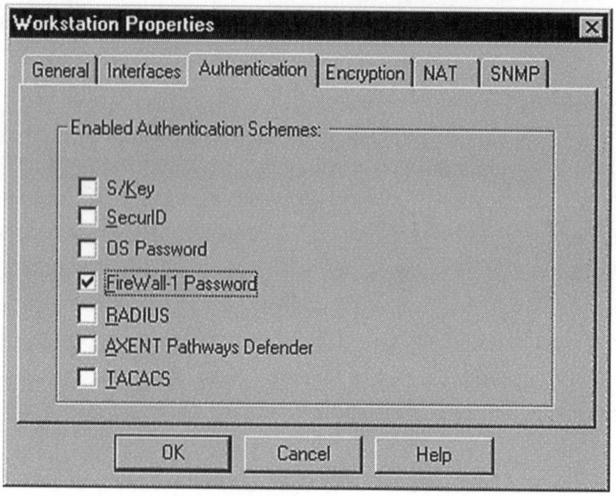

Figure 17-13
Assigning user
authentication
schemes.

response. (See the discussion on user authentication methodologies in Chapter 3.)

Building the Rule Base

When all pertinent network components are defined, including the firewall enforcement points, the rule base required to administer the enterprise security policy is then constructed. FireWall-1 utilizes a stateful inspection engine to process packets. (See Chapter 8 for information on stateful packet filter architecture.) Stateful packet filters process packets by examining each rule in the rule base in sequence. Consequently, the rules composing the security policy must be defined in the appropriate order. (See Chapter 11 for a review of rule-base logic.)

To support the network components defined previously, a security policy will be translated into the appropriate rule base. The following is the security policy for this example:

1. Allow inbound traffic to the internal network after successful user authentication.

2. Permit internal clients to make unrestricted HTTP connections, but allow retrieving only, not sending of files, via FTP connections.

From the main management screen (Figure 17-2), choose the Edit menu, then select Add Rule-Top. Notice that a default rule appears, as shown in Figure 17-14. In FireWall-1, the default rule, or the "implicit-drop" rule, denies all traffic through the firewall. As a result, a rule base must be developed and installed on all security gateways protecting the internal network.

To translate the first policy statement into a rule, begin by right-clicking in the Source box on row number 1. The pop-up menu shown in Figure 17-15 appears. In the pop-up menu, select Add Users Access.

Figure 17-14
Getting started.

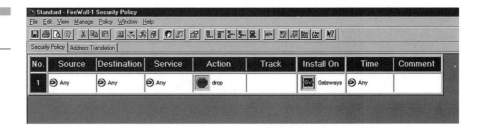

Figure 17-15
Building the first rule.

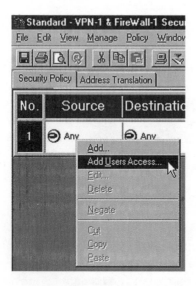

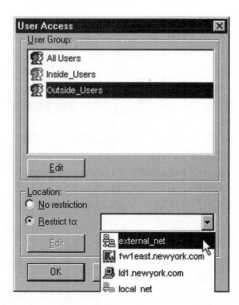

Then select `Outside_Users` when the User Access dialog materializes. Also select `Restrict to` and `External_net` from the associated drop-down menu. This action reduces the chance of spoof attacks when external access to the internal network is restricted.

To complete the first rule, right-click in the Destination box, choose `Add`, and then select the Web server *www.newyork.com.* (Recall that this server was defined as a network object earlier.) To continue, perform the following actions for the remaining rule categories:

1. *Service*   Add `Authenticated`.

2. *Action*   Add `User Auth`.

3. *Track*   Add `Long`.

As an interim and recommended step for testing purposes, change the HTTP option to `All Servers`. Normally, user authentication should be defined for each individual firewall server for the most effective security. When the administrator double-clicks on the User Auth icon, this operation can be initiated through the dialog that appears in Figure 17-16.

Finally, leave the Install On field set to `Gateways`. Also, don't modify time restriction, and in the Comment box, describe the rule as `Inbound Users`. The resulting rule should look like the depiction in Figure 17-17.

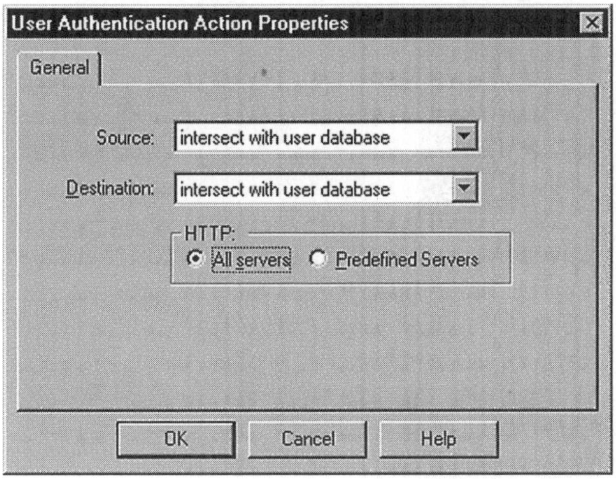

Figure 17-16
User authentication
testing procedure.

Figure 17-17
The first security
policy rule.

In preparation for translating the second policy statement into a new rule, a new resource must be defined. The second policy statement specifies unlimited HTTP access, but retrieval of data only for FTP operations. When working with resources in FireWall-1, you actually are working on the content level of the service in question, which in this case is FTP activity. Content security is concerned with inspecting data at the highest protocol level. This ensures finely tuned access control to network applications and resources. For each connection through the security gateway, FireWall-1 allows the administrator to control access according to the fields that belong to a specific service, such as URLs, filenames, FTP PUT/GET commands, and Type Of requests.

To add a new resource begin by selecting the Manage menu from the main management screen (Figure 17-2). From the options, select Resources and then New from the dialog screen featured in Figure 17-18. From the drop-down menu, choose FTP. Upon completion, this operation will limit FTP activities to file retrieval only.

The next screen you will see is the FTP Definition dialog, shown in Figure 17-19. At the previous screen, notice the name FTP No Put has

Figure 17-18
Constructing a new resource.

been entered and the Exception Track is designated as Log. A comment, which indicates what the new service is for, is also entered. The next step actually enables the feature. In Figure 17-20, notice the actions taken at the dialog. The wildcard "*" is left for the Path, and the box next to GET is checked.

To recap, this operation says that the client can retrieve (GET) files via FTP but will not be allowed to send (PUT) files at the FTP server.

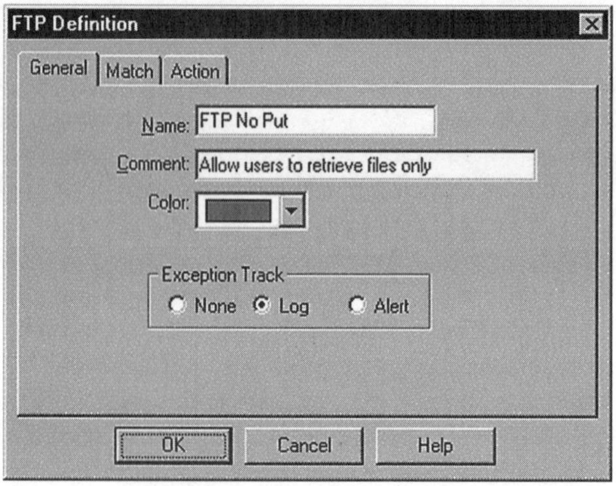

Figure 17-19
New resource definition.

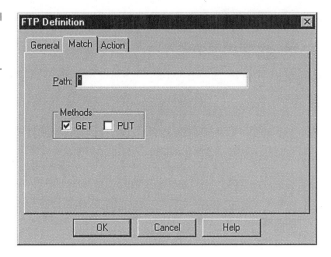

Figure 17-20
Designating specific
FTP activity.

With the new service defined to FireWall-1, the second rule can be built. Going back to the main management screen where the rule base is being built, select the button Add rule after current rule. Note that this rule could have been added before the first rule, if warranted. However, adding it after the first rule is the proper action desired. For the second rule, the headings should be responded to as follows:

1. *Source.* Local_net

2. *Destination.* External_net

3. *Service.* HTTP, FTP No Put

4. *Action.* Accept

5. The remaining categories are the same as the previous and the comment is Outbound Users.

Providing the Service box (Item 3) with the variables HTTP and FTP No Put requires a right-click in that box to select HTTP and a second right-click to select the FTP entry. Figure 17-21 depicts the resulting dialog screen when Add with a Resource is selected in response to the second right-click. This screen says for the FTP service, attach FTP No Put as the resource. The resulting rule is depicted in Figure 17-22, which follows.

Since the two-rule security policy is completed, you are now ready to install the resulting rule base to the FireWall-1 security gateway(s). From the main management window (Figure 17-2), select the Policy menu. Figure 17-23 shows the Install User Database menu. This dialog

Figure 17-21
Selecting Service with
Resource function.

Figure 17-22
The individually
developed security
policy rules.

Figure 17-23
Installing the rule-
base operation.

Figure 17-24
Firewall install
pseudo-rule warning.

VPN-1 & FireWall-1 Warning

Warning: In addition to the rules you explicitly define in
the Rule Base, your Security Policy includes directives
that are implied by properties set in the Properties Setup
window.
You can view these directives in the form of rules by
selecting Implied Pseudo Rules from the View menu.
You can change the directives by changing the
appropriate properties in the Properties Setup window
(Choose Properties from the Policy menu).

☐ Don't show this message again.

[OK]   [Cancel]

will show all available firewall enforcement points with a check mark
next to them. If you are administering to multiple firewalls, this screen
enables the administrator to deselect the firewalls that should not
receive the new security policy. To proceed, select OK.

FireWall-1 responds with a warning that "pseudo rules" are in effect
in addition to the two explicit rules that you created. (See Figure 17-24.)
FireWall-1 automatically generates pseudo, or implicit, rules from the
related security properties and combines these with the explicit rules
created by the network administrator into the overall rule base. To view
the rule base complete with implicit and explicit rules, select View from
the main management screen. The resulting rule base is depicted in Figure 17-25. After reviewing the pseudo rules, you can return to the
explicit rule by deselecting `Implied Pseudo Rules` under the `View`
menu.

There you have it. You have just walked through a straightforward
process of configuring a firewall with the FireWall-1 system. As you may
suspect, Firewall-1 also allows this firewall deployment to be tested. To
test this configuration, access *www.newyork.com* through your Web
browser. If everything is functioning correctly, you should be prompted
in accordance with the dialog screen shown in Figure 17-26.

Upon completing authorization procedures, you will be allowed into
the Web site (Figure 17-27), signaling the "rite of passage" through the
FireWall-1 security gateway.

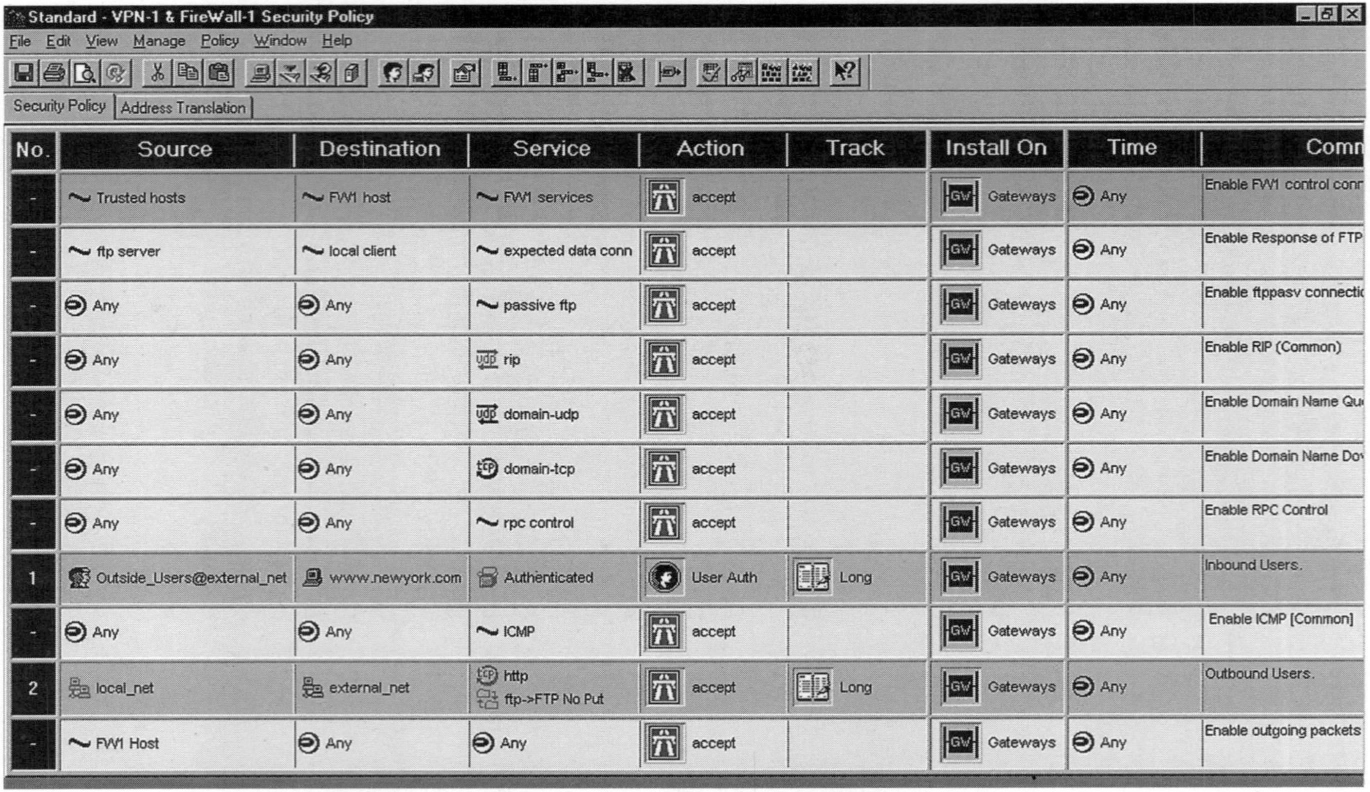

Standard - VPN-1 & FireWall-1 Security Policy

File Edit View Manage Policy Window Help

Security Policy | Address Translation

No.	Source	Destination	Service	Action	Track	Install On	Time	Comment
	Trusted hosts	FW1 host	FW1 services	accept		Gateways	Any	Enable FW1 control control
	ftp server	local client	expected data conn	accept		Gateways	Any	Enable Response of FTP
	Any	Any	passive ftp	accept		Gateways	Any	Enable ftppasv connectio
	Any	Any	rip	accept		Gateways	Any	Enable RIP (Common)
	Any	Any	domain-udp	accept		Gateways	Any	Enable Domain Name Qu
	Any	Any	domain-tcp	accept		Gateways	Any	Enable Domain Name Do
	Any	Any	rpc control	accept		Gateways	Any	Enable RPC Control
1	Outside_Users@external_net	www.newyork.com	Authenticated	User Auth	Long	Gateways	Any	Inbound Users.
	Any	Any	ICMP	accept		Gateways	Any	Enable ICMP [Common]
2	local_net	external_net	http ftp->FTP No Put	accept	Long	Gateways	Any	Outbound Users.
	FW1 Host	Any	Any	accept		Gateways	Any	Enable outgoing packets

Figure 17-25 The Firewall-1 full security policy.

Figure 17-26
Firewall-1 user login
prompt.

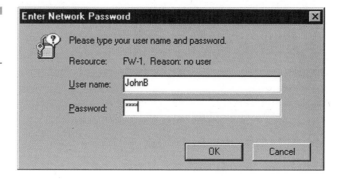

Figure 17-27
The Web site behind
the perimeter.

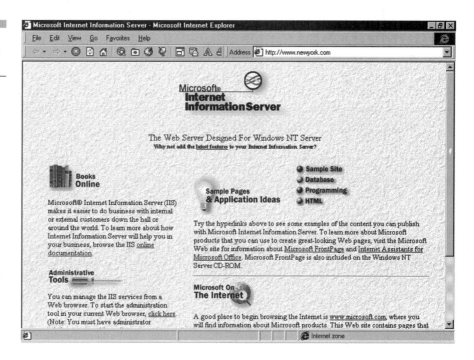

18

Let's Configure a VPN

Configuring a firewall with FireWall-1 is a straightforward process. The security afforded by a firewall gateway is primarily access control. A configured firewall may also provide security mechanisms such as anti-spoofing, address hiding, and translation and code stripping for Java applets and ActiveX controls. Although security provided through a firewall may be adequate in certain situations, this book has demonstrated that a firewall alone is not sufficient security if the Internet is the communications backbone. A firewall and VPN solution offers the strongest potential for security if the Internet is involved. A VPN, through tunneling, encryption, and authentication, provides total privacy in a public communications medium such as the Internet. In this chapter, we configure FireWall-1's companion in arms, VPN-1. As the next pages will demonstrate, configuring, VPN-1 is also a straightforward process.

Setting the Stage

This chapter expands the firewall scenario in the previous chapter. Chapter 17 demonstrated the steps involved in configuring a firewall for the network's New York office. It also depicted how user authentication is selected and administered and how a rule base is installed to the firewall enforcement point. This section describes the steps needed to deploy a VPN between the two corporate offices in New York and Los Angeles. The steps required to build a VPN are similar to those required to build the firewall. The Los Angeles firewall will be defined as an *external* network object to the New York network, which is considered the *internal* network. Next, encryption schemes will be selected to establish the VPN over the Internet. The appropriate rules will be built and added to the rule base, and a test will confirm the accuracy of the configuration effort. The overall steps required for building the VPN are as follows:

1. Define any *additional* network objects on each gateway.

2. Specify encryption domains for *locally* defined firewalls. This involves:
   - Defining the encryption domain
   - Specifying the appropriate encryption method in the Firewall-1's object properties box
   - Generating the encryption keys by editing the encryption properties box
   - Initiating the key update process

3. Specify encryption domains for *remotely* defined firewalls. This involves:
   - Defining encryption domain
   - Specifying the appropriate encryption method in the Firewall-1's object properties' box
   - Editing the encryption properties box, i.e., set the property to `remote` and retrieve the public keys from the peer gateway

4. Add VPN rule to rule base.

5. Define encryption properties for VPN rule.

6. Install security policy.

7. Test the implementation.

8. Configure and install the session authentication client on the mobile/remote users' Win 95 client workstations.

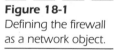

Defining Network Objects

The purpose of this chapter (as well as the previous one) is to demonstrate the relatively straightforward process of configuring a firewall and VPN. As in the previous chapter, some assumptions are in order. This section focuses on the steps required to build the related VPN only. Information regarding other preparatory steps required to configure this or other VPN-1 applications is omitted. The information featured in both chapters is obtained from a preview guide, which could actually be utilized to simulate a live test of FireWall-1 and VPN-1. Therefore, do not use this chapter to configure VPN-1. For proper configuration, you will need other information not contained in these two chapters.

VPN-1 supports LAN-to-LAN and client-to-LAN VPNs. This chapter provides the steps involved in establishing both implementations. The names of the two firewall enforcement points are *fw1east.newyork.com* and *fw1west.losangeles.com*. The first firewall was defined as a network object in the previous chapter. Thus, to begin the process, the West Coast firewall must also be defined as a network object.

From the main management screen (shown in Figure 17-2), select Network Objects in the Manage menu, then select New. The Workstation Properties dialog box appears. (See Figure 18-1.) Since the new object is being configured from the perspective of the internal network in New York, notice that the Location field External is selected, the Host type Gateway is selected, and the FireWall-1 installed box is checked.

Figure 18-1
Defining the firewall as a network object.

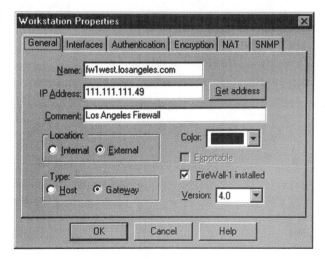

Figure 18-2
Defining access for
valid IP addresses
(West Coast).

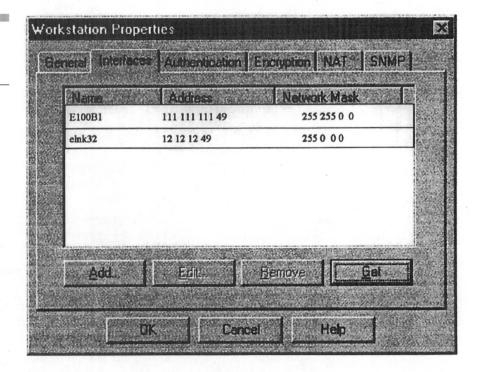

As was done for the East Coast firewall, select the Interfaces tab. This is where the allowable IP addresses for each of the two firewall interfaces are defined. Select the Get button. The IP addresses for the network adapters for the West Coast should appear. (See Figure 18-2.)

The second IP address listed in Figure 18-2 is the internal address for the West Coast firewall. A double-click on the entry summons the Interface Properties dialog. When this happens, the Valid Addresses field is set to `This Net`, as was done in Chapter 17. This operation is repeated again for the *external* IP address. To validate the external interface in anticipation of access from the East, the Valid Addresses field is set to `Others`. (If necessary, refer to Figure 17-12 to review the operation.)

Designating Encryption Domains

So far, all the required adjustments have been made to the East Coast firewall. Before modifications to the West Coast firewall are initiated, the office in the East must be defined as an *encryption domain*. An encryption domain includes all the hosts that are involved in the VPN,

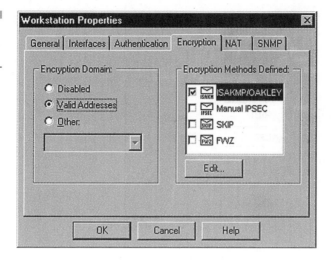

Figure 18-3
Defining VPN-1
encryption domains.

including the security gateway or firewall. To choose the encryption scheme, select the Encryption tab in the Workstation Properties dialog. Figure 18-3 states that for all valid addresses going out of and coming in to the network in New York, use ISAKMP/OAKLEY (Now IKE) encryption. Note that the encryption scheme is selected on the right.

With this selection, pressing `Edit` summons the dialog depicted in Figure 18-4. In this screen you actually select the encryption algorithm and the hash function desired for data integrity operations through the digital signing process.

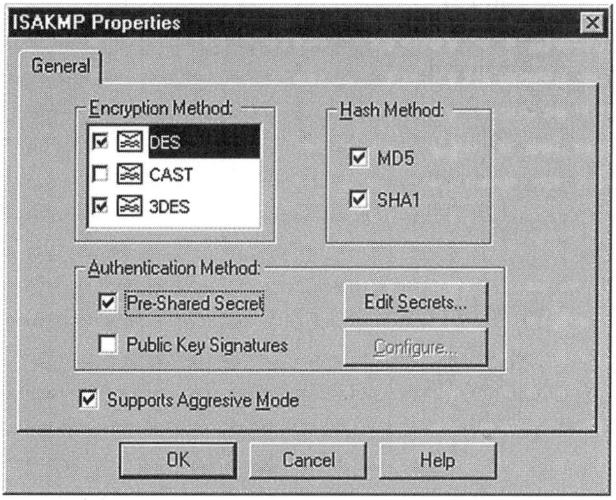

Figure 18-4
Selecting encryption
and hash algorithms.

Figure 18-5
Peer assignment of
shared secrets
procedure.

Notice that this dialog allows you to select whether you are working with or without a certificate authority. Obviously, for a VPN pretest, a CA is not necessary. Thus, for this example, Pre-Shared Secret is selected. The preceding encryption operation defines the encryption domain for the network. This operation (Figures 18-3 and 18-4) is performed next for the New York firewall *fw1east.newyork.com*.

When all network objects for this domain have been completed, the last step is selecting or assigning a "pre-shared secret" for the West Coast firewall: *fw1west.losangeles.com*. This activity is initiated by clicking the Edit Secrets button. In response, the Shared Secret dialog captured in Figure 18-5 materializes. Highlighting the West Coast firewall peer and selecting Edit enables the shared secret to be entered. Selecting the Set button assigns this key to the Los Angeles firewall and completes the operation.

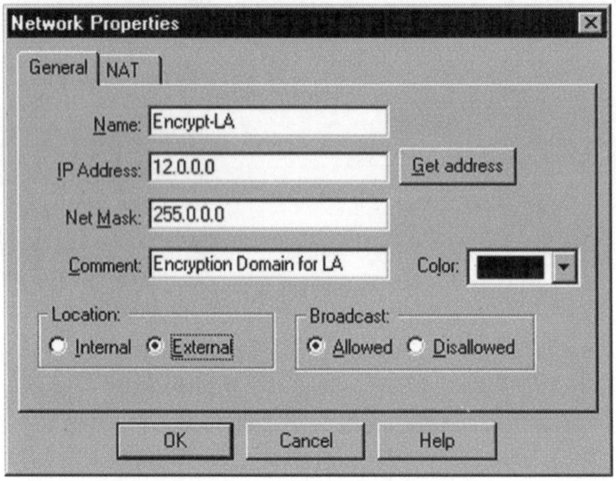

Figure 18-6
Defining the remote
network in a LAN-to-
LAN connection.

Defining the *internal* network of the Los Angeles site is the last modification required on the New York firewall. From the main management screen, Figure 17-2, select `Manage`, `Network Objects`, and, finally, `Network` to summon the Network Properties dialog. The internal network at the West Coast site is provided the name `Encrypt-LA`. (See Figure 18-6.) The IP address and subnet mask are entered accordingly.

Defining More Network Objects

The previous series of steps created one side of the VPN relationship— the objects that will participate in the East Coast side of the VPN. It also defined the West Coast's network as the potential partner in the VPN relationship. The next series of steps will define the objects on the West Coast network that will participate in the VPN relationship. Similarly, the East Coast network will be defined as the VPN partner for the West.

As initiated for the East, the West Coast firewall is defined as a workstation object from the perspective of the West. To do this, the Manage menu is selected from the main management screen, followed by `Network Objects`, `New`, then `Workstation Properties`. (See Figure 18-7.) The Get Address button summons the IP address for the New York firewall.

Figure 18-7
Defining the East Coast firewall as a network object.

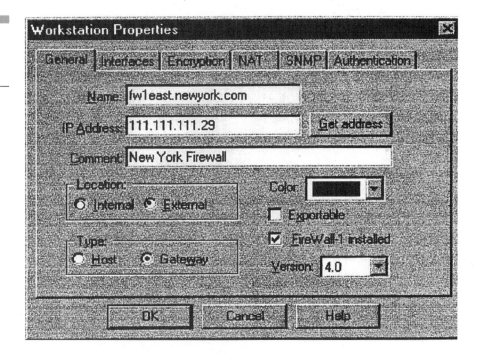

Figure 18-8
Defining access for
valid IP addresses
(East Coast).

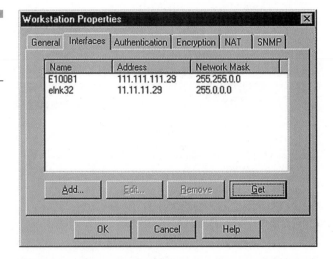

After the East Coast firewall has been defined as an external workstation object to the network in the West, defining the external interfaces to the newly created workstation object (firewall) for valid IP
addresses is next. In the preceding screen, the Interfaces tab is selected.
The second-row entry in Figure 18-8 is the IP address for the internal
interface. When selected, the internal interface `This  net` is chosen
under options for Valid Addresses. Actually, this operation is not shown
in either Figure 18-8 or 18-9. However, the operation is completed by the
dialog shown in Figure 18-9. Instead of selecting "Others" as shown,
"This net" would be chosen instead. Then, to validate the external inter-

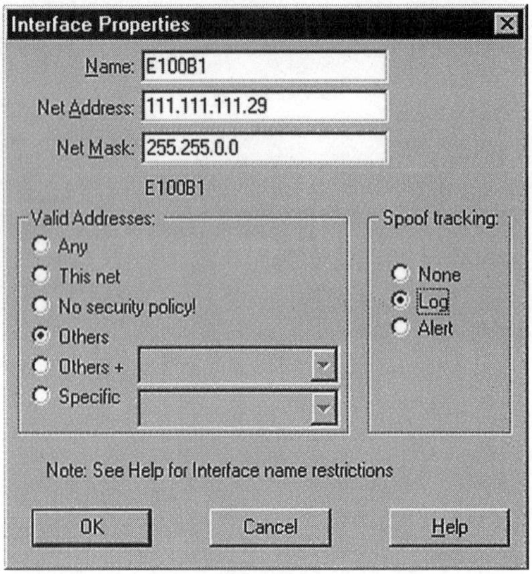

Figure 18-9
Validating access for
external users (IP
addresses).

face, the first-row entry is selected and `Others` is highlighted under Valid Addresses. (See Figure 18-9.)

After the East Coast firewall is defined as a network object to the West, the West Coast firewall must also be defined as a network object. Thus, the steps reflected in Figures 18-7 through 18-9 must also be followed for this firewall as well. The settings for *fw1.losangeles.com* are as follows:

1. *IP Address.*   111.111.111.29

2. *Location.*   Internal

3. *Type.*   Gateway

4. *FireWall.*   1 installed, Version = 4.0

5. *Internal Interface.* This Net

6. *External Interface.* Others

Finally, the Los Angeles LAN must be defined as a network object, and the internal network of the New York site must be defined on the Los Angeles firewall. From the main management screen, select `Manage`, `Network Objects`, and `Network` to access the Network Properties dialog. The setting for the Los Angeles LAN are `12.0.0.0` for IP Address, `255.0.0.0` for Net Mask, and `Internal` for Location. This step, represented in Figure 18-10, is repeated for the internal network

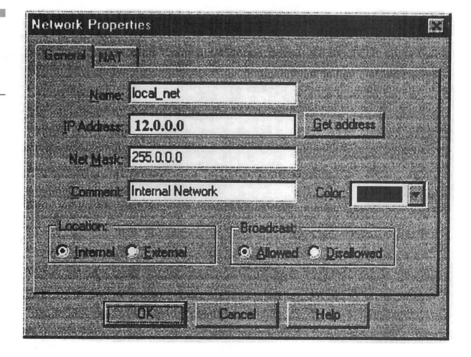

Figure 18-10
Defining the West Coast LAN (Network Properties dialog box).

at the New York site on the West Coast firewall. The settings are `Encrypt-NY` for Name, `11.0.0.0` for IP Address, `255.0.0.0` for Net Mask, and `External` for Location.

Designating Encryption Domains (West Coast)

After defining the West Coast network objects that will participate in the enterprise VPN, encryption schemes are defined. Encryption for the East Coast firewall must be defined from the perspective of the West as well as for the West Coast firewall. Starting with the Workstation Properties menu, the `Encryption Tab` is selected. (See Figure 18-11.) Under Encryption Domain, `Valid Addresses` is selected and the `ISAKMP/OAKLEY` (IKE) method is checked. In addition, as previously chosen for the East, in order to match up, `Pre-Shared Secret` is the authentication method also chosen for the West. (See Figure 18-12.)

Assuming that encryption for the East Coast firewall was handled first, encryption should be initiated for *fw1west.losangeles.com* in order to complete this step. The final step in assigning encryption domains is to actually designate the West Coast's shared secret to the East Coast firewall. (See Figure 18-13.)

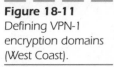

Figure 18-11
Defining VPN-1 encryption domains (West Coast).

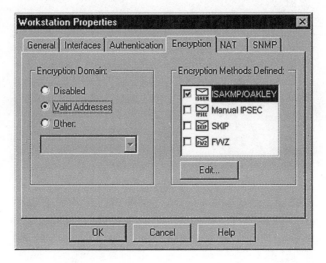

Figure 18-12
Selecting encryption
and hash algorithms
for the West.

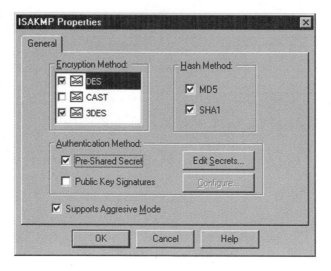

Figure 18-13
Peer Assignment of
Shared Secret (East
Coast).

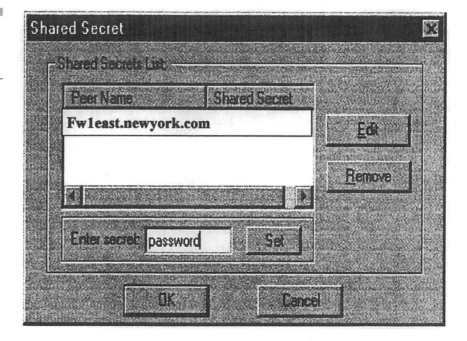

This completes the process of defining the encryption domains and encryption in the East and West ends of the VPN. In the next section, the actual security policy rule base is built to enforce the VPN on each of the respective firewalls.

Building the VPN Rule Base

The network objects that will participate in the coast-to-coast VPN were defined to VPN-1. Initiation of the rule set requires the definition of only two rules for each of the security gateways. To do this, the following steps are required:

1. On the New York firewall, discard the existing security policy. The easiest way to do this is to create a new one. Choose `File`, `New....` Enter a name (such as `VPN-NY`), and click OK.

2. Right-click in the Source box and add `fw1east.newyork.com`. Repeat this step, and add `fw1west.losangeles.com`.

3. Repeat Step 2 in the Destination box.

4. Under Service, add `ISAKMP`, and for Action, choose `Accept`. Set Track to `Long`, and enter `ISAKMP encryption rule` in the Comment field.

5. Add a second rule below the first. For Source, enter `local_net` and `Encrypt-LA`. Do the same in the Destination box. Change the Service to `Any`, and Action to `Encrypt`. Track should be set to `Long` once more, and the comment can be `ISAKMP VPN rule`.

Figure 18-14
Selecting ISAKMP
properties.

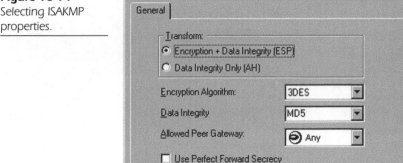

6. The last step is to right-click on `Encrypt` in the Action column, choose `Edit Properties...` (`ISAKMP/OAKLEY` should be preselected), and then click `Edit...` once more. (See Figure 18-14.)

7. Here you can specify the type of transform and encryption algorithms used. You may also want to invoke perfect forward secrecy. Whatever options you set here must be set identically on the Los Angeles firewall or the VPN negotiation will fail.

To complete the process, Steps 1 through 7 above are repeated for the Los Angeles firewall. In Step 5, use `Encrypt-NY` instead of `Encrypt-LA`. The resulting VPN rule set for the New York firewall is captured in Figure 18-15, and the Los Angeles firewall's rule set is depicted in Figure 18-16.

After these two rule sets are installed on their respective firewalls, the resulting VPN can be tested. For example, *www.newyork.com* may be accessed through your Web browser. Expect a slight delay while encryption negotiations are being managed through ISAKMP. After this, the home page featured in Figure 17-27 appears. To confirm the operation of the VPN, initialize the Log Viewer from the management console (in New York). The Log Viewer produces a report featured in Figure 18-17.

Figure 18-15
The New York firewall's VPN rule set.

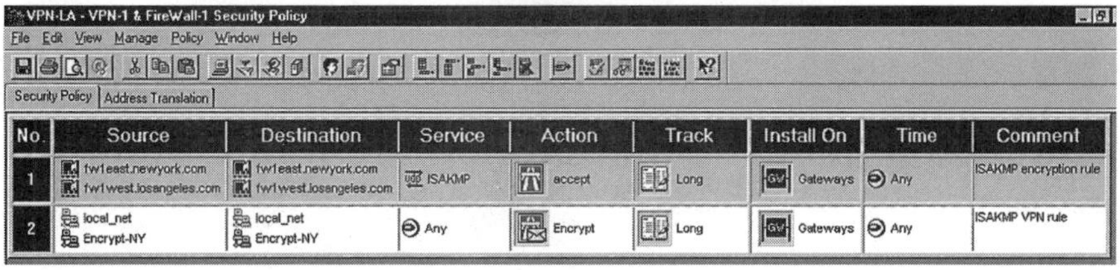

Figure 18-16
The Los Angeles firewall's VPN rule set.

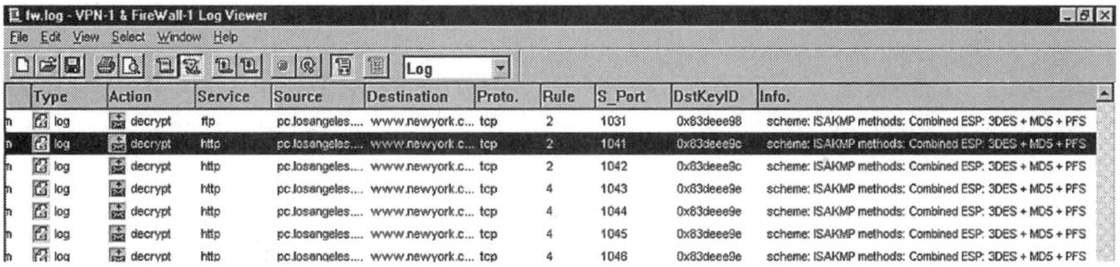

Figure 18-17
Verifying VPN operations through the Log Viewer.

Notice that the most recent log entries show `Decrypt` under the Action column. The Info column details the type of encryption scheme and options used. You've just configured a VPN.

Client-to-LAN Implementation

Establishing a client-to-LAN VPN with VPN-1 is also a straightforward process. VPN-1's client-to-LAN solution is called SecuRemote. SecuRemote enables remote office or nomadic users to access the enterprise network securely. Windows 95 and NT users connect either directly to the server or through Internet service providers. VPN-1's client-to-LAN implementation does the following:

1. Encrypts data before it leaves a remote computer.
2. Transparently encrypts any TCP/IP communications.
3. Interfaces with any existing adapter and TCP/IP stack.
4. Enables access for FireWall-1 SecuRemote users through the rule base editor.
5. Enforces security features, including authentication servers, logging, and alerts, on FireWall-1 SecuRemote connections.
6. Includes support for dynamic IP addressing, which is necessary for dial-up communication.
7. Includes stronger authentication using Diffie-Hellman and RSA algorithms, as well as strong encryption using FWZ-1 (Check Point's proprietary encryption and tunneling protocol) and DES.

Assuming that all necessary modifications are initiated, the process starts again with the New York firewall. Beginning with the main management screen, select the Manage menu. From this menu select `Network Objects` and activate the Workstation Properties dialog for the East Coast firewall. On the General tab, the option `Exportable` should be selected. The importance of this will be described shortly. (See Figure 18-18.)

To demonstrate the flexibility of VPN-1 and SecuRemote, a different encryption scheme will be employed. Thus, the encryption options of *fw1east.newyork.com* must be edited. While still at the Workstation Properties dialog, select the Encryption tab. (See Figure 18-19.) Now deselect `ISAKMP/OAKLEY` and substitute with `FWZ`.

Figure 18-18
Preparing the firewall
for remote access.

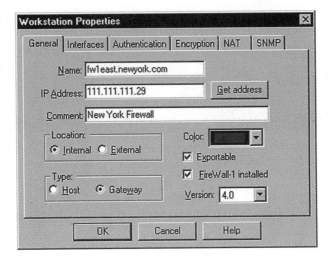

Once the new encryption method is selected, the actual encryption keys must be generated. Click on Edit to summon the FWZ Properties dialog depicted in Figure 18-20. Again, the properties' screen provides the administrator with the option to indicate whether or not a CA is being employed in the VPN. Since this example assumes no CA is being utilized, VPN-1 must perform the certificate authority key-generation function. Notice that Local is selected, and to produce the keys, Generate is selected next.

VPN-1 requires only seconds to produce the encryption keys. An OK acknowledgement, and the CA's key is installed. Recall that one of the

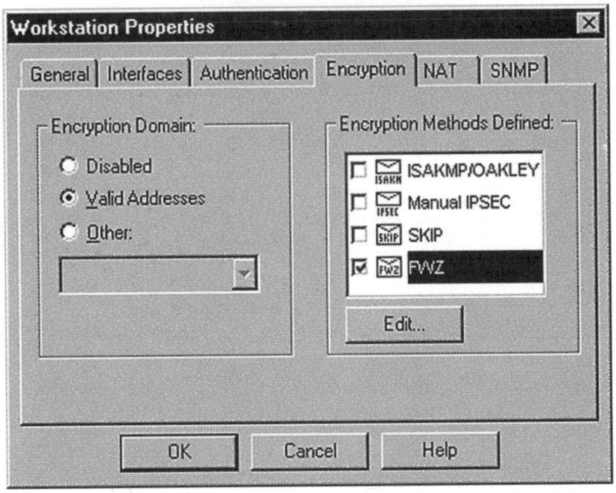

Figure 18-19
Selecting a new
encryption method.

Figure 18-20
Generating encryption keys.

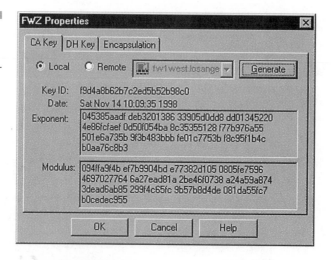

functions of the CA is to sign digital certificates in order to validate a user's identity for the use of a set of public keys. Without the use of an "actual" CA, the VPN-1 administrator provides this function.

While at the FWZ Properties dialog, the key for the SecuRemote client is generated next. Choose the DH Key tab and select Generate once more. After responding Yes to an interim step, the newly generated key becomes available. (See Figure 18-21.) This completes the necessary preparation for the New York firewall to support a SecuRemote user.

Figure 18-21
Generating user encryption keys.

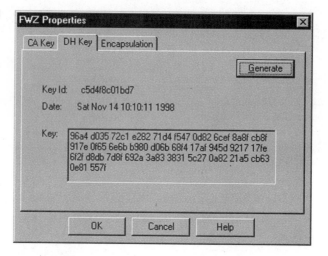

Figure 18-22
Assigning encryption
to remote users.

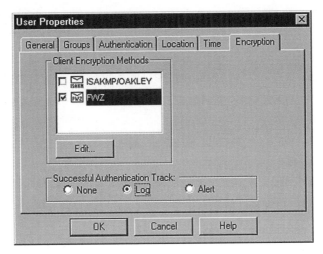

In order for the SecuRemote client to gain access through the firewall, the VPN-1 user account must also be properly configured. In this example, the user in question is JohnB. Recall that JohnB was created in the last chapter and added to the group Outside_Users. Configuring JohnB's account is a snap. Figure 18-22 shows the User Properties dialog. After selecting the appropriate user, the appropriate encryption scheme must be initialized for JohnB. Deselect ISAKMP/OAKLEY and select FWZ. For Authentication Tracking, select Log. You're done.

Building the Client-to-LAN Rule Base

VPN-1 affords enterprises the ability to designate a firewall enforcement point as the SecuRemote or remote access server. The final step in preparing for remote access is building the appropriate rule set and installing it to the firewall. The steps involved are as follows:

1. Choose File, New.... Enter a name (such as SecuRemote-Test).
2. Right-click in the Source box, select Add Users Access, and select the Outside_Users group.
3. Right-click in the Destination box and choose local_net.

Figure 18-23
The client-to-LAN
rule set.

4. Set the Service to Any, the Action to Client Encrypt and the Track to Long. If you wish, enter a comment.

5. See Figure 18-23 for the finished rule, which is installed to the remote access enforcement point.

   That's a wrap.

APPENDIX A

RSA EXAMPLES

Invented by Ron Rivest, Adi Shamir, and Leonard Adleman in 1977, RSA is a public key cryptosystem for both encryption and authentication. It works as follows: Take two large primes, p and q, and find their product: $n = p \times q$ (n is called the *modulus*). Choose a number, e, less than n and relatively prime to $(p-1) \times (q-1)$, which means that e and $(p-1) \times (q-1)$ have no common factors except 1. Find another number, d, such that $(e \times d - 1)$ is divisible by $(p-1) \times (q-1)$. The values e and d are called the *public* and *private exponents*, respectively. The public key is the pair n,e; the private key is n,d. The factors p and q may be kept with the private key or destroyed.

It is difficult (presumably) to obtain the private key d from the public key, n,e. If one could factor n into p and q, however, then one could obtain the private key d. Thus, the security of RSA is related to the assumption that factoring is difficult. An easy factoring method or some other feasible attack would break RSA.

Here is how RSA can be used for privacy and authentication (in practice, the actual use is slightly different):

RSA privacy (encryption): Suppose Kim wants to send a message m to Bob. Kim creates the ciphertext c by exponentiating: $c = m^e \bmod n$, where e and n are Bob's public key. She sends c to Bob. To decrypt, Bob also exponentiates: $m = c^d \bmod n$; the relationship between e and d ensures that Bob correctly recovers m. Since only Bob knows d, only Bob can decrypt.

RSA authentication: Suppose Kim wants to send a message m to Bob in such a way that Bob is assured that the message is authentic and is from Kim. Kim creates a digital signature s by exponentiating: $s = m^d \bmod n$, where d and n are Kim's private key. She sends m and s to Bob. To verify the signature, Bob exponentiates and checks that the message m is recovered: $m = s^e \bmod n$, where e and n are Kim's public key.

Thus, encryption and authentication take place without any sharing of private keys: Each person uses the public keys of others and his or her own private key. Anyone can send an encrypted message or verify a signed message using only public keys, but only someone in possession of the correct private key can decrypt or sign a message.

GLOSSARY

access control   An inherent feature of firewalls that restricts access of external users to only certain applications, domains, or areas of the internal network. Access control protects not only the data but also the enterprise's entire repository of intellectual property. This ensures that users access only the information they need, but nothing more.

ActiveX   Microsoft's object linking and embedding (OLE) technology specifically designed to challenge Java for development of multimedia types of applications for network applications. ActiveX is not a programming language per se. Rather, it is a specification for packaging programs written in virtually any programming language for transmission and execution via computer networks, including public networks such as the Internet.

algorithm   A set of mathematical or systematic steps used as a formula for performing repetitive or problematical functions, such as an encryption algorithm used for scrambling cleartext into ciphertext.

authentication   A critical step in establishing secure network communications, it involves verification of an entity at the initiating end of the communication channel. The entity may include a user, host, application, and other network nodes, such as a router or security appliance. Authentication methods are classified by two categories: weak and strong. Weak authentication involves the use of an identification mechanism and password, typically transmitted in cleartext. Strong authentication usually entails transmitting user IDs and passwords in encrypted test, or ciphertext.

demilitarized zone   The area of an enterprise LAN/WAN that operates outside of its security or perimeter defenses. Examples include external Web sites and FTP sites for various information dissemination purposes.

digital signature algorithm   A digital signature algorithm is essentially a hash function operation used to authenticate an entity at the end of a communication's channel. SHA-1 is an example of a digital signature algorithm.

extranet   Technically, an internal enterprise network that extends online access to business partners, suppliers, or best customers in order to achieve a competitive advantage. Initially, *extranet* was synonymous with *virtual private network*. However, a VPN is one of several cost-effective mechanisms for supporting the extranet's communication backbone by utilizing the Internet.

firewall security appliance The next generation of firewall implementations. Firewall security appliances are self-contained enforcement units (black boxes) that are distinguishable by how they are deployed in the network. Typically, firewalls operate on the network's perimeter. Firewall appliances, on the other hand, are designed to work within the network's infrastructure. Thus, they perform a bridging or pass-through function, as opposed to a gateway or routing function. A security appliance, designed without keyboard, mouse, file system, or administrative login, is configured and managed by a remote management system. Once deployed the appliances establish and protect network *security zones*.

fractional T1 High-volume digital telephone service that is contracted at fractions or increments of the full T1 bandwidth. Fractional T1 speeds commonly run at bandwidths including 128K, 256K, 384K, 512K, 768K, and 896K. In essence, most trunk speeds can be purchased in fractions of their fully rated bandwidth.

hardened operating system A hardened OS is one that has been stripped down to its bare essentials and has utility and related applications, which represent security holes patched or removed.

hash function A one-way operation that takes a variable-sized stream of data and derives a fixed-length number that represents the data. One-way hash functions are cryptographically secure and cannot be reversed without the associated hashing algorithm. Through hash functions, it is mathematically infeasible to find two different messages to produce the same hash value.

ISDN (Integrated Services Digital Network) A low-end digital telephone line. ISDN is available in two basic formats: Basic rate interface (BRI) with two 64K Bearer (B) channels and one 16K signaling D channel. BRI is used for small branch offices and home offices. In action, the two 64K channels bond to provide a switched 128K connection to a LAN or ISP.

intranet An internal corporate or enterprise network that employs Internet protocols for development of network applications. Intranets utilize TCP/IP for the WAN protocol, and HTTP, FTP, SMTP, UDP and other Internet-based standards to establish Web-based applications, such as Web sites, multimedia presentations, newsgroups, online chat rooms, email, and information exchange.

key escrow   Involves employing independent security agents that keep your private and master keys securely locked away in a safe facility off site. Key escrow is gaining in popularity with enterprises for protection against a disgruntled employee making off with master encryption keys. The federal government is also advocating this system because it gives them an avenue for obtaining your keys in the interest of national security. In practice, the keys are divided in half, and each half is kept in separate, unrelated escrow agents for added security.

latency   The normal delays that transmissions experience while traversing a communications medium or other connecting interface. For example, when packets are processed by routers to determine an optimal transmission pathway, the transmission undergoes some delay or latency as the router decides how to send the packet on its way.

public data network   Essentially, a communications backbone tying together enterprise LANs into a WAN. PDNs, such as the kind offered through UUNET or CompuServe, enable secure long-distance communications between geographically dispersed locations of an enterprise.

public key encryption   An asymmetric key algorithm that employs two keys: a public or encoding key and a private or decoding key. In a public-key cryptography system, users disseminate their public keys, and their correspondents obtain these keys to encode messages sent between them.

security association   A relationship between two or more entities that describes how security functionality should be utilized to communicate securely.

T1   Also known as a *trunk line*, T1 is one of the highest-speed digital telephone line services commercially available. Trunk lines are popular because they offer the highest bandwidth, are always available, and are very reliable. A full T1 line provides up to 1.544 mbps of bandwidth speed.

T3   The highest-rated trunk line is a T3 line with rated bandwidths, or trunk speed, of 45 mbps. Both T1 and T3 lines can be purchased at full bandwidth or at clear channel functionality.

throughput   What a user sees on the display in response to the input and output stages through which information travels within a communication and/or processing system in response to user commands.

virtual network   Network that tunnels data (packets) without any form of encryption and does not provide any privacy whatsoever. In this scenario, the resulting network is more appropriately called a *virtual network* (VN), since data are being transmitted in cleartext.

virtual private network   A VPN utilizes encryption, tunneling protocols, and authentication to establish secure and private communications over a public communications network, such as the Internet. VPNs deliver security at the packet level by encapsulating (tunneling) header information and packet payload data with encryption for privacy and/or hash functions for data integrity. VPNs are typically extended with the complementary functionality of firewalls.

Web of Trust   A community of users owning private/public key sets that vouch for each other's identity. A public key becomes valid when someone who knows the owner and signs the owner's public key with his or her public key. If enough users sign one person's public key and enough people sign another's public key, chances are that both individuals have a signer in common, or someone who knows both individuals. When this happens, one can trust that both individuals are who they claim to be, hence the Web of Trust.

X.25   A wide area networking communications protocol used primarily in the international arena. X.25 is widely used to support packet switched networks in PDNs.

INDEX

311

X

Z

About the Author

David Leon Clark is an Information Technology Consultant and has been working in the IT industry since 1978. He has worked with UNISYS, General Electric Information Services, Litton Computer Services, and Tandy. He has developed information technology interventions and workshops for Fortune 100 companies.